Apr 2015

DEATH OF CAPTAIN AMERICA

A NOVEL OF THE MARVEL UNIVERSE

ADAPTED FROM THE GRAPHIC NOVEL
BY ED BRUBAKER AND STEVE EPTING

DEATH OF
CAPTAIN
AMERICA

A NOVEL OF THE MARVEL UNIVERSE

LARRY HAMA

CAPTAIN AMERICA: THE DEATH OF CAPTAIN AMERICA PROSE NOVEL. Published by MARVEL WORLDWIDE, INC., a subsidiary of MARVEL ENTERTAINMENT, LLC. OFFICE OF PUBLICATION: 135 West 50th Street, New York, NY 10020. Copyright © 2014 Marvel Characters, Inc. All rights reserved. ISBN# 978-0-7851-8996-1

Printed in the U.S.A.

ALAN FINE, EVP - Office of the President, Marvel Worldwide, Inc. and EVP & CMO Marvel Characters B.V.; DAN BUCKLEY, Publisher & President - Print, Animation & Digital Divisions; JOE QUESADA, Chief Creative Officer; TOM BREVOORT, SVP of Publishing; DAVID BOGART, SVP of Operations & Procurement, Publishing; C.B. CEBULSKI, SVP of Creator & Content Development; DAVID GABRIEL, SVP of Print & Digital Publishing Sales; JIM O'KEEFE, VP of Operations & Logistics; DAN CARR, Executive Director of Publishing Technology; SUSAN CRESPI, Editorial Operations Manager; ALEX MORALES, Publishing Operations Manager; STAN LEE, Chairman Emeritus. For information regarding advertising in Marvel Comics or on Marvel.com, please contact Niza Disla, Director of Marvel Partnerships, at ndisla@marvel.com. For Marvel subscription inquiries, please call 800-217-9158. **Manufactured between 1/6/2014 and 2/17/2014 by SHERIDAN BOOKS, INC., CHELSEA, MI, USA.**

First printing 2014
10 9 8 7 6 5 4 3 2 1

CAPTAIN AMERICA CREATED BY JOE SIMON AND JACK KIRBY
INTERIOR ART FROM CAPTAIN AMERICA #25-42 BY STEVE EPTING, LUKE ROSS, MIKE PERKINS, BUTCH GUICE, ROBERTO DE LA TORRE, RICK MAGYAR, FABIO LAGUNA, ED MCGUINNESS, DEXTER VINES, JASON KEITH AND FRANK D'ARMATA
COVER ART BY STEVE EPTING
BACK COVER ART BY ALEX ROSS

Marie Javins, Editor
Design by Nelson Ribeiro

Senior Editor, Special Projects: Jeff Youngquist
Associate Managing Editor: Alex Starbuck
Assistant Editor: Sarah Brunstad
SVP Print, Sales & Marketing: David Gabriel
Editor In Chief: Axel Alonso
Chief Creative Officer: Joe Quesada
Publisher: Dan Buckley
Executive Producer: Alan Fine

Acknowledgments

Much thanks, of course, to Ed Brubaker and Steve Epting who wrote and drew the bulk of the *Captain America* comics arc from which this book is adapted.

Marie Javins went above and beyond the call of duty in shepherding this project and correcting my lapses in grammar, as well as curbing my tendency to expound on arcane minutiae.

I am grateful to Stuart Moore and Axel Alonso for having the faith in me to go the distance with the material, and I thank them for their support and patience throughout my learning process.

Jeff Youngquist is one of the most competent editorial people I have ever worked with. His comments and suggestions were always on the mark, and his ability to track down the most elusive reference was nothing but amazing.

Joe Simon and Jack Kirby were the creators of Captain America, and their contribution to that character and comics in general is monumental. To list all the others who contributed to Cap's canon and lore would require quite a few pages, but Stan Lee would top the list for sure.

The late Mark Gruenwald not only held the record for the longest writing stint on *Captain America*, he set down the unwavering moral compass point at the core of who Steve Rogers is, and he did it simply by saying "Cap wouldn't do that" whenever anybody dared to "bring the character into line with modern morality." We miss you, Mark, and we won't let the shield fall in the mud.

DEATH OF
CAPTAIN
AMERICA

A NOVEL OF THE MARVEL UNIVERSE

PROLOGUE

LIGHTNING dances across the New York City skyline. Johann Schmidt watches it with detached indifference from his Midtown penthouse. He is old, and he has been "reborn" a number of times, but his hatred remains unabated. He is, after all, a product of his hatred, and it is what really sustains him.

It has been a long, arduous journey since he was a young bellhop knocking on Adolf Hitler's hotel-room door in that giddy time before the Nazis blitzkrieged their way into Poland to ignite the cataclysm we call World War II. The Führer himself redubbed Schmidt "der Roter Totenkopf," the Red Skull, and put him charge of all terrorist and sabotage activities for the Third Reich.

This appointment propelled the former bellhop to the vanguard of the National Socialist propaganda machine, and in a sublime twist of fate, spurred the United States to utilize the sole product of their secret Operation: Rebirth project, Steve Rogers, in the same way. Enhanced to a level of strength, speed, and perception far above a normal human, Rogers became Captain America. Along with his teen sidekick, Bucky, he took the fight against fascism to the battlefields of Europe and became the Red Skull's lifelong foe.

The Red Skull refocuses his vision to contemplate his own reflection as he stands at the sliding terrace doors that look out on the city. The city that is also home to Captain America. The crimson death's-head mask is a terrifying visage, but it was meant to be, and he has grown used to it—prefers it, even. The former Nazi wills himself to relax—his hands involuntarily forming fists—as he remembers his magnificent dreams of conquest brought to ashes by the Amerikaner Schwein in the red-white-and-blue costume.

How many times had he seen that verdammt shield carom through his soldiers, minions, and allies? How often had Captain America and his adolescent protégé unraveled his diabolically clever schemes, and destroyed devices that were the fruits of years of research and development? The injustice rankles, but he does not concede. The defeats are temporary setbacks. Did he not precipitate the events that led to Bucky's death in the explosion of the drone aircraft stolen by Baron Zemo?

The Red Skull is momentarily bemused. Satan's words from Milton's Paradise Lost spring to his mind. "All is not lost, the unconquerable will, and study of revenge, immortal hate, and courage never to submit or yield." The reflection in the glass grins back at him. Yes, the tide is turning in his favor. He has regained possession of a Cosmic Cube, a matrix of interdimensional energy small enough to fit in the palm of one's hand, but powerful enough to warp reality. Soon, he will inflict extreme suffering upon Captain America, that insufferable icon of democracy, and everything he stands for will be brought low and trampled in the dust.

The Cosmic Cube is the key. It has been five years since Aleksander Lukin offered the Winter Soldier to Red Skull in exchange for the Cube. The Winter Soldier being the resuscitated and enhanced James "Bucky" Barnes, who had been turned into a Soviet assassin by Lukin's guardian and mentor, Vasily Karpov.

Lukin had inherited all of Karpov's secrets and treasures, and had risen high in the ranks of the KGB, acquiring the assets and contacts he needed to go rogue and remake himself as the oligarchic head of the Kronas Corporation. Lukin shared Red Skull's hatred of Western democracies, and he lusted after the Cosmic Cube because he thought it could advance his own plans for world dominion: another reason why Red Skull would never agree to the trade.

Having control of Bucky Barnes would have provided Red Skull with another dagger to twist in Captain America's heart—and some interesting genetic material to play with, as well—but giving up the Cube? That would be like sacrificing his queen too early in an even chess match. General Lukin played an arrogant offense, but why give him any advantage at all, nicht war?

The Red Skull reminds himself that Lukin has been known to press risky gambits with no apparent regard for the endgame. An infant with a straight razor—

The telephone rings.

"Hello, Johann, this is—"

"I know who you are, Aleksander Vasilievich. And I knew you would be calling as soon as your spies reported in. I am holding the Cosmic Cube even as we speak. Such a thing of ephemeral beauty, having no past and no firm foothold in the present. It glows with the light of the future. That future will be mine, and not yours, Lukin."

"I am prepared to increase my offer, Herr Schmidt."

"If you had anything I wanted, I would simply take it."

"I'm sorry you feel that way."

"Is that a threat? You are more of a fool than—"

The Red Skull turns away from the glass to stare at the

molybdenum steel door of his rooftop sanctum. Still locked and intact. Then why is Lukin prolonging a pointless conversation? Unless…

The pain is so acute he thinks he's having a heart attack. As he starts to fall, he sees the blood spray from the exit wound in his chest onto the white carpet. He knows there is a bullet hole in the glass behind him. He marshals his unconquerable will before the Cube slips from his fingers.

The glass slider opens, and a man in black wearing Russian paratrooper boots steps into the room. He picks up both the Cube and the phone.

"The subject is terminated, General. And the artifact is secured."

At the other end of the connection, Aleksander Lukin's elation is cut short by the realization that there is another presence in his consciousness. Horror and revulsion grip him as more than eight decades of vile memories goose-step through his mind and a voice like a death rattle whispers, "Checkmate, Herr General."

PART ONE

HIGH CRIMES
AND TREASON

ONE

S.H.I.E.L.D. didn't give me a number and take away my name. That's not protocol in the U.N.'s Strategic Homeland Intervention Espionage Logistics Directorate. I'm still Sharon Carter—even if all the suits, techs, and field ops call me "Agent 13."

As a senior field agent, I am authorized to wear the distinctive black armored body suit with white accessories and carry the regulation advanced plasma pistol. But being an old-fashioned girl, I still keep the original-issue .30-caliber machine pistol and a 9mm Beretta under the floorboards in my closet.

I get my hair "done" in the East Village at a place that still charges less than twenty bucks for a cut, and where the languages of choice are Russian and Mandarin. They don't realize I can understand most of what they say, but that doesn't bother me at all.

Most of the guys who come on to me when I'm in civvies figure it's no great loss if I reject them. That doesn't bother me, either. I was never a big one for casual romance. But I have known love, and I know that it comes with as much pain as joy.

I'm good at my job, even if I've made mistakes—like getting involved with somebody I work with. That's what got me in trouble with my boss, Deputy Director Hill. And that's how I got stuck with a mandatory psych eval. Minimum ten sessions—with the psychiatrist's report counting heavily toward whether I get benched, suspended, charged, or reinstated.

Hill will get her way, no matter what.

The shrink I was assigned at Admin turns out to be pretty cool. He doesn't steeple his fingers, and he doesn't display any tics when I purposely say things to rock his socks. I find myself liking him and trusting him for no discernable reason. Maybe that's a good sign. The fact that he looks like Martin Luther King Jr. with a shaved head helps, too. He makes me verbalize stuff I might otherwise suppress or deny. I get through nine sessions by holding my cards close and never even peeking. But the tenth session is the high-stakes pot, and both of us know it.

"So, Agent 13, can you elucidate your anger issues with Deputy Director Maria Hill?"

"She played me. She leveraged my relationship with Cap—Steve Rogers—because she wanted him to go against his own principles to support the Superhuman Registration Act. And this was *after* she sicced the Cape-Killer Squad on him. Some name, huh? Cape-Killers. Powered suits of armor to go after people who'd been 'heroes' before a lily-livered Congress passed the Registration Act to appease the paranoids."

"Captain America is and always has been an active agent of the United States government, and you were the official liaison between him and S.H.I.E.L.D. You had a prior history with this man, and you were aware of the regulations forbidding such involvements, yet you blame Hill—"

"I managed to work with Steve—Captain America—for a long time without any, um, *incidents*. We're both pros. I didn't expect anything more to come of it. Maybe I was naïve to think it wouldn't go that way. But suddenly, it just *was*."

I know if I tell the shrink what he wants to hear, he's going to submit a more positive report that will look good in my personnel file. But what's the use of that? I know Steve would disapprove, and the thought of that makes me feel all hollow inside. Everything is so *complicated*. At first, I was in favor of the Registration Act. That hero-related tragedy in Stamford that resulted in kids dying shocked me to the core. I've never had much use for costumed heroes except for Cap and Falcon. I stood by and watched as Steve built a resistance movement, and saw him fight tooth and nail against his best friends. He paid a terrible price for putting himself above the law. When I tell the shrink all this, he suggests that I didn't want to betray the man I love.

There isn't a whole lot of use in explaining that every soldier knows two contradicting facts: Orders come before friendship, and there are few stronger bonds than those between comrades-in-arms. Most civilians don't get how we juggle those concepts because they've never been there and can't comprehend how people who have survived combat together feel about each other. It's why soldiers only tell *real* war stories to other soldiers.

It's the shrink's job to ferret all this out. So when he calls, I show him my hand. But I don't flip over my hole cards.

"In the end, Agent 13, you still betrayed him. Do you want to talk about that?"

"Steve had been underground for weeks. Every security agency and all the registration-compliant costumed heroes were searching for him, but we had a secret dead-drop for getting messages to each other. I arranged to meet him on a rooftop, and it just wasn't in his nature to suspect me of luring him into a trap. I'd never felt so dirty as when he kissed me there in the moonlight, and I kissed him back. Afterwards, in a tawdry safe room nearby, in the warm afterglow, he told me I wasn't going to change his mind. He said people had been turned into walking targets just for knowing him when he'd decided to make his identity public a few years ago, and some of them had been killed. It meant he could no longer partition his life or have any semblance of normalcy. 'I accepted that because Captain America is who I am, but I wouldn't wish it on anyone else,' is how he put it. So I told him it was still breaking the law, and the rule of law was what our country was founded on. He countered by telling me our country was founded on *breaking* the law, because that law was wrong. And then he quoted Ben Franklin and Thomas Paine."

"And during all of this, you knew a Cape-Killer Squad was on its way to the safe room?"

"I thought I could win him over. I thought if I could just talk to him face-to-face, I could at least make him reconsider. It was a desperate move to buy some time. I should have known Steve was willing to die for what he believed in, and I didn't want the man I loved to die."

"Agent 13, you have admitted to serious breaches of the Code of Conduct in your After-Action Statement. You did scramble the GPS tracer in your communications unit, and you did give the wrong address to the S.H.I.E.L.D. agents? You knew the agents would kick down the door of an empty apartment? You put love before duty. How do you resolve that ethical quandary in your head?"

"I'd planned to send a signal to the Cape-Killer Squad if I failed to persuade Steve. I really did. But when it came down to it,

I just couldn't. I don't know why. It's not like me at all. I'm a good soldier. I stood up and swore all the oaths. But when I was alone there with Steve, I asked him to stay, and I told him that I loved him—God, I hadn't said that in years. It just spilled out, and there it was in the room with us."

The shrink says exactly what I expect, that verbalizing what I'd bottled up was a healthy thing. His face is unreadable when he says it. I guess it's a basic requirement for psychiatrists. I'm a pretty damned good poker player, and I can usually spot some sort of giveaway, but there's not a glimmer there. Still, I trust the man, and I ask him outright if I'm no longer fit for duty. He tells me he doesn't know yet, and we should meet again in two days.

I'm very relieved, because I love my job despite everything.

As I go out the door, he tells me one last thing: "I don't believe we're done with you yet, Agent 13."

INTERLUDE #1

THE psychiatrist waits four hours after Agent 13, a.k.a. Sharon Carter, leaves his office. He performs a passive electronic sweep to make sure she didn't plant any bugs, and then takes the elevator to the main floor and leaves the S.H.I.E.L.D. administrative building by the night door, sweeping his card at the turnstile and waving to the guard. On the dimly lit street, he doubles back on himself twice to make sure he isn't being tailed and hails a cab to take him across town. It's past midnight, and traffic is thin. Exiting the cab, he walks several blocks, doubling back three times before he hops into another cab that deposits him at the gate of a small cemetery. The psychiatrist happens to have a key to the gate, but he waits until the street is deserted before he enters.

On the tree-shadowed path that runs between the tombstones, the Red Skull casually joins the psychiatrist on his late-night ramble. The psychiatrist doesn't seem as confident as he was with Sharon Carter.

"Did it have to be a cemetery?"

"Would you prefer I expose you to your colleagues instead, Doctor? I think not. Much more advantageous for them to believe you are being gnawed by death-watch beetles in some unmarked grave."

The psychiatrist turns off the nanotech holographic projector built into his belt buckle. The 3-D holo-mask that disguised his real features flickers for an instant, then disappears, revealing the bearded face of Doctor Faustus. The so-called "Master of Men's Minds" wedges a monocle over his left eye before he answers. He ignores the Red Skull's question.

"It disgusts me that I must disguise myself as a mongrel subhuman. I am frankly surprised that this ruse defies the security system of the S.H.I.E.L.D. Administration Building. It would not pass scrutiny on the Helicarrier."

"That will not be required. Does all go as planned?"

"Sharon Carter has no idea that I have been tampering with her thoughts and memories. Carter is extremely vulnerable at this time, and that makes the implants take root and establish themselves with credibility. When the time comes, Agent 13 will be right where we want her."

The Red Skull is already walking away and doesn't bother to turn his head when he replies to Doctor Faustus.

"She had better be, or it will be *your* fat head on the block."

T W O

THE black-clad masked man sprinting across the rooftops
in the dead of night still thinks of himself as a boy. That's because
he was so young the first time he died, and he has spent more than
two-thirds of his time on Earth in cryogenic stasis. The combat
boots on his feet came from a special lot made for elite Russian naval
infantry paratroopers during the Soviet era. The pistols in his nylon
shoulder holsters are 1911AI government-model .45 automatics
from a production run shipped to Russia during WWII that have
been retrofitted with high-spec heat-treated recoil springs and
tritium night sights. The numerous spare magazines are stainless
steel and loaded with jacketed hollow-point ammo. The body armor
built into his fire-resistant combat togs is an experimental Swiss
design, lightweight and flexible. He has knives, grenades, garroting
wire, nerve-toxin injectors, and other lethal devices jammed into
belt pouches, pockets, and hidden compartments. But the deadliest
weapon he possesses is his left arm.

The man who thinks of himself as a boy was born
in Shelbyville, Indiana, in 1925, and the name on his birth
certificate is James Buchanan Barnes. His mother is a mystery to
him; he barely remembers his father, who was killed in a training
accident at Fort Lehigh in Virginia. After he was unofficially
adopted as the camp mascot, he had a whole battalion of
substitute fathers and older brothers. One of them was Private

Steve Rogers, who went to war as Captain America and took the camp mascot along with him.

Bucky.

That's what the soldiers at Camp Lehigh called him, and that's how he answered to Captain America. He had forgotten all that for a long time. But now, as he crouches behind a roof ventilator assessing the security cams and defensive sensors of the seemingly derelict building across the alley, the restored memories flicker through his mind like old newsreel footage. Often, during the war, after sustained gunfire, his hearing had been degraded by temporary tinnitus, and his vision had been constricted by the "adrenaline tunnel," so the memories seem like silent movies shot through a narrow lens. Some of the more ghastly images speed by as if the Grim Reaper were riffling a deck of hellish flash cards: soldiers run over by Tiger tanks, the bloated bodies of a French family in a gutted farmhouse, partisans hanging from lampposts, a head rolling down a cobbled street, wounded men begging to be shot, a weeping *babushka* pushing a wheelbarrow piled with dead grandchildren, screams reverberating from inside a burning Sherman, a forest with dead paratroops dangling from shroud lines like Christmas ornaments. And those were snapshots of battles *won.*

The man who thinks of himself as the boy-soldier Bucky pops his head out from behind the ventilator and instantly notes the sensor units on the target building that are his most immediate threats. He bides his time to ensure his recon wasn't spotted. This patient wariness is the result of intensive training received during the Cold War.

"Cautious" was never an adjective one could apply to

Captain America during the conflict the Soviets called "The Great War Against Fascism." Never one to sneak up on a foe, Cap would charge Waffen SS machine-gun nests head-on, deflecting bullets with his Vibranium shield. Bucky would be right behind, trying to suppress flanking fire with his Thompson gun. Having no shield of his own, the boy sidekick had to trust wholly in Cap's ability to fend off all the incoming lead. His faith was bottomless.

All that changed for Bucky over the English Channel while he clung to the wing of a stolen top-secret drone-aircraft prototype.

The grown-up boy-soldier sticks his left arm out from behind cover. It is a cybernetic prosthetic strong enough to bend steel bars and punch through armor plate. One of the weapons it contains is a low-yield EMP generator capable of shutting down close-proximity mechanical devices controlled by solid-state electronics. The man in black has amped up the power setting to reach the spy-cam circuits and motion sensors across the alley. There is no hesitation on his part as he leaps across the gap separating the two buildings. He grabs a window ledge six floors above street level, out of the search fields of all the rooftop sensors.

The man who was once Bucky hangs motionless by his mechanical arm as he mentally clicks on the safety of his EMP weapon. This is not the original arm the Soviets fitted him with in the bad old days. This is a vastly improved model that even includes a holographic disguise suite, making it seem like a flesh-and-blood limb to the casual observer. Sometimes, he has ghost-memories of his own arm. Now, he remembers the mission to Baron Zemo's castle, during the war—the drone over the channel, and Captain America yelling at him to let go and abort the mission. But there was stupid pride at work there. A desire to prove himself to the mentor he admired so much. He had hung on too long; the drone self-destructed, blowing off his arm and plunging him into icy waters.

Everybody presumed he was dead. The recovery of his body by a Russian K-Class submarine was never reported to the Allies because of a tactical decision made on the spot. The boy-soldier remembers floating down a dark tunnel toward an ethereal white light, then abruptly being pulled back.

He now understands he was plucked from the brink of death by a Soviet intelligence officer named Vasily Karpov, who had the foresight to have him put into cryogenic suspension until that time when Russian medical technology had advanced to a state in which revival, reconstitution, and prosthetic improvements were possible.

The boy returned to the land of the living as an enhanced super-soldier with his memory selectively wiped. Reprogrammed to be loyal to Mother Russia, Karpov, and later to Karpov's heir and protégé, Aleksander Lukin. This super-soldier was deployed to the West as an assassin and saboteur by a directive of the Executive Action Department X of the KGB (*mokrie dela*, i.e. "wet-works") and assigned the code name "Winter Soldier."

The man who thinks of himself as a boy and was once called the Winter Soldier processes these memories in mere moments. He knows he has a thirty-second window before the security backup system reroutes feeds to standby sensors. It takes him fifteen seconds to unfasten the grill over the ventilation port with a mini electric screwdriver, and he is well inside the duct system when the backup sensors come online behind him.

Bucky is now inside a top-secret S.H.I.E.L.D. substation.

He drops from an interior ventilation duct into a deserted corridor and makes his way through the labyrinthine complex like a fast-moving wraith. The techs and operatives might sense something behind them in the more densely occupied passageways or catch a flitting motion in their peripheral vision, but there is nothing to be seen when they turn.

When he was the Winter Soldier, he would not have thought twice about breaking the neck or cutting the throat of anybody who impeded his way during a mission. He had killed hundreds and felt no remorse. But that was before Lukin sent him to retrieve the Cosmic Cube and he had his first encounter with Agent 13. Sharon Carter had informed Captain America of the Winter Soldier's amazing resemblance to Bucky, and Cap had taken it upon himself to track down the boy-soldier-turned-assassin and make amends for leaving him to his fate on the drone over the channel. Captain America prevailed, recaptured the Cube, and turned it on the Winter Soldier, telling him, "Remember who you are."

But "who you are" is more than memories of events. It is ethics, morals, loyalties, obligations, faith, and all the lines in the sand you have drawn to protect your integrity and self-esteem. Who can imagine the avalanche of despair, anguish, and guilt that overwhelmed a patriotic kid who had been turned against his own country? Bucky had crushed the Cube and teleported away.

The techs and operatives have nothing to fear from the seasoned killer darting from doorway to doorway behind them. Not that he wouldn't defend himself if attacked, but his techniques would be debilitating rather than lethal. There might be pain and scarring, but no new bodies on the morgue slab.

In one of the lowest levels, a secure door slides open in a mainframe-access room where cooling units are humming constantly and breath turns to frost. A black-gloved finger taps in a twenty-digit access code and scans in a hologram of Nick Fury's thumbprint. The small square of floor beneath his feet glides silently down into the sub-subbasement and an alternate command center known only to S.H.I.E.L.D. agents at the directorship level.

The figure standing at the monitoring station in the command center is wearing a director's uniform and an eye patch. A facial-recognition scanner would identify him as Nick Fury— former director of S.H.I.E.L.D., veteran of three wars, and black belt in Taekwondo. Although Bucky is careful to approach from an oblique angle so his reflection on the monitor screens doesn't give him away, his first punch is easily blocked. The fight that ensues is brutal, brief, and silent but for the dull thuds and grunts of the combatants. The man who was once the Winter Soldier punches past a combination inside block and palm block to hit a secret switch on the temple of his opponent. The single eyeball rolls up, and a computer-generated voice announces, "Emergency shutdown activated." With that, the Nick Fury Life Model Decoy turns itself off and sinks to its knees on the tiled floor.

Bucky pulls out a S.H.I.E.L.D.-issue encrypted holographic communicator and activates it on channel-hopping security mode. A flickering image of the *real* Nick Fury appears in front of Bucky, but his voice emanates from the communicator.

"So Sharon's intel was on the money? I haven't been to this substation in years. Wasn't even aware it was still operational."

"Yeah, I got in slick as a whistle, and this automaton version of you was right where she said it would be."

"Let's get on with it, kid. Inject the nano Trojan horse where I showed you."

Bucky peels the face off the robotic Fury to reveal the access ports to the organic memory banks and pushes the plunger on the nanobot injector. The lone eyeball in the mechanical head revolves and locks forward when Bucky plugs a cable into a data-input port. "It's weird," he mutters. "This thing even *moves* exactly like you."

"It's the new advanced-model L.M.D., and it probably thinks it *is* me. The current honchos don't mind that one bit. All the soldiers and rank and file believe it really is me, and it's a damn convenient blame-dump if the whole Registration and Cape-Killer thing goes south on 'em. Plug that cable into the console next to the monitor. The output port with the red triangle next to it."

Bucky follows Fury's instructions, and dense pages of code start scrolling quickly down the monitor.

"What does this do?" Bucky asks. "Are you in their system now?"

"I never left the system, kid. I may be hiding out, but I ain't blind and deaf. But now, whenever this L.M.D. stand-in logs in, I'll be able to access him, and I'll have eyes and ears on the Helicarrier."

Other screens light up on the console. More data, and sped-up video. Scenes of a major scrum between Captain America's resistance and Iron Man's pro-registration supporters flash by. It is a visual documentation of the superhuman Civil War that tore the costumed community in half. Bucky watches it, dumbfounded.

"What are they *doing?* I know I'm still in the dark about most of these guys, but it looks like they've all lost their minds. How can Cap be letting this happen?"

"Let it happen? Kid, Cap is trying to *stop* it. Just like I am. And now, maybe you, too."

Bucky stares morosely at a screen on which Captain America is going head-to-head with Iron Man. He can see that neither man has his heart in it—both pulling punches, holding back their full powers. The Civil War holds no logic or reason to him, but neither does any war that he can think of. Personal ambition, nationalism, greed, and humanity's hardwired fear of the "other" collide in an ethical vacuum, and wholesale slaughter results. He sees no safe path out of the minefield and is reluctant to jump into the thick of it.

"It's different for me, Colonel. Because of what I've done."

"They hijacked your body, kid, and used it for their own purposes. That wasn't *you*."

The man who killed for the *Rodina*, the Mother Land, takes a hard look at the holographic image of Nick Fury. When Bucky was Cap's sidekick, Fury was already a grown man—a sergeant leading a small unit of elite troops called the "Howling Commandos." There are few left alive who can remember the world seen through Bucky's eyes—and the eyes of Fury, Captain America, and the Red Skull. The entire world was at war then, with two conflicting ideologies allying to crush the axis of fascism. Millions dead, and nothing much has changed—except for a noticeable loss of innocence and the steady erosion of optimism. Fury appears middle-aged, rather than elderly—a result of the experimental Infinity Formula that saved the then-sergeant's life during the last year of the war, a snippet of data the former KGB assassin remembers from a briefing at the *Lubyanka*, the KGB headquarters building in Moscow.

"I came here to do this job for you because I owe it to Cap.

I'm not signing up for another hitch here, sir. I heard that speech Senator Wright made when they passed the Registration Act. He made a big deal out of the Philadelphia bombing, the terror strike I conducted as Winter Soldier. So that makes me partially responsible for this mess."

"All the more reason to pitch in on making it right, Bucky."

"I'll think about it, Colonel Fury."

The monitors on the console freeze on images of Aleksander Lukin passing through the gates of the Latverian embassy. Bucky taps the screen.

"That's the evil S.O.B. who unfroze me every time he needed something blown up or a chop-job done. What's he doing hooking up with Doctor Doom?"

The Fury hologram is evasive.

"You leave Lukin to me, kiddo. The screen freeze means the download is done, so it's time for you to get out of Dodge."

"Consider me gone. Are we still a go on that other thing?"

"Affirmative. I am blacking out the pertinent S.H.I.E.L.D. satellites and surveillance cams in five minutes, so time it to be in place by then. Blackout will max at two minutes before security backups kick in, so do the dirty and lam out on the double."

It takes four minutes and thirty-seven seconds for Bucky to exfiltrate from the S.H.I.E.L.D. substation and make his way to the location designated by Fury. A small recon squad of Cape-Killers arrives ten seconds later, dispatched to investigate the surveillance-cam sighting of a rogue superhuman. It takes less than ten seconds for the squad leader to ascertain that the suspect they have surrounded on the dark and lonely street corner is a holographic decoy. Before they can report the ruse to headquarters, a cross-channel communication disruptor is tossed into their midst, followed by a smoke-generator grenade and an optical-nullification strobe. This is a situation for which they have no protocols; when they realize there is an armed hostile attacking them, they make the mistake of blindly opening fire. The ordnance they are expending is designed to combat superhumans and is equally effective against armored power-suits. With communications down, there is no way to order a cease-fire.

The last man standing attempts to reload his weapon, but it is already too late. The attacker appropriates one of the squad's assault weapons and shreds the last Cape-Killer's armored suit, destroying the power pack. With the servos and motors shut down, the suit is nothing but a very heavy containment device. With the oxygen regulator no longer functioning, the Cape-Killer begins to lose consciousness and falls to the pavement. Seconds pass, he can breathe again, and he hears a voice.

"I'm unlocking his helmet and removing it. I guess you can reverse-engineer it and figure out a way to fight a whole army of 'em, huh, Colonel? I'd love to see Tony Stark's face when that happens."

The Cape-Killer tries to blink his eyes back into focus as the helmet is lifted away. The face looming over him starts to resolve into something vaguely human when a black-gloved fist smashes down, and everything goes black.

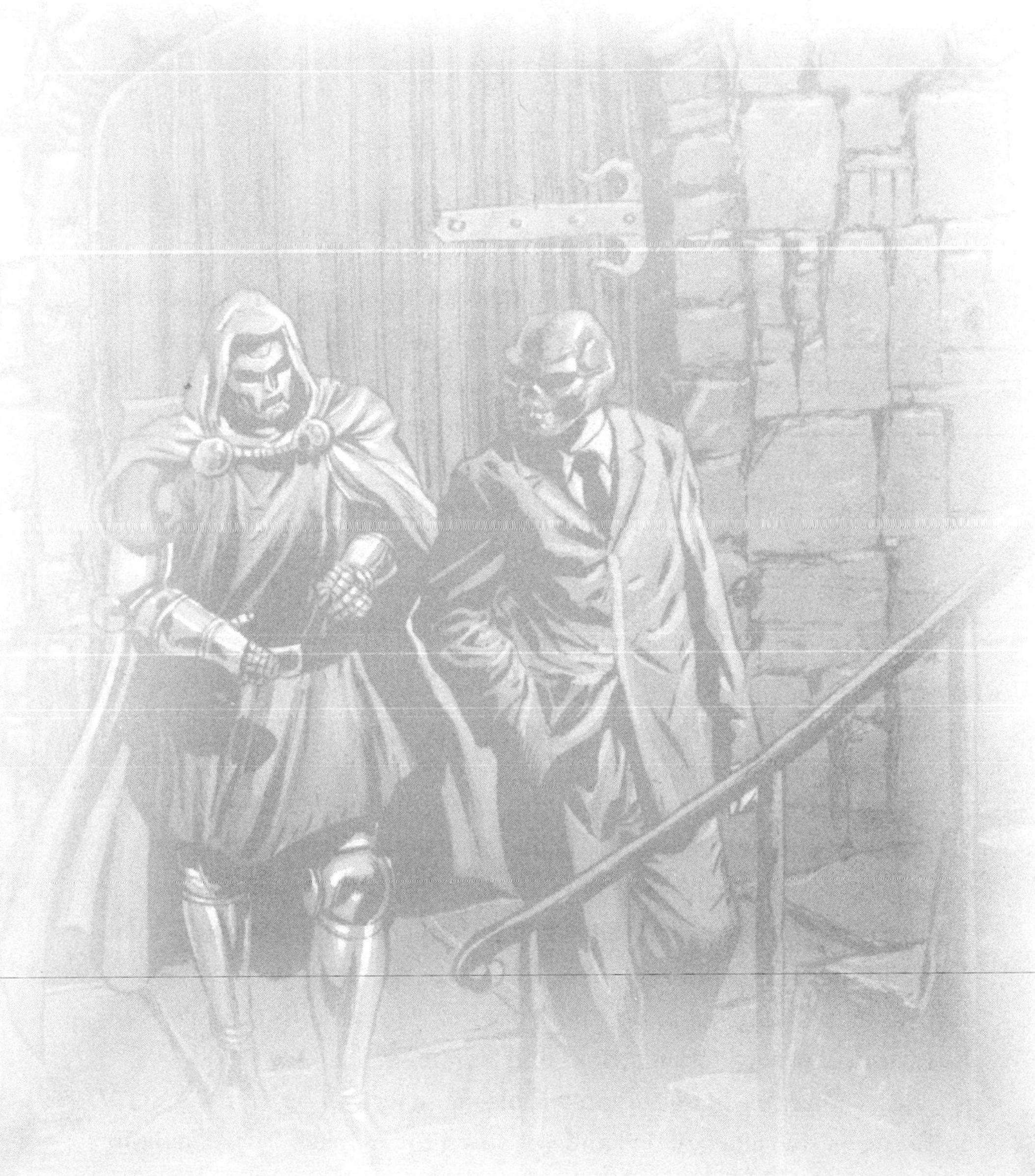

INTERLUDE #2

ACROSS the Atlantic, in his baronial castle in Latveria, Victor von Doom gazes with mild disdain upon the Red Skull—who is, after all, nothing but an elevated thug who rose to power on the coattails of jackbooted fascists. Acknowledging the Red Skull's Machiavellian skills and technological prowess is one thing, but accepting him as an equal is out of the question. One must have *standards*, mustn't one? Toleration is a step below acceptance, and Doctor Doom grudgingly grants that accommodation only because it is to his advantage to do so.

The Red Skull is not impressed with the ruler of Latveria. He sees Doom as the offspring of Gypsies, lording it over a debased population; a megalomaniac with a taste for grand opera and a fascination with mysticism that belies his scientific training.

They both desire something the other has, and this is the root of their present accord. They are standing in Doctor Doom's laboratory, which is equipped with a bewildering mixture of modern technology and the paraphernalia of a medieval alchemist. If the space it occupies looks like a dungeon, it is because that is exactly what it used to be. There are centrifuges and computer terminals where torture racks and iron maidens once stood.

They exchange whatever pleasantries can be exchanged between two icons of evil and get down to business. The Red Skull speaks first.

"Have your people found what I told them they would find in that dig in Germany? Are you satisfied with the result?"

"Yes, Skull. We are quite pleased. And you shall have what you requested. Doom is true to his word."

"Do you believe it now? That you had a previous existence in Eisendorf five hundred years ago? That you were the legendary Baron of Iron?"

Doctor Doom fingers a component on his workbench that was once part of a temporal-displacement machine. He knows the dangers of time travel—the multiple realities that it creates, and the disruption to the order of the cosmos.

"That is not what I *was*, Skull. That is what I shall *become*. What we found in the Eisendorf excavation is an anomaly in the time stream. It is a node in an infinite loop that I shall tap into one day and unlock unimaginable secrets. The device you want shall be delivered to the Kronas lab. You understand it can be used only once?"

The Red Skull smiles under his mask.

"That will be all I require, von Doom, to ensure this Civil War is just the beginning of my enemy's suffering."

THREE

DEPUTY Director Maria Hill requested my presence on the Command and Operations Bridge of the S.H.I.E.L.D. Helicarrier, which I reckoned was a good thing. If a head honcho is planning on giving a subordinate a good drumming, or informing them of charges being brought or a demotion being handed down, they usually ask them into their office and close the door.

Not to be confused with the attack bridge, which is topside along one edge of the flight deck, the Command and Operations Bridge looms over the Internal Command Center just forward of the main hangar deck. It's basically a giant catwalk that affords the command element an unimpeded 180-degree view forward through a Vibranium-infused tempered glass "greenhouse," and visual access to flat-screen situational displays and holographic real-time event models along the bulkheads.

So there I am on the open catwalk with my boss, in plain view of hundreds of techs and crew-people who keep the massive attack platform humming and in the air. Deputy Director Hill has strategically placed herself on an elevated platform of the catwalk so I have to look up at her. The panorama of New York City from five thousand feet stretches vertiginously behind her, providing backlighting that diffuses the age-lines around her eyes. No fool, she. No idle chitchat, just straight to the point.

"You are being reassigned, Agent 13. There will be no

administrative actions, no reprimands in your personnel file, and your security clearance will remain at ultra-ultra. You're very lucky that the shrink at Admin filed a glowingly positive report on your evaluation. The tea-leaf readers at Risk Assessment also gave you a clean bill of health despite your insubordination last month."

I figure I'm getting off a lot easier than I expected, so I keep my neutral face on while I thank her respectfully. But she can't let it just lie there. No, that would be too easy.

"It goes against my instincts, Sharon, but I'm going along with the consensus here. I'm considering this a one-time offense, and you are damn well going to make certain that it is."

Nice passive implied threat there. Neat move using my given name instead of my number. Bet she picked that up from a book on how to be a successful manager. She's waiting for a reply, a reassurance of compliance or a gesture of obeisance. I'm just not in the mood to suck up, so I simply tell her that I was conflicted, but I'm not anymore. Just the facts, ma'am. She seems to take a quiet delight in informing me of my new assignment. Her eyes flick left and right, and she leans close to whisper, "You're joining our new task force that will be hunting down Nick Fury."

Great. Now my job is tracking down my *real* boss, the guy I report to off-the-record, and my best chance for helping Steve get through the current situation. Talk about piling stressors on top of stressors. I've got a lot to keep close to the vest and under my hat right now, and I get one step closer to blowing it every second I spend in the company of people like Maria Hill and Tony Stark. I'm trying so hard to conjure up those chilling alpha waves I don't notice there's somebody standing in the corner of my tiny "stateroom" in the Bachelor Officer Quarters until after I enter and relock the door.

"Anything wrong, Agent 13?"

It's Nick Fury. Or at least the Life Model Decoy of him they have walking around so all the brass with "ultra-ultra-plus" clearances can pretend he's still around, and being all cooperative and such, when he's actually hunkered down in an undisclosed location surrounded by passive jammers and not-so-passive booby traps. I have to watch myself here. Is this the L.M.D. that Winter Soldier turned? I know there are a number of Nick Fury decoys, but could this be one of the ones that isn't co-opted and reporting back to the one-eyed Colonel? My answer is noncommittal. In fact, it's a question.

"Why are you here?"

The robotic Fury raises its eye patch to reveal a retinal scanner.

"I was scanning your quarters for surveillance devices. There is a need for my controller to have a meeting with you. Please step forward to confirm your identity."

I pass the test, the patch gets lowered, and the communications interface kicks in, turning the L.M.D. into a disconcerting Nick Fury-proxy with all the gestures and tics of the real thing.

"Hey, Sharon, we got a real problem here."

"You're telling *me*, Colonel Fury? I think she knows I've been in contact with you."

"Maria Hill doesn't know squat. She *suspects*. But hell, she suspects everyone I was close to. She's even got Dum Dum Dugan's bathroom bugged. I wouldn't wish that surveillance assignment on Baron Strucker."

Conversing with an L.M.D. in proxy mode is off-putting. I keep forgetting, and try to make eye contact. There's also a slight time delay, which makes me suspect the encrypted signal is bouncing off a satellite. I cut him off abruptly.

"With all due respect, you are not listening, sir. She just put me on the team that's supposed to track you down. And now you send your double-agent L.M.D. to my B.O.Q. stateroom for an information exchange that could have been safer with a dead-drop?"

The Fury duplicate curls his lip, raises one eyebrow, and scratches the back of his head. Somewhere, the real Fury is doing the exact same thing. He's gesturing at me to sit down, like there's a long story coming.

"Kiddo, you're the one who ain't listening. I said we got a problem, but it's not Maria Hill."

I sit.

"First off, you still got that early model S.H.I.E.L.D.-issue neural-neutralizer pistol?"

"Yes, it's locked in a safe in my bedroom. Cut to the chase, Fury. Who is it?"

"It's Cap."

It's a long story, all right—full of dramatic tension, good intentions, and bad things happening to good people. Shakespeare would be proud. "Full of sound and Fury," you might say, but signifying a lot. At the end of the story, he gives me instructions that make everything I've done for him so far seem like a walk in the sun. Not just bending the rules and insubordination—chargeable willful acts that violate three national-security acts, the U.N.

Charter, several local statutes, and a dozen articles of the S.H.I.E.L.D. Uniform Code of Justice. But Fury reads me like a book, and he has me firmly behind the eight ball. Big Mama Thornton and Janis Joplin were right about what love is: It's a ball and chain.

Fury tells me there's a bundle for me in my desk drawer before he shuts down communications and the L.M.D. reverts to being the not-so-exact duplicate that he is. I wait until the robotic Fury lets himself out of my stateroom before I dare to open the drawer. What I find there is what appears to be a remote-control unit that has a "safety" cover over a red button under an unlit light marked "armed." The other item is a "black box" about the size of a USB memory stick.

I spend an hour in-processing my new assignment. I get one printout of my official S.H.I.E.L.D. orders assigning me to my new duties; a new security card; a list of access codes, passwords, and mission-specific acronyms I have to memorize; and a reminder to be at the team operations briefing in one of the wardrooms at 0800 tomorrow. That's the easy part. Finagling a trip-ticket and checking a S.H.I.E.L.D. Mark V Flying Car out of the hangar deck takes some doing. I have the black box I got from the Fury L.M.D.—I think Fury hands them out like burger-chain toy giveaways. It's a nontraceable cross-channel jammer that amplifies nearby wavelengths to overpower spy cams and mics. It will also spoof the GPS built into the Flying Car, as well as the one in my communicator. It tells Central Processing that I'm in Hoboken when I'm really in a part of downtown Brooklyn that hasn't been infested with hipsters and still has a rundown warehouse district.

I turned on the infrared dampers, Doppler deflectors, and

passive cloaking as soon as I crossed the East River, so it's not easy
to spot my Flying Car as I creep past water tanks and cooling vents
on the darkened rooftops. I really wish the S.H.I.E.L.D. techs had
chosen a less conspicuous model than an Aston Martin Vanquish
convertible. But at least the seats are comfortable, and the sound
system takes no prisoners.

The shockwave from the explosion buffets the car one
second before I hear the big whomping thud. Shattered glass tinkles
for a two-block radius. My GPS destination is the blast's epicenter.
Right where I'm supposed to find Cap. I have to fight the controls
to stabilize the Flying Car since it switches over to helicopter-style
inputs while in hovering mode, turning the steering wheel into the
cyclic and the fake gearshift into the collective. Above eighty mph
forward speed, the controls revert to fixed-wing mode. I position
myself where I can just see down into the alley, but keep most of
the vehicle hidden from any eyes down there. A steel door has
blown out, and black smoke is billowing from inside. A single figure
staggers out of the burning building.

A figure with a big, round shield.

But there are others leaping down into the alley from fire
escapes and running in from the street. Menacing figures wearing
armored suits and brandishing overkill weaponry.

The Cape-Killer Squad is too intent on their target to see
me. Their target is Cap, and they've got him cornered. I personally
doubt they have a chance against Cap since Winter Soldier was
able to wipe up the street with them. But that incident has made
the Cape-Killers jumpy and their already itchy trigger fingers even
itchier. The squad facing Cap is a reinforced heavy-weapons unit

authorized to load 60mm "Hulk-Buster" rounds and hyper-velocity armor-piercing micro-projectiles. Their built-in loudspeakers echo in the alley.

"Captain America, you are ordered to surrender by authorization of orders from the president! Put the shield down, and raise both hands palms forward and open! You are already injured, so don't force us to open fire."

What? He's *wounded?* I have to bank severely to get a clearer view. There's blood trickling from his nose, and he's unsteady on his feat. Those are symptoms of concussion, inner-ear imbalance, and worse. He was in an enclosed space during an explosion, so he's got temporary tinnitus degrading his hearing. There's a good chance he can't understand the orders and ultimatums he's being given. Cap answers the Cape-Killers, but doesn't comply.

"I've had this conversation with you people a few times already. Hasn't Director Hill shown you the videos of those encounters?"

It really looks like the fools are going to unload on Cap. Two or three are yelling at the same time, which is never a good sign in a group of nervous armed men. I roll out over the alley, point the nose towardthe ground, and goose the throttle while I grab the "remote" I got from the Fury L.M.D. I flip open the safety cover, which makes the "armed" light glow; point it at the Cape-Killers; and punch the red button—all while plummeting straight down. Just before impact, I execute another roll and pull back hard on the wheel, which brings me level and burns off drop velocity. The Cape-Killers are all twitching on the alley pavement like a bunch of dying cockroaches.

I know I don't have to slow down for Cap to be able to hop on board. I floor it as soon as I feel the jolt of him dropping into the shotgun seat and grab altitude. I tell him there're more armored suits on the way, and we have to make ourselves scarce. He's looking back, concerned.

"What did you do to them? Are they hurt?"

That's just like him. No hello kiss, no "thanks for saving me, sweetie." But worrying about the welfare of hard men who were ready to kill him, that's what tops his priority list. I wave the remote at him, with the safety reengaged.

"They're just stunned and unconscious. Electromagnetic overload pulse—broadcast directly into their suits via their commo systems. Fury got his hands on one of their helmets and reverse-engineered a way to disable them without killing the grunts inside."

He pulls off his cowl, and his eyes are clear and bright as they stare back at me. If I had to name the shade of blue they are, I'd say "uncompromising." I'd like nothing better than to be driving through the night with Steve in an open-top sports car, but that's in another reality. In this one, I'm aiding and abetting a fugitive in a twenty million dollar piece of classified hardware. I keep my eyes on the altimeter and artificial-horizon indicator, but I can feel those uncompromising eyes drilling into the side of my head.

"Is that why you flew to my rescue?" he asks. "Because Nick Fury ordered you to?"

I'm annoyed and don't want to answer. I ask my own question.

"What happened back there before the explosion?"

He's not annoyed. He's more disappointed—which, coming from Cap, is like fifty lashes with the cat-o'-nine-tails. I swallow hard and listen.

"I'd been spinning my wheels too long, and I let this whole

conflict steer me off course. I made up my mind it wouldn't take me over, wouldn't let me accept an imposed status quo, wouldn't let me ignore my duty. Back before the war—the *big* war—I stood up in a windowless room in Fort Hamilton, faced the flag, and took an oath to 'defend and protect the Constitution of the United States of America.' There is no expiration date on that oath, no escape clause, no rider of 'limited liability.' I don't care if I'm the only one who sees it that way. It's my own weight to carry—to paraphrase Father Flanagan, 'It ain't heavy, it's my country.'

"So I said to hell with Tony and S.H.I.E.L.D., and all of them. The Red Skull is my priority, and I aim to keep him square in my sights. That psychopath made his televised statement a week before Nitro blew up a whole neighborhood in Stamford and killed all those innocent civilians, a week before Tony and Reed Richards decided to build a gulag for noncompliant super heroes in the Negative Zone. Organizing the resistance to the Registration Act blinded me, but a one-eyed man saw everything more clearly. Nick Fury never let up on his hunt for Red Skull, and this is the first time in a dog's age that he's picked up anything resembling a scent. Fury intercepted a transmission from A.I.M. to the Skull that originated in the warehouse back there in Brooklyn."

I feel compelled to butt in.

"Advanced Idea Mechanics used to be part of Hydra, but split off in the sixties. They're anarchistic tech-savants, one-stop shopping for state-of-the-art nasty hardware. But they can't extrapolate the results of their actions. Red Skull has been a frequent client of theirs."

Immediately, I feel foolish for having told him something he already knows. Why do I keep trying to impress him? I want to bang my head on the steering wheel.

"A tenuous connection," he says, "but it was all I had, so it was worth following up. I got there to find that Nick wasn't the only one who overheard that message. I caught the rear end of a Hydra assault force entering through the alley door. They only left two guards at the door, so I bounced my shield off their heads, appropriated one of their acid-green pajama-suits, and took a stroll through the premises. My guess is that Hydra was taking advantage of the ongoing chaos to make a power grab, and a rival group like A.I.M. was an obvious target. Hydra was too late, though. The facility was deserted and stripped. All the burn boxes were still smoking, as were the mainframes. Distinctive stench of thermite in the air, and the drop pits full of acid were still bubbling.

"The last place they would wipe would be the security station, and that's where I lucked out. The timed self-destruct module had failed. One of the fatal flaws in A.I.M. technology is overengineering—and the more complexity you have, the more chances for things to go wrong. Playbacks of security videos from labs and workstations were up and running on the bank of displays. None of the doors to those facilities was wide enough for M.O.D.O.K., so who was working here? And why was he or she reporting to Red Skull? I was pretty shocked when a face I knew appeared on one of the screens, but the room filled up with Hydra goons at that moment."

"They spotted my non-Hydra red boots right away, and it was all downhill from there—mainly for *them*. There were hordes of them, crawling out of the woodwork like green-and-yellow termites. They're very good at shouting slogans, but not so good at hand-to-hand combat. Opening fire on full automatic in closed quarters was not to their advantage, either. When you're grossly outnumbered, friendly fire is your friend. Their leaders are fitted out with Semtex underwear and have orders to self-destruct if they determine a mission has been compromised. If he hadn't announced his intentions, I doubt I would have been able to get my shield up in time."

I tell Cap that Fury had found out that the A.I.M. cell got tipped off and flew the coop. Fury also had hard intel that Hydra was on the scene, but he had no way to warn Cap because all their communication is through dead-drops. Sending a backup was his only choice.

"But why send you?" he asks. "I thought you were conflicted?"

"I got off the fence after they blew a hole in Goliath's chest."

Cap stays silent until after we cross the East River and make our way over the rooftops of Tribeca. I know a few dark alleys off Hudson Street where I can drop him off without being seen. I switch to hover mode and flare in to touch down lightly. Cap pulls his cowl back on but doesn't open the door.

"Those Cape-Killers showed up awfully fast after the explosion."

I'd been thinking the same thing. He goes on.

"Tony and Reed have cut unholy alliances with some pretty nasty characters. Bullseye and Green Goblin are world-class psychotic sociopaths..."

There's real anguish in his eyes when he asks, "You don't think they'd use Hydra, do you?"

I level with him. What else can you do with Captain America?

"I wouldn't have thought so, but I didn't think *any* of you would have done half the things you've done recently. Where does it end, Steve? After you and Tony Stark beat each other to death?"

"It won't come to that," he says as he steps away from me, out into the alley. "You know, I found out something important before Hydra interrupted me. I know who was using that A.I.M. facility. And if he's in league with Red Skull, we've got bigger problems than any of my differences with Iron Man."

I watch Captain America walk away, not knowing this is the last I will see of him until after he sacrifices his freedom to end the Civil War.

INTERLUDE #3

THE Kronas Corporation Tower is an artless pile of steel and glass that is to architecture what fife-and-drum corps are to music. Its lack of a pleasing aesthetic is intentional. It is meant to project power and authority without standing out too much from its neighboring skyscrapers in Midtown Manhattan. Hidden behind the gleaming façade are areas and entire floors sealed off from the casual visitor or average employee. Armored, soundproofed, and shielded by electronic baffles, they house armories, training halls, military-style command centers, and advanced-technology laboratories.

In one of those laboratories tucked into an unmarked level between the twelfth and fourteenth floors, the Red Skull is giving an introductory tour to the new director of research, who had formerly been ensconced at an A.I.M. facility in Brooklyn.

"The best that money can buy, Herr Zola," the Red Skull grins. "You will be able to finish your work here under our direct protection."

The holographic face projected inside the chest of the robotic body answers in a computer-generated voice.

"I prefer to operate under my own supervision, but this will suffice for now. I note your use of the collective pronoun. Am I speaking to Red Skull, Aleksander Lukin, or the pair of you in concert?"

The death's-head grin never wavers, but the tone of voice grows colder.

"The Red Skull is firmly in charge here, but Lukin is necessary for autonomous bodily functions. He is no more than a building superintendant locked in the utility basement." He pauses briefly, and the sham camaraderie returns. "Since the nature of some of your work here is related to your...*condition*—that is, the process by which you transfer your consciousness from one robotic body to another; perhaps we can discuss the actual mechanics of that process some time over a glass of schnapps and a vial of gear lubricant?"

The mechanical construct that houses Arnim Zola's intellect swivels the psychotronic ESP box that sits where a head would be on a human. The single unblinking red visual sensor in the middle of the box focuses on the Red Skull.

"Ah, but we know the discussion you pursue will be about your *own* condition, Herr Schmidt." The robotic voice manages to convey a modicum of *Schadenfreude*. "But I do not reveal data essential to my continued existence. I thought I had made that clear to you many years ago when you were funding my work in Central America. You may taste of what I create for you, but you shall not be privy to the recipe."

The Red Skull assumes the face of acceptance, but what is inside his head is another matter.

"Your terms are quite satisfactory, as long as I get what is needed. Your importance to this project is paramount. My master plan would not get very far without the unique genius of Arnim Zola."

The face in the robot's thorax never blinks. The lips move, but the jaw does not.

"And what is the plan this time, Johann?"

"We're going to destroy Captain America and everything he holds dear!"

"Oh, that one again?"

FOUR

RECENT events have played out so drastically that my perception of time has taken a real beating.

I can barely believe that Steve Rogers, the hero known around the world as Captain America, has been incarcerated like a common criminal for all these weeks. It makes me angry, sad, and ashamed all at once. I'm angry with the government for currying to paranoia, sad that the citizenry let it happen, and ashamed of myself for not doing more to stand up for the man I love.

America has a long history of turning its back on its heroes after their shelf lives expire. The Rough Riders who followed Teddy Roosevelt up San Juan Hill came home with malaria and ended up quarantined in a tent hospital at the far end of Long Island, where hundreds died while wealthy summer residents whined about being indisposed by sick soldiers. The doughboys who survived the trenches and mustard gas of World War I marched on Washington when Congress reneged on the bonuses they were promised. President Herbert Hoover ordered the Army to disperse the marchers, and American soldiers did so by opening fire on the veterans. GIs who were sprayed with Agent Orange in Vietnam and exposed to toxic substances during the Gulf War waited years for settlements, and many died before they received a single penny. So much for heroes, huh?

Every American knows the story of Steve Rogers—the

skinny, sickly kid who grew up on the mean streets of New York City back during the Great Depression. How he saw the best and worst this great country had to offer. How he sat, enraged, watching newsreels of the Nazi *Blitzkrieg* devastating Europe. How he was declared "unfit" and designated "4-F" when he tried to enlist.

We know how a general in charge of a secret project code-named "Operation: Rebirth" recognized the courage, determination, and honor within that young Steve Rogers. That general, Chester Phillips, asked him to take a risk far greater than parachuting behind enemy lines or storming a beachhead into fields of intersecting machine-gun fire. Steve was supposed to be the first of a whole army of super-soldiers made possible by a serum invented by Dr. Abraham Erskine. That serum had never been tested on a human; for all anybody knew, the side effects could be lethal. That didn't put Steve off one bit. It just made him more determined to go ahead and take the risk if it meant possibly saving thousands of American soldiers' lives.

We all know that everything went wrong when a fanatical Nazi spy sabotaged Operation: Rebirth and shot Dr. Erskine dead before the scientist had a chance to record the latest changes to the formula and treatment, rendering it impossible to recreate. Steve Rogers would be the country's first and only super-soldier, the sole hero who had to march on in place of the many others who might have been.

I'm standing in Foley Square in Lower Manhattan in sight of the long steps that lead up to the classical Grecian pillars of the Federal Courthouse. A crowd has been gathering there since dawn. It's what you might call a polarized gathering. Some are holding signs calling Cap a traitor. Others have preprinted placards reading, "FREE CAPTAIN AMERICA." Most of the truly hateful signs are misspelled: "Hang the Trayter!"

Some in the crowd want blood. They sat in front of their home entertainment centers watching the Civil War on plasma screens with surround sound while ingesting great quantities of cholesterol and sugar. They saw the live telecast of the climactic battle during which Captain America threw down his mask, gave up the resistance, and surrendered to the authorities. Their pointy little heads had been inflamed by AM-radio pundits, and now they're demanding "justice" with all the moral authority of a lynch mob.

Others remember the Captain America who fought the good fight and never budged an inch on his core beliefs. They respected the Captain America who could not be swayed by fickle public opinion or bought by special interests. They loved the Captain America who clearly put *We the People* before himself.

I'm firmly in the latter camp, but I'm so far ahead of the pack that they can't even see my back. I'm not standing here waiting to catch a glimpse of a tarnished icon as they parade him through the "perp walk" to face arraignment before a federal judge. I'm standing here armed and ready. I am determined that Captain America is not going to spend another day behind bars.

I hear Nick Fury in my earpiece, telling me it's a risky plan, but it's going to work. I tell him I don't need a pep talk. I need backup I can count on.

"I've got a real hotshot watching your six, kiddo."

"One guy? He'd better be good, Colonel..."

"Next best thing to Cap himself."

I'm thinking there's a big gap between Cap and second best, but my boat has sunk before it got out of the slip if I can't trust Fury's judgment. So I wait, and the crowd gets antsy. There are senior citizens here who were probably kids when the newsreels of Cap were playing in all the theaters. Their opinions were formed when they were young, and they aren't about to change them at this late date.

Movie newsreels were long gone before I was born, but my Aunt Peggy had a 35mm projector. She'd wheel it into her living room, and we'd sit there on winter evenings watching reel after reel of "The March of the News" in grainy black and white—me in my Doc Dentons, and her in a pink chenille robe. There wasn't a lot of footage of Cap in real action—for obvious reasons—but there were plenty of shots of him talking to the troops before a big mission or visiting the wounded in field hospitals. The looks on the faces of those war-weary GIs told the whole story. They all knew Cap would take a bullet for any of them. They all knew he was one of their own.

It wasn't until years later that I found out Aunt Peggy had worked with Cap when she was in France with the Resistance and briefly fallen in love, the only way you can with bombs and artillery shells hitting all around—with wild abandon. All I knew when I was a kid was that she liked to watch those old newsreels over and over, even though they made her cry.

I didn't understand those tears until I was a young S.H.I.E.L.D. agent, and I came face-to-face with the man she'd lost. He moved like an Olympic athlete and fought like a heavyweight champ. And for all the combat skill and awesome power he exuded, you could still look in his eyes and see nothing but compassion and honesty. Like Peggy, I fell in love immediately—even though I knew that life would take us down different paths, and whatever happiness we could have would be offset by pain and tears.

My mind gets snapped back to the present by a ripple of expectancy in the crowd. A superhuman-detention van is coming down the street between two armored cars. It's trailed by unmarked SUVs full of U.S. marshals.

A door that could have come off a bank vault opens at the rear of the van, and it takes two burly guards to help Cap down because the strength-dampening restraints they've put on him make it an effort just to walk. They've also replaced his Vibranium-laced costume with a cheap imitation that won't stop their bullets if they need to get tough with their prisoner.

The press weenies are elbowing their way to the front, cameras held high, and shouting out questions—

"Was Tony Stark right?"

"Are you supporting the Registration Act now?"

"Have you resigned as Captain America?"

Cap is half a head taller than the biggest marshal, so I can see his blond head moving within the cordon of blue jackets heading from the van to the courthouse steps. I begin to shove my way closer. I've got the authority of my S.H.I.E.L.D. uniform to help clear the way. Part of the mob is chanting "traitor!" A young girl yells, "We love you, Cap!" Something goes flying through the air. It's a rotten tomato. It hits Steve right in his face. He can't wipe it away because of the restraints. All he can do is look back in the direction it came from. There's no hate in that look, just a calm sense of pity. The marshals are alert now. Their eyes scan the crowd, and their hands rest on the butts of their pistols. One of them looks directly at me. I shift sideways, ducking down, but continue to press forward. I pop up to get my bearings and see Steve shifting his gaze from over his shoulder to the back of the marshal in front of him. Crowd density is thicker the closer I get—I'm less than ten feet away, and I can see that what Cap has been staring at on the marshal's back is a red laser spotting dot. *The kind of dot that sits on the point-of-aim of a high-power sniper rifle.*

I fill my lungs to shout out, but Steve yells, "Look out," and throws himself forward to cover that red dot with his own body. I hear the wet slap of the bullet hitting Steve in the back before the rifle shot echoes across Foley Square, and red blood sprays across blue marshals' jackets on the white courthouse steps.

"Sniper!"

I don't know whether it's me shouting that, or somebody else. There's an eerie second of silence, then pandemonium. The U.S. Marshals, NYPD, and Homeland Security converge on Cap as everybody else flees in panic. My black-and-white S.H.I.E.L.D. outfit marks me as authorized law enforcement as a protective wall of blue gets thrown around Cap. They all let me through, and I'm just a few feet away. A marshal shouts out, "The sniper's up there," and points across the square. Everybody turns to look in the direction of that pointing finger except me. I'm focused on Steve.

Three more shots ring out.

I see Steve diffused through a fine red mist. He sees me now and calls my name, pink bubbles at his nostrils and scarlet froth at the corners of his mouth. I'm holding him and blinking away tears. Arterial blood is pumping out of new bullet holes. I try to recall my trauma training. I need a piece of plastic to plug the sucking chest wound. Why isn't anybody helping? Why is Steve looking at me that way? Why does everything feel so wrong?

The ambulance siren is getting close. One of the marshals has taken off his T-shirt and is trying to stop the bleeding with it. Steve is struggling to say something. I tell him to shush, don't make the effort, save your energy. I realize he's telling me to make sure the crowd gets away out of the field of fire. He's bleeding out on the courthouse steps, and he's worried about others.

"Hang in there, kid." It's Nick Fury in my earpiece. "You stick with Steve. The EMTs will say you can't ride in the ambulance with him, but you flash your S.H.I.E.L.D. ID and tell them you have clearance."

"What went wrong, Colonel Fury? The plan—"

"No plan survives the first five seconds of combat, Sharon. I sicced your backup on the shooter; there's somebody else on that case, too. You keep yourself together and make sure the bad guys don't try to get in an insurance shot at the hospital."

I'm holding Steve's hand, and I don't plan to let go.

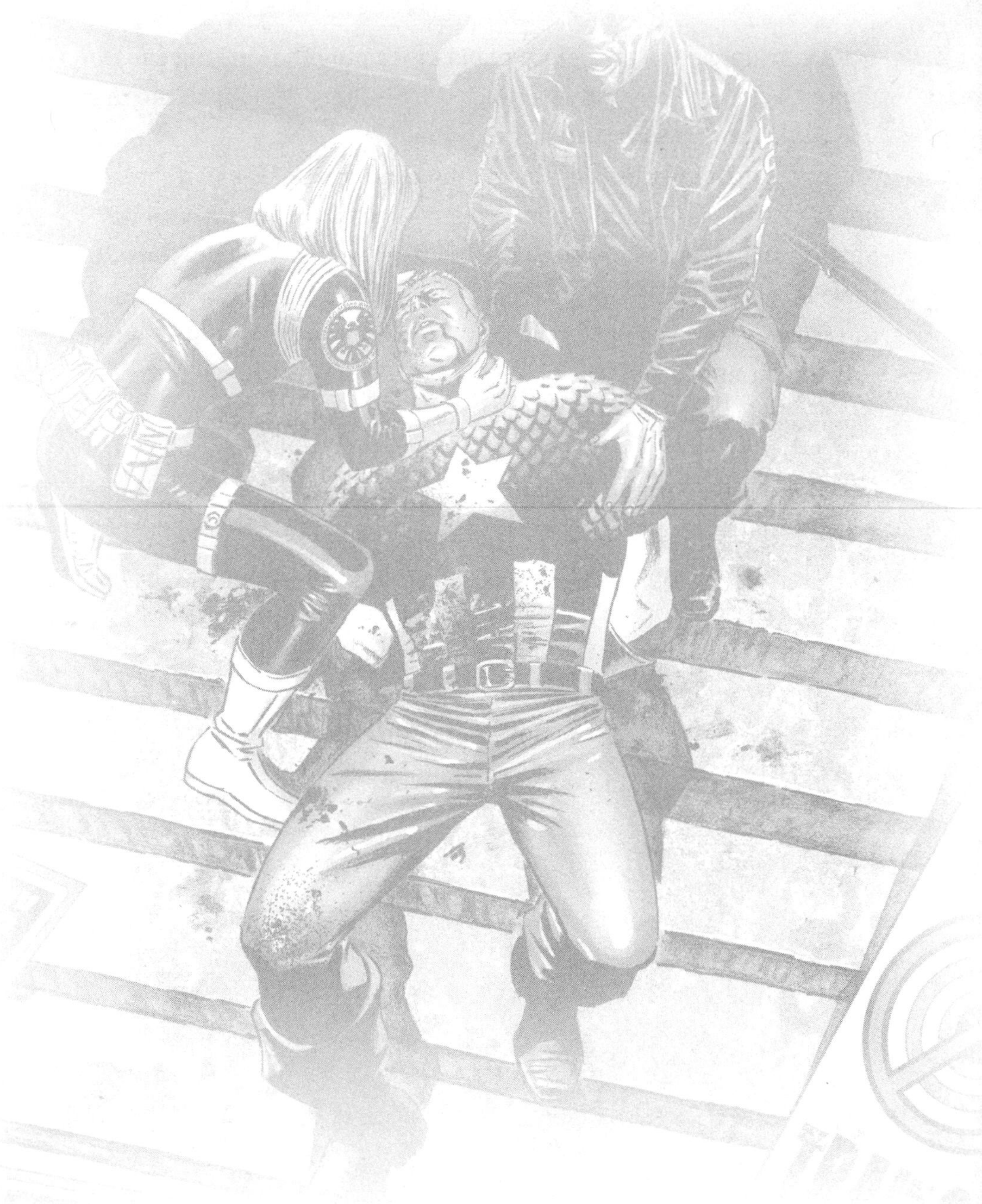

FIVE

THE man who had been leaning against the lamppost on the other side of Foley Square when the shots rang out looks like he could be a mob enforcer, an undercover cop, or an incredibly fit hipster. What he is, is an ex-KGB assassin.

James "Bucky" Barnes came dressed for action in his Winter Soldier togs, with a loose black leather jacket worn on top for discretion's sake. He's sprinting up the fire stairs of the building across the street from the '30s office tower in which he saw the muzzle flash. Nick Fury had told him he was just there as backup, and Sharon Carter was the main act. There was supposed to be a plan. He taps his earpiece and hopes it sounds irritating on the other end.

"Is this your plan, Fury?" he asks as he kicks open the roof door.

"No, damn it, Bucky—this is something else. You saw the flash? The shooter is up in—"

"I saw it. I'm on it."

"I'll check in with you later, kid. I gotta talk Sharon through maintaining security on Cap on the way to the ER at Mercy."

Emergency room? Steve's not dead. There's still a chance. There's still hope.

Bucky builds up speed racing across the rooftop, then pushes off from the parapet. Forward velocity and body streamlining carries him two stories down and across the street to crash through the window where he'd spotted the sniper firing. He rolls to his feet with a locked-and-loaded .45 in his fist.

Nothing.

He rotates, holding the pistol in a modified Weaver combat stance, visually searching the room in quadrants as per his training. There's a scoped 7.62X54mm Dragunov (SVD) rifle left carelessly on the floor of the vacant office. The shooter has taken the spent cartridge with him, but the stink of smokeless powder is still in the air. Fury's voice crackles in the earpiece.

"Talk to me, kid."

"The shooter policed his brass and got in the wind. Can you access a satellite and track his exit? There's a broken skylight right above me."

"I've got that working right now. Will get back to you when I have him pinpointed."

A winged blur in a red-and-white costume hurtles down from the smashed skylight, knocks the pistol out of Bucky's hand, grabs him by the collar, and almost takes him down to the floor. Bucky holds his ground and pushes back, ready to take back the initiative, but sees that his attacker is the Falcon—one of the Avengers, and another longtime former partner of Captain America.

"I would have thought judging by appearances was beneath you, Falcon. Is that what you learned from Steve?"

The red gloves tighten on Bucky's leather collar, but not too tight. There's hesitation now. Some thought damping the rage. Bucky points with his head at the rifle and the smashed-in window.

"If I was the assassin, why would I enter this place by crashing though the window? Why would I still be here with the smoking weapon while the spent cartridge is missing? And why wouldn't I have squeezed the trigger on my second pistol by now?"

It dawns on Falcon that what he feels pressing into his side is the muzzle of a .45 automatic identical to the one he knocked out of Bucky's hand moments before. The two men had both thought of Steve Rogers as an older brother, and neither wants to be a Cain to the other's Abel. Falcon lets go and steps back. Suspicion has not completely left his face.

"I had my own memory tinkered with, so I think I have an inkling about where you've been. And Cap always stood up for you, even when it looked like you'd gone over to the other side. I'm not pushing my own issues with you if we're on the same wavelength here."

Falcon watches Bucky closely as he thumbs up the ambidextrous safety catch on the .45 and holsters it. He notices the hammer is left cocked and locked over a live round in the chamber. Bucky retrieves his primary .45 from where it fell on the floor. He notes that Bucky drops the clip, inspects the breech, performs the safety checks to make sure the sear wasn't damaged by the impact before he reloads it, reengages the safety, and tucks the .45 back into the empty holster. A good soldier never deviates from weapon procedures. Is Bucky still a good soldier? Cap thought so. That will have to do for now.

"Are you on your own, Barnes? Or did somebody send you?"

Bucky shrugs off his leather jacket and puts on his Winter Soldier mask.

"I'm here on Nick Fury's say-so."

"You sure it's really him? Word is that it's an L.M.D. taking his place."

"He's the genuine article. In fact, he just told me where the shooter is. Can you fly and carry me at the same time?"

The lift and thrust generated by Falcon's cybernetically controlled wings and magnetic drive are more than adequate to carry Bucky high into the darkening sky. Bucky points out the news helicopter that a S.H.I.E.L.D. spy satellite spotted as it swooped down to pick up the shooter. It's exactly where Fury said it would be.

"That's it. Nobody questioned another news chopper out for an event like this. By the way, you've never had the power cut out on you while flying, have you?"

"Black Panther built in two backups for every system in my flying harness. 'Built to last in Wakanda.'"

Falcon is trying to approach the helicopter from its blind spot, but a black-and-white skull mask is peering back at them. Not the Red Skull—one of his henchmen, Brock Rumlow, the mercenary called Crossbones. The helicopter tilts forward, trading lift for speed as Bucky draws both of his pistols and slips off the safeties.

"Whoa," says Falcon. "I thought we were supposed to take them *in*, not *down*."

Bucky opens fire.

"I'm forcing them to set down. Every helo pilot knows how to auto-rotate and land after a catastrophic engine failure."

The big .45-caliber slugs rip through the engine cowling. Black smoke swirls in cyclonic twists in the rotor wash as oil and hydraulic fluid spew into the wind. The helicopter drops to rooftop level as lift bleeds off. The pilot tells the big mercenary with the death's-head mask that the controls won't work without hydraulic pressure. He hears Crossbones say, "The hell with it." And when he looks, the door is open and the copilot's seat is empty.

Falcon has barely registered the big, black, leather-clad form barreling at him before it slams into Bucky and rips him from his grip. He sees Crossbones and Bucky plummeting toward the rooftops below, locked together, trading blows. But a glance in the other direction tells him the crippled helicopter is slewing toward a crowded housing project. Falcon makes his decision and follows the helicopter.

The laterally downward velocity of the two black-clad combatants is checked somewhat by a billboard touting the registration law. Their landing amid water tanks and chimneys would have killed normal men, or left them crippled. These two are far from normal, and they've both been through worse.

They roll apart, spring back to their feet, and face off. Brock Rumlow knows exactly whom he is fighting.

"Winter Soldier, is it? Don't tell me you think you're a good guy now?"

The punch the powered prosthetic arm delivers is faster than the eye can see, and it sends Crossbones flying.

"Not exactly," Winter Soldier replies as he follows up with a roundhouse kick and a flurry of jabs.

Brock Rumlow had come up through the street gangs on the Lower East Side. He's no stranger to savage beat-downs—although he's usually the pitcher, not the catcher, since he came into his size. Now, the punches and kicks are coming too fast for Crossbones to block, and his arms and legs are starting to go rubbery. Between the devastating barrages, Winter Soldier interrogates the mercenary.

"Where's the Red Skull? I know he's pulling your strings!"

"Go die," Rumlow grunts through bloody teeth. "Oh, wait. You already did."

Winter Soldier delivers a right hook that sends Crossbones crashing to the tarred surface of the roof just as Falcon lands on the parapet. His hard-light wings retract into his flying harness as he steps down to face Bucky.

"You took your time getting here," Barnes says.

Falcon jerks a thumb toward the housing project.

"Had to keep that helo from impacting negatively on low-income families. You have to consider collateral damage if you want to be a good guy, Bucky. And you need to get out of here before the Cape-Killers show up. S.H.I.E.L.D. just ramped up their alert status to 'red,' and they'll be flooding the nabe with their people pretty damned soon."

Winter Soldier kicks the supine Crossbones in the ribs.

"I'm gone. But keep an eye on this trash until somebody comes to haul him away. Gunpowder residue will show up on his hands. Forensics should be able to match his boots to the prints in the vacant office on Foley Square."

He pauses before he disappears over the edge of the roof.

"Get over to Mercy Hospital and watch Cap's back. I'd do it myself, but—hell, you know."

Crossbones is beginning to moan and clutch his ribs when the first Cape-Killers arrive.

INTERLUDE #4

MOST New Yorkers are savvy about violence on the streets. They back away from their windows when they hear a commotion outside, lest they get hit by a bullet marked "to whom it may concern." The few who actually witnessed the fight between Winter Soldier and Crossbones assumed that what they saw was another action movie being filmed, or cosplayers taking their hobby too far.

One witness knew exactly what was going on. Her name is Sinthea Schmidt, sometimes known as "Sin" and always known as the Red Skull's daughter. Her relationship with Crossbones could, by some stretch of the imagination, be called romantic—if your idea of romance is a straight-razor fight between the Marquis de Sade and Ilse Koch, "She-Wolf of the SS."

She had ascended to the roof to watch her paramour's helicopter escape and seen the interception. Ten blocks away, the figures plummeting from the helicopter were little more than dots in the darkening sky. They were out of her line of sight after they had gone through the billboard, but she was certain that Crossbones would have survived. It was a matter of whether he could best whoever it was that had shot down the helo.

Right now, she is very angry, which is her usual condition after speaking to her father. Red Skull had wanted a son and heir, and had been about to fling the newborn Sin into the sea when the woman who would become Mother Night intervened and volunteered to raise her. The parameters her father had set for her upbringing were uncommonly cruel, and her childhood had been a black hole of anger and exultation in the pain of others. Not only had she stared into Nietzsche's abyss and had it stare back at her, the abyss had engulfed her and become her friend.

The card Sin had extracted from the cheap, prepaid cell phone she had used for that communication has already been crushed under her heel and flung off the roof. She had reported that Crossbones was in danger of being taken into custody, that she needed to go to his aid. Red Skull, being pragmatic and ruthless, had ordered her to continue with what she had been ordered to do. She had bitten her lip and said, "Fine."

Sin must let the rage simmer out of her before she can even move. Her father always has to have his own way. He has a tremendous ego, but someday his chickens will come to roost—and she will be there to gloat. For now, she bides her time and follows his orders.

Sin covers her bright-red shag with a curly black wig, adjusts the fit of her light-green scrubs, and goes down the stairs under the big lit-up "Mercy Hospital" sign.

The security around the ER and trauma center is dense, wary, and trigger-happy. Civilian visitation has been curtailed, and hospital staff IDs are double-checked and matched against shift rosters. Everybody entering the emergency room must pass through a metal detector, and there are no exceptions. Sin is wearing the ID badge of Bridget Connaught, a brunette nurse who is currently double-bagged and duct-taped in storage units in

Bayonne, Elizabeth, and Newark. Young Ms. Schmidt took Bridget's place on the day she was supposed to transfer to Mercy from All Souls in the Bronx, three days ago. Her superiors have noted that her startling lack of procedural knowledge is offset by a remarkable coolness under fire even when dealing with the most gruesome trauma cases. The ER doctors know she won't flinch if asked to "hold this," "clamp that," or "push that back into place."

The S.H.I.E.L.D. security team double-checks "Bridget's" ID and is about to run a facial-recognition scan when a passing surgeon says, "That's Nurse Connaught. She's okay." When the ER resident comes out of the trauma center to seek out the woman in the black-and-white uniform who rode the ambulance with Steve Rogers, Sin is wheeling a used "sharps" bin through the waiting room. She hears the doctor tell Sharon Carter that Rogers has been pronounced dead. She sees Carter collapse into a plastic chair and weep into the Falcon's chest. Sin feels no empathy at all for Carter's anguish and loss. She despises her as a weakling who sucks up sympathy from gullible men. She is glad to be the agent of even more pain for her.

On her third pass through the waiting room, Sin panics momentarily when she sees Falcon sitting alone. A quick scan reveals the door to the women's lavatory still swinging closed.

Red Skull's daughter enters the ladies room. Her white shoes squeak on the tile. Sharon Carter is at a sink splashing cold water on her face.

"Excuse me, ma'am. The doctor asked me to tell you something."

Carter is drying her face with a paper towel.

"Which doctor would that be?"

"Doctor Faustus."

Sharon whips around to face the nurse. Her face looks familiar, but there's something wrong with the expression. It's not the mask of professional detachment or the feigned look of sympathy. There is malice, and a certain glee when she speaks again.

"He says, 'Remember.'"

Sharon Carter's reaction to the two trigger phrases is immediate. Her body goes rigid, and her eyes roll up in her head.

Sinthea Schmidt knows what she triggered, and she can imagine the sights and sounds that are flashing through Sharon Carter's mind. The courthouse steps. The shot ringing out across Foley Square. The spray of blood. Steve Rogers collapsing. The crowd running in confusion and that moment when all eyes were turned toward the window from which the shot was fired. That moment when Sharon Carter obeyed the command Doctor Faustus had implanted in her and fired three very special bullets into Captain America.

Sharon collapses into the corner of the lavatory, so stunned by the revelation that she doesn't notice the nurse going out the door or the smirk upon her freckled face.

PART TWO

CONTEMPLATIONS
OF MORTALITY

SIX

VAL insisted on walking with me to the wake, so I couldn't refuse. Her full title and name is Contessa Valentina Allegra de la Fontaine. Most S.H.I.E.L.D. personnel call her Contessa—but she told me to call her "Val" years ago, and that sort of stuck. She calls me "Sharon," with the ghost of an "a" at the end. It makes me feel a little glamorous when I hear her say it that way. Val had a long-running thing going with Nick Fury in the wild and wooly days, and I've always liked her, which would seem to be two good reasons to confide in her. But I don't.

The neighborhood we're walking through is the one Steve Rogers grew up in. Working-class Irish, Polish, Jewish, and Ukrainian with abutting neighborhoods being Italian, Chinese, Puerto Rican, and African-American. You don't have to walk more than two blocks to get a *pierogi*, a *knish*, or *colcannon*. I can picture how it looked when Steve was a kid: boys playing skully with bottle caps on the street, and girls chalking hopscotch boards on the sidewalk. I wouldn't romanticize it as a melting pot, but it was surely a place where diverse cultures rubbed shoulders and managed to get along. The kind of place where the promise of what America was supposed to be was never taken for granted. The true hometown of Captain America.

Val can read people like a book, which is one of the reasons she was recruited to be an agent. She can tell I want to let something out, but I'm not ready just yet. I don't even know for sure what exactly happened, and how it's possible Doctor Faustus hijacked my mind. Does that mean I've been a tool of the Red Skull all this time? The guilt and frustration I feel are overwhelming, but I have to deal with it. I have to find out how this happened to me, and I have to make it right. I owe that to Steve.

I'm mumbling inanities, and she has the European grace to change the subject by asking how my meeting with Director Tony Stark went. Dum Dum Dugan had told her it hadn't gone well.

I'm so emotionally drained and exhausted that I tell her the whole story without edits.

It wasn't a "meeting" in the strictest sense. It had come to me on the S.H.I.E.L.D. grapevine that Stark had Steve's body secretly removed from the hospital morgue, and it was now lying in the Helicarrier cryo-lab like some sort of damned *specimen*. I went storming over there to find the new director waiting to intercept me at the bulkhead hatch to the lab. Stark was wearing the black-and-white S.H.I.E.L.D. combat togs, which ticked me off even more. Slim chance he was ever going into a fight wearing anything but his Iron Man suit.

He was standing in front of the pressure hatch, blocking the way. I wasn't about to let him sweet-talk my outrage away. My indignation was righteous and full-blown. I said things I shouldn't have ever said. Stark was all explanations and rationality delivered with that maddening sympathetic superiority that comes from being too smart and too rich.

"We had no choice other than bringing his body here," he said. "Steve was the only successful product of the Super-Soldier program. The information in his cells is protected by several national-security acts."

That just ramped up my anger.

"Steve wasn't a 'product.' He was your friend, Tony."

For a moment, it looked like Tony Stark had a conscience. I wasn't feeling like being nice and understanding. I was hoping his guilt was stabbing him through the heart. Like mine was.

"Something happened," he said. "I didn't want to shock you."

He put his eye to the retinal scanner, and the hatch slid open.

Tony dismissed a half-dozen guards, and we entered an autopsy suite. The form under the sheet looked so small and shriveled, I was struck by the thought that death lays us all so low in many ways. But no—it was too small. I started to say this must be a mistake, that it couldn't possibly be Steve. But then Tony pulled down the top of the sheet, and I saw it really was him. Steve Rogers as he would have been had he never taken the Super-Soldier Serum: a scrawny old man with a sunken chest and white, thinning hair.

"Somehow, the Super-Soldier Serum reversed itself when he died. Obviously, this is not something we want released to the general public."

I held Tony Stark responsible. Didn't Iron Man spearhead the call for enforcement of the Registration Act? It was that gleaming red-and-yellow suit on all the posters, wasn't it? Wasn't Stark the main reason Steve Rogers had been taken into custody? And now, Stark is director of S.H.I.E.L.D., and Steve is stretched out cold on a slab. I told him all that, and he said he'd been trying to do the right thing, that it was killing him to see Steve that way.

I lost it at that point.

I slapped him across his face as hard as I could and told him he didn't get to say that.

Val stops walking and turns to me.

"You did not!"

"I did."

"But why would *you* feel guilty?"

Did I say that out loud? I must have. Sometimes when you tell the truth, too much of the truth comes out. I pretended not to hear and went on.

"Then I resigned."

"Sharon! What will Nick say when he finds out?"

"He wouldn't be Nick Fury if he didn't already know. Wherever the hell he's hiding out this week. He's more elusive than the Scarlet Pimpernel."

"But to *resign*—life without S.H.I.E.L.D.? Whatever will you do?"

I open the door to the bar.

"Without Steve, what's the point?"

The bar is twice the size of a regular neighborhood watering hole. and all the ceiling fans, wood paneling, and fake stained glass make me suspect the owners were betting on a gentrification that never happened. It being shunned by tourists and trendsetters was the main attraction that turned it into a place for costumed heroes and their ilk to unwind in civvies and anonymity. The joint is packed tonight, but the usual noisy camaraderie is muted. There's no music playing on the sound system, and the big flat-screen over the bar is turned down low on a news channel. Val is surrounded by friends as soon as we enter, but people are avoiding me. Either they're uncomfortable with the personal nature of my pain and loss, or they sense my unwillingness to engage. These are quirky individuals with keen perceptive powers, but they're generally lacking in social skills. Add to that the tension arising from the fact that some of the people in the room were actively hunting others in the room not too long ago, and you get a bad situation waiting to happen. There's no "celebrating a life" here. There's just loss, and the awful understanding that someone you had thought would always be there is gone forever. I know there has to be a healing and a letting go, but it seems too early for me. The wounds are too raw.

I have the same stupid, impersonal conversation three or four times with people I barely know who buy me white wine and tell me to "call sometime." I feel relieved when I spot Sam Wilson leaning on the bar and looking lost. It's hard for me to think of him as the Falcon when he's wearing a designer suit instead of a red-and-white costume. He's one of the closest things to family that I have. I haven't spoken to him since the funeral, and I never thanked him for being there with me in the waiting room at Mercy Hospital. I give him a big hug and tell him his speech was beautiful.

"So what's this about handing in your papers at S.H.I.E.L.D.?"

That's the first thing he asks. I don't have to reply. He can see in my face that it's true.

"Sharon, you're one of the best field agents on their roster. Steve wouldn't have wanted you to throw your career away."

I tell him I don't think I can stomach taking orders from Tony Stark, and I'm just no good anymore. He says it wasn't my fault. Inside, I'm screaming, "Yes, it was my fault." And when he tells me there was nothing I could have done, I almost blurt out everything that's bottled up inside me.

It's Rick Jones who saves me from spilling the beans. He walks over, beaming, telling me I haven't changed at all. Rick had been a substitute "Bucky" for only a short time, but he had remained close to Cap ever since. Rick had even been a pallbearer at the funeral; in his eulogy, Sam had pointed him out as one of the few who knew what it was like to have called Captain America a partner. Sam, concerned and sincere as always, asks Rick how he's holding up. There's grief in his eyes, but Rick tells Sam he's good and apologizes for interrupting.

Sam Wilson takes the opportunity to make his escape.

"I'm just on my way out. Sharon, I'll call you tomorrow, okay?"

He's gone before I can think of anything to say, and I'm left fumbling for words to fill the awkward silence. The rule in these situations is to avoid eye contact, mumble, and take deep breaths. Rick throws away the rules as he looks directly at me and says, "He really loved you. You knew that, right?"

In a paranoid moment, it seems like all the conversation has stopped in the bar, and everyone has turned to await my reaction. I'm afraid to look around to confirm this. It takes all the control I have to answer him.

"Yes. I knew. Thank you for being...a friend."

I make my excuses, gather my shreds of dignity, and walk as calmly as I can to the ladies room. I lean against the sink and fight back the sobs. When I look in the mirror, the words come back to me. "Doctor Faustus says remember."

What have I done? What have I done? What have I done?

"Damn it. Damn it all to hell."

INTERLUDE #5

IN the executive penthouse suite atop the Kronas Corporation Tower, Sin aims her pistol at the flat-screen TV that takes up half a wall. A news channel is broadcasting live from the candlelight vigil in Central Park where thousands have gathered to pay tribute to Captain America. The newscaster notes that hundreds of similar vigils are taking place across the country, and the crowds represent advocates and opponents of the Superhuman Registration Act. The man taken into custody at the scene is referred to as the "lone gunman" or the "alleged assassin." Sin screams at the screen.

"His name is Brock! Give Crossbones some damn credit, why don't you?"

The Red Skull tells his excitable offspring to put her gun away and assures her that Crossbones' sacrifice will be rewarded. She pouts and does as she is told. Sin may be a willful child, but she is aware of consequences—her father's views on parenting owing more to Dr. Moreau than to Dr. Spock.

"I've chosen my subordinates for the rest of your plan," she says as she leaves the room. "I'm ready to move forward."

The feelings the Red Skull holds for Sin have nothing to do with love or paternal duty—more like the pride of ownership he feels for certain effective weapons. He has no qualms about putting her aside once she is no longer of use to him. Sentimentality is for the weak. Sin's mother had been chosen for her breeding qualities, and Red Skull had felt nothing but anger when she died birthing a daughter instead of the male heir she was expected to bring forth.

After descending on his private elevator to the secret lab, Red Skull strolls the corridors, confident there are no unauthorized visitors to this, the most secure section of Kronas Tower. He remembers the pleasurable perambulations he took through his research labs during WWII—the smell of blood, the screams. He wasn't sharing a body with an ex-Russian general then. He didn't have to expend energy keeping another consciousness at bay.

Doctor Faustus steps out of the lavatory as Red Skull comes down the hallway to the research suites. It does not escape the Red Skull's attention that Faustus used a paper towel to open the door, but he still does not deign to shake the man's hand.

"I was just on my way to see you," Faustus says as he shoves the moist towel into the pocket of his pin-striped suit. "I was wondering if you will be in my office for the session tonight?"

"I will be where I need to be, when I decide to be there, Faustus."

"Don't ask for my help, then spit in my face."

"If I didn't need you, I'd rip your guts out through your throat for speaking to me like that."

"If we didn't need each other, I wouldn't speak to you at all."

The blast-proof sliding doors to Arnim Zola's lab open with a hydraulic hiss, and a robotic voice cuts off the exchange.

"Forgive me for interrupting this battle of egos, but perhaps you would care to see the progress I have made before you break out the dueling sabers?"

Red Skull and Doctor Faustus follow Arnim Zola through

the lab. They pass a row of his identical robot bodies—all plugged into maintenance and monitoring devices, but none displaying the holographic face that marks Zola's inhabitance. Zola sometimes transfers his "self" into a spare body so he can fine-tune the one he usually "wears."

Zola opens an armored door and leads his guests into the chamber where Doctor Doom's device is throbbing and emitting pulses of blue light. Only a short while ago, it had been an inert mass of metal, glass tubing, and wires. Now, it is radiating an energy field that distorts light around it, creating the illusion that the room is tilting.

"You have cracked the device's inner workings?" asks the Red Skull.

Zola adjusts a setting to damp the 60-cycle hum. The proximity of the device is causing the hologram on his chest to flicker.

"Not entirely, Herr Schmidt. But what Victor von Doom can invent, I can reverse-engineer, given proper time and resources."

Zola, being entirely robotic, does not experience the vertigo and nausea the device is inflicting on the two humans. He continues, unaware of their distress.

"Once I totally understand how it functions, I can adapt the technology to suit our needs. Where Doom sought only isolated moments, all of the past and future shall be open to us."

Red Skull trips the switch that turns off the device and gathers his composure. He feels better already, but Faustus continues to look out of sorts. Skull snaps at Zola. "*Our* needs? *Us?*"

A relay clicks somewhere inside Arnim Zola's mechanical frame, and an "obsequious filter" is activated on the speech generator.

"Excuse me, leader. *Your* needs, of course."

Red Skull takes Doctor Faustus by the arm and leads him out of the lab.

"Come, my good doctor. General Lukin and I have a meeting this afternoon with the secretary of the treasury, and your presence is required."

SEVEN

PASSENGERS on the Lexington Avenue subway line are unaware that the last stop of the downtown #6 train is the beginning of a track loop that passes through the abandoned City Hall station that has been closed to the public since 1945. Part of the station has been bricked off from the still-operational tracks, but the power lines that serve the station are the same that power the signals and switches, so the lights in the station still work. It is now the scene of the secret wake for Captain America—the one held by the "other side" in the Civil War, those who couldn't go to the funeral or the official wake.

Falcon had changed into his costume when he left the bar, flown downtown, and entered the subway via a maintenance access door in the basement of the Municipal Building. Unlike the official wake, the mourners at the secret wake are mostly dressed in their crime-fighting togs, but without their masks. No imported beer on draft, ten-year-old single malts, or platters of crudités here. It's strictly a BYOB affair with six-packs in coolers and chips being passed around still in the bag.

Luke Cage is there with his wife, Jessica, and their newborn. He is about to say something to Falcon, but he has to wait until an uptown train finishes squealing past on the tracks behind the bricks.

"I saw your funeral speech on TV, Sam. Thought it was something special. Wish I could have said a few words myself."

"That was a bum deal, Luke. It wasn't right—not having you all there. It was worse at the other wake. Felt all wrong, you know?"

"Everything about this feels all wrong. Like seeing your name on the list of registered heroes."

"That was the ticket price for having my say. Otherwise, it would have been nothing but the people who were tracking him down. And Tony Stark..."

"That was weird, Sam. Seeing Stark break down like that. Considering—"

Danny Rand, a.k.a "Iron Fist," gets in his two cents.

"I almost felt bad for him, but then I remembered that it was Stark who sent me to that concentration camp in the Negative Zone."

"I don't have a lot of love for Tony Stark right now," Falcon says. "But he wasn't the one who killed Cap."

Luke Cage isn't convinced. There's more than a little antagonism in his voice.

"Tony Stark set Steve Rogers up like a duck in a shooting gallery with that perp walk. I don't know if Stark meant to or not, but it sure looked like Cap lost heart after that face-off with Iron Man. Why else would he take a hit like that?"

Peter Parker drops down from his perch near the top of a pillar. He's got on his black Spider-Man suit, and he has his own opinions.

"I don't think so. I've been over the footage a thousand times. Ran enhancement programs and watched them again. Cap spots the laser dot on the marshal in front of him, turns, and somehow figures out where the shooter is. Then, he deliberately pushes the marshal out of the line of fire and takes his place under the laser dot. That was the first shot. The crowd went nuts, and that's when the rest of the shooting started. With the strength-dampening restraints, it probably took everything Cap had to just walk up the steps, but he was still a hero right up to the end."

The station goes quiet long enough for everyone to hear water dripping from the overhead air vents. Spider-Woman breaks the silence by raising a bottle of Merlot.

"Is it time, then?"

Plastic cups are topped off and raised in salute. The questioning eyes all turn to Falcon, who has no hesitations about what to say.

"Here's to Steve Rogers. He was one of the first of us, and he will always be the best of us."

"The best of us," is the response that echoes around the station. As the cups are drained, a cell phone chirps. Sam Wilson answers and stares at the text message. Luke Cage asks whether there's someplace else he has to be.

"Yes, damn it."

The Falcon pulls on his mask and leaves his second wake of the night.

The bar is on the other side of town and is the sort of establishment Sam Wilson would feel uncomfortable walking into while wearing street clothes. It's the type of place that sells beer in longneck bottles and shots of cheap rye to an all-male clientele that is blue-collar, disaffected, and white. The bartender is leaving, shouting into his cell phone at a 911 operator as Falcon enters. The dust is still settling, and the patrons who remain conscious are moaning or whimpering. The television above the bar is playing a rebroadcast of the funeral.

Bucky is leaning on the pool table staring at the blood on his gloved hands. Falcon rolls the eight ball across the table and sinks it in the side pocket. Bucky looks up, and there are tears in his eyes.

"Damn, Bucky. When Fury said you were in the deep doo-doo, I didn't think you'd be taking out the entire bar. Please tell me it's a Hydra front, or an A.I.M. monitoring station…"

"Nope. They were just morons."

Falcon's gaze drifts up to the television.

"That's what started it," Bucky explains. "I came in here to watch it and have a beer. I just wanted to see my best friend's funeral. The guy I hadn't had the guts to face for the past year. And now he was gone, and I couldn't even show my face when they put him in the ground. The bartender called it a 'freakin' tragedy.' The guy two stools over said it was more of a cover-up, that Cap wasn't really dead. Then, a big lug with a Navy tattoo who was chalking up a cue-stick pipes in saying the tragedy was burying him in Arlington—that it was for heroes, not traitors. When I told him to say it again, he started parroting that talk-radio line of tripe—that Cap turned against the will of the American people and dishonored the uniform he wore.

"I sort of lost it right then, Sam."

Falcon doesn't say a word.

"Yeah, I know what Cap would have done. He'd have tried to reason with the guy. He'd have told him just because the majority of citizens believe something doesn't make it right. He'd have said the majority of Americans once believed in slavery and opposed women's suffrage. And he'd have walked away from the confrontation before it went physical.

"But I'm not Cap."

Bucky looks around at the devastation he has caused.

"I can't help thinking Steve would be ashamed of me right now, and that makes me miss him more than anything. Through the worst days of the war—when I wanted to throw out the rule book; when I was looking into the abyss, and the abyss was looking right back at me—Cap was my conscience, my moral compass, and my confessor. And now I have nothing."

Falcon takes Bucky by the arm and turns him toward the door.

"We need to get you out of here, Bucky. The cops will be here any minute."

As Bucky lays a roll of bills on the bar, Tony Stark's attempt at a eulogy gets replayed on TV for the umpteenth time that night. Bucky can't tear his eyes from the screen and Stark muttering, "It wasn't supposed to be this way," breaking into tears, and walking away from the podium. Falcon is tugging hard on his arm, but Bucky isn't moving.

"Are you coming or not?"

The man who used to be Captain America's teen sidekick acknowledges to himself that he can't bring Steve Rogers back to life. He can't be the hero Cap wanted him to be. But he knows he can do one thing.

He can kill Tony Stark.

The man who used to be the Soviet Union's most skilled assassin lets the hero in the red-and-white costume lead him to the door as sirens approach in the night.

"Okay. Let's roll," Bucky says.

EIGHT

THE line for the new Captain America exhibit at the American History Museum in Washington, D.C., stretches around the block. Tony Stark had been on network news telecasts in the morning announcing that the uniform and shield used by Steve Rogers would be on permanent display there, and that there would be no "new" Captain America. The title, the mantle, and the equipment were to be retired.

The man who had been closer to Captain America than anybody else on the planet has stood in the queue for more than two hours. The security is tight, but Bucky is not worried. Nick Fury's upgrade on his prosthetic arm included a jamming device for metal detectors, an airborne-molecule neutralizer for dogs, and a false-image array for X-ray machines. Nothing short of a pat down will reveal the two pistols, combat knife, grenades, and other lethal devices concealed about his person.

He enters the exhibit room in a controlled group of ten. Guards are posted to prevent visitors from touching the bulletproof glass that encases the artifacts. The room was intended to convey the respectful atmosphere of a shrine, but a trace of carnival sideshow has infiltrated the design.

Bucky is still seething from the remarks Tony Stark made on television—such hypocrisy and gall, after what he did, to call Cap "the finest man I ever met." And to say it was "a national tragedy that he was taken from us," after he was responsible for Cap being on the federal courthouse steps and in the sniper's sights. The bronze plaque noting that the exhibition was made possible by a donation from Stark Industries makes Bucky clench his fists with rage.

The exhibit's centerpiece is Cap's uniform and shield. A brass rail keeps the public at more than an arm's length—but to what end? Nothing short of a low-yield nuke could damage the Vibranium-laced costume or the solid Vibranium shield. An elderly woman is standing nearby, regarding the relics as if they were the Shroud of Turin and the Holy Grail.

"He saved my father's life during the war. Him and Bucky and the Invaders."

With a start, he realizes she is younger than he is.

"Oh, really? Where?"

"The battle of Saipan. My dad never stopped talking about it."

Bucky doesn't tell her he and Cap weren't even close to the Pacific Theater at that time. Saipan had been a living hell, and he surmises that her father felt more comfortable making up stories about costumed heroes than telling his child what he really experienced. Every soldier knows better than that. So the man who was both a boy-soldier and the Winter Soldier does not trample her memories. He knows he could never do that to anybody else.

What Bucky also knows is that as fine a tribute as the exhibit is to Captain America, Tony Stark is full of crap.

The shield in the display case is a fake.

It might fool everybody else, but it can't fool somebody who saw it up close for so long. It can't fool somebody who could probably tell you what it *smells* like.

And that means that Tony Stark is lying through his teeth.

The promise about not letting anybody else wear the suit or carry the shield is no promise at all. It's all a sham. They'll wait a year a two—then, with the public clamoring for a new Captain America, Stark might even clone him. As long as they have the real shield stashed away somewhere, they won't be able to just let it sit. They'll grow a clone, or zap some steroid-pumped yahoo with gamma rays or jack him up with some new serum. Any way they do it, it'll be a "good soldier" who buys into their worldview and does what he's told. He'll never stop to question right or wrong. He'll never think about the collateral damage. James Buchanan Barnes is not about to let that happen. He's not letting some unworthy stranger carry it.

But where's the real thing? Where is S.H.I.E.L.D. hiding Captain America's shield?

NINE

THREE in the morning, and I choose to shoot myself in the bathroom, sitting on the edge of my tub. Stupid, huh? Who's going to be the beneficiary of my consideration? My landlord? Lots easier to get blood and brains off tile than shag carpet and wallpaper. The muzzle is under my chin, there's a round in the chamber, and the hammer is cocked. I'm saying to myself, "Go ahead and squeeze the trigger, Sharon."

Obliteration is the way to go. Ceasing to exist neatly solves all the problems and erases the pain. But why can't I do it? I lower the gun, and I see Doctor Faustus in the mirror over the sink.

"No, there won't be an easy way out of this, Agent 13. You can't pull the trigger any more than you can tell your friends what you've done. Or rather, what I made you do."

I tell him to shut up. I smash the mirror with the butt of the pistol. Doctor Faustus laughs at me from a hundred shards of mirror, and I scream at him to get out of my head. The upstairs neighbor starts thumping on the floor. He'd have been doing a lot more than thumping if I'd sent a bullet up through my head and into his toilet.

Cool it, Sharon.

Yeah, right. Can't even off myself with any sort of proficiency.

Stumbling into my dark living room with a cocked-and-locked pistol in my hand, I see somebody coming through the open window from the fire escape. My training kicks in, and I snap the gun up into a two-handed combat grip and start to take up the trigger slack.

"Freeze, or I'll shoot."

More of that good training. Always give them a warning or you get spit-roasted when you go before the review board for a bad shooting.

It's Sam Wilson, in full Falcon regalia. I guess flying in through a fifth-floor window makes more sense than standing on a stoop and pushing a buzzer when you're wearing red-and-white tights and a mask.

"Damn, girl," he says. "It's just me."

"What the hell, Sam—I almost shot you."

"I noticed. You okay?"

"Are you kidding? I'm a wreck. Steve is dead, my career at S.H.I.E.L.D. is over, I have no friends, and I can't...sleep."

Watch it, girl. You almost told him you can't even kill yourself.

"No friends? What am I, chopped liver? And you know damn well there are others who would take a bullet for you."

Bullet? Bad choice of words, Sam. But I can't say anything, can I? Best to steer clear of any subject where I might have another slip of the tongue. I'm trying to hold my gun at my side as casually as possible, but Falcon is looking at it and probably wondering why I had it in my hand coming out of the bathroom. I push the de-cocking lever and shove the gun down into my sweats.

"So. Something heavy must be going down to bring you through my window at this hour. Is it more bad news?"

"I was worried about you. Is everything copacetic?"

That's the code word Fury gave me to activate the black-box jammer. "Copacetic." Another bad choice of words, but nothing that will raise a red flag at the surveillance analyst's chowder and marching society. I reach outside the window, pull the loose brick, extract the plastic-wrapped gadget, and turn it on. Falcon waits for the red activation light to come on.

"I just got the word from Fury. He needs you and me to do a job for him."

"Fury always needs somebody to do a job for him."

"More personal this time. Winter Soldier went off the grid yesterday. Looks like he's getting set to kick over the poker table, and we need to keep him cool."

I feel a migraine coming on, but this sounds like a good excuse to get out of the apartment and distract me from my own wallowing pit of depression. I tell him fine and duck into my bedroom to change into something I can fight in. I ask Sam to brief me through the open door.

"Fury says Bucky has been accessing S.H.I.E.L.D. databases to find out where they're hiding Cap's shield. The one on display in D.C. is a replica. The real McCoy is here in Manhattan. Not long after the location data was compromised, one of Fury's weapon caches got pilfered. So Winter Soldier is now below the radar, seriously armed, and out for blood. Every way I figure it, the shield is a means to an end, not the end itself."

"What's that supposed to mean?"

"Another big load of data that got downloaded was about Tony Stark. Fury thinks Bucky is out to whack the head honcho of S.H.I.E.L.D."

That's something I wouldn't mind doing myself, but I'm

keeping my hole cards facedown until I sort out the Doctor Faustus predicament. I pull on a pair of boots, strap a holster over my jumpsuit, load up with spare ammo clips, and I'm ready to go.

"Are we flying, or taking a cab?"

TEN

ONE percent of hunting is the kill. Two percent is the chase. Ninety-seven percent is the stalking—or in some cases, the waiting. In the computer age, much of the stalking is done online and requires extensive hacking skills. A good deal of the Winter Soldier's formal KGB training was in the computer-science department at the elite Foreign Intelligence Training Institute in *Chelobit'evo* just outside Moscow, in a building that was supposedly an insane asylum. He had been drilled to anticipate and plan for future needs, so he installed a "backdoor" into their database that he can still access. That access provided him with a password algorithm cracker that enabled him to penetrate both the S.H.I.E.L.D. internal network and Nick Fury's secret trapdoor into that same system.

Winter Soldier was able to remotely hijack the Nick Fury L.M.D. already co-opted by Fury himself and use it to forcefully enter a secret S.H.I.E.L.D. laboratory in Long Island City. There had been a confrontation between the robot Fury and two agents that resulted in the destruction and exposure of the L.M.D. and sent both agents to the Helicarrier infirmary's ICU. Before the L.M.D. went off-line, it confirmed the presence of Captain America's shield at that facility. Tony Stark reacted by doubling the security at the lab and began formulating plans to move the shield to a more secure location.

Two blocks from the substation, Winter Soldier observes

the activity there through range-finder binoculars. He has removed bricks from the parapet to create a peephole that doesn't silhouette him against the sky. A black tarp blends his prone body into the tar roof for the benefit of satellite cams. The lenses of his binoculars have been shaded to prevent reflected glare from betraying his location. Tony Stark may be a technical wizard and a smart businessman, but he's in the minor leagues when it comes to sneaking into places. And you can't prevent somebody from doing something unless you have a pretty good idea of how to do it yourself.

Still, Bucky has to hand it to Stark, if he was the one who came up with the plan for moving the shield. There are four armored transport vehicles leaving the loading bay of the lab at the same time. The ruse is meant to give the impression that three of the vehicles are decoys, and the fourth one is carrying the prize. It might have worked if there had been an attempt to camouflage the four departures, but their very openness is the giveaway to the mind of the trained assassin. He makes no move to follow any of the vehicles, but shifts his focus to the roof of the lab where he catches the glints off a dozen pairs of binoculars that are scanning the rooftops or following the vehicles.

Winter Soldier barely moves one hand to hit the redial button on a throwaway cell phone that calls another throwaway phone on a rooftop four blocks away from the other side of the lab. The other phone's ringtone triggers a remote that releases a prone black-clad mannequin on casters to roll down the slight incline of the flat tar roof toward the fire stairs. The response is immediate. Scores of Cape-Killers and tactical-support vehicles converge on the mannequin. At the same time, a garage door next to the lab loading bay opens. A single car emerges and drives away at a speed well within the posted limit. The car has the outward appearance of an Aston Martin Vanquish, but the whine of the revving engine is not even close to the throaty roar of a 362.2-cubic-inch V12.

It's a S.H.I.E.L.D. flying car.

Egress routes in four directions from the roof had been plotted out well in advance. The Winter Soldier takes the one that will bring him the closest to the where he estimates the car will be within the next five seconds; he swings down from roof-access ladder to fire escape to lamppost and hits the street just as the flying car leaves the asphalt with tires rotating to airborne mode.

Bucky has upgraded the capacitors and coils of the EMP generator in his left arm to triple the output. He only has to crank the power halfway to burn out all the flying car's control circuits and bring it down hard on a row of parked cars. When he pries open the crumpled door of the fake Vanquish, a black-booted foot kicks him hard in the face. He notes the accuracy and power behind the kick. He also notes that it is a very feminine size 6.

The next series of kicks come in a precise flurry; Winter Soldier blocks with his cyber arm, but he must retreat three steps to do so. The kicker exits the wrecked flying car in a blur of black leather, landing on her feet like the trained ballerina and martial artist she is.

Black Widow.

The Winter Soldier had known her as Natalia Romanova. He helped train her for the KGB's Department X. That had been right after the war, during the worst of the Cold War paranoia. She had gone on to further training in the Red Room, another of Comrade

Karpov's pet programs. The Black Widow was the Soviet's second most effective assassin until she defected to the West. Now, she faces off against Winter Soldier with Captain America's shield strapped to her back.

"Natasha Alianovna."

He uses the diminutive and the patronymic, indicating familiarity and affection, but he has not let his guard down. He knew there was a Black Widow working with S.H.I.E.L.D.—but that had been the name of the *program*, not necessarily an individual.

"I thought you'd be an old woman by now."

She smiles but does not lower her guard, either.

"You, of all people, should not need to be told about the wonders of Russian biotechnology. Now, why are you after the shield? Who are you working for, *Zeemneey Soldat*?"

"I don't work for anyone anymore, Natasha. I'm here for an old friend."

Black Widow is taken aback. Of course. All the clues add up.

"So it wasn't just a rumor back then—about who you *really* were, about how Karpov found you floating in the English Channel."

"It was more like a joke that everyone was in on except for me. Not anymore, though. Karpov and Lukin made me over for their own purposes, but now I'm going to be what I was always supposed to be."

His words ring true to her, but she knows he was trained by the most devious minds at the *Lubyanka* on Dzerzhinsky Square. She knows where her own allegiance lies and what her duty is. But she is burdened by memory.

"Walk away, Soldier," she says. "I don't want to hurt you."

He shifts his stance to lead with his left.

"That's funny, I was just about to say the same—"

She strikes before he finishes the sentence, executing a *grand jeté* that morphs into a flying kick as she fires electrostatic bolts from her Widow's Bite bracelets.

The 30,000-volt charges are grounded out by Winter Soldier's prosthetic arm as he draws one pistol as a diversion, then kicks her so hard she hits a brick wall ten feet above the sidewalk.

The most effective assassin of the Soviet era draws his other pistol and opens fire at the second most-effective assassin. Microscopic electrostatic suction cups on Black Widow's boots and gloves allow her to cling to the wall as bullets bounce off the shield. The man who used to be Captain America's sidekick stops shooting as soon as he realizes what the jacketed lead is ricocheting from. That moment of hesitation is the only opening Black Widow needs to launch a counterattack—springing off the wall, lashing out with a roundhouse kick that would have resulted in major cranial trauma had it connected.

Police sirens are wailing, their Doppler effect indicating convergence. 911 lines have been jammed with reports of "shots fired." Without a doubt, S.H.I.E.L.D. tactical teams and Cape-Killer squads will beat the cops to the scene. Winter Soldier knows he has less than ten seconds to neutralize his opponent, take possession of the shield, and make his escape. In two of those seconds, he flashes back to a time when Natalia Romanova reminded him of what it was to feel human. Another second elapses as he wishes he was on another of Karpov's missions, and that there was a stasis tank waiting for him to wipe away his memories. One more second to repress sentiment and strengthen resolve before he feints with his right, and then connects hard with his left.

Winter Soldier unstraps the shield from her back and makes his escape before her unconscious body hits the pavement. Four seconds later, the first Cape-Killers arrive on the scene.

Two blocks away on a warehouse rooftop, Sharon Carter and Falcon watch the police arrive. The cops get shunted aside as S.H.I.E.L.D. situation-management teams spirit away Black Widow and sanitize the site.

"The kid doesn't waste any time, does he, Sharon?"

"That kid is older than your grandfather, Sam. You got any idea what plan 'B' is?"

"You feel like talking to S.H.I.E.L.D.?"

"Not in the slightest."

"Then we have to start tracking him on our own. Right now."

Black Widow wakes up in the MRI suite of the Helicarrier infirmary with Tony Stark standing over her. He's telling her that she has a concussion, but she wishes he would stop talking so she can remember the dream that is already fading away. It was a remembrance more than just a dream, enhanced and romanticized with all the bad parts edited out. The Winter Soldier sneaking in through her bedroom window all those years ago, the night before she was sent away to marry the test pilot Shostakov. She remembers the first kiss and the last, because they were the sweetest and the most bitter; all the kisses in between are fragments of lost feelings she can never recover. She can barely conceal the resentment in her reply to Stark.

"You knew he was out there. You knew Winter Soldier was out there, and you knew who he really was. And you didn't think I needed to be briefed about that?"

"Until he told me, nobody but Steve Rogers believed that Bucky was still alive—and he wanted it kept quiet, so I respected that."

Stark reaches out to Black Widow, but she flinches.

"I also wasn't aware that you two had a history."

She knows where her loyalties lie, but she also knows that what's personal is personal. And the director of S.H.I.E.L.D. has no valid reason for knowing the secrets of her heart. She prevaricates by stating the unadorned facts.

"We trained together for a few weeks, then I never spoke to him again."

But she did not forget.

Stark crosses his arms, which is a convenient way of doing something with his hands after she has rebuffed his attempt at human contact.

"I think Winter Soldier is working for Nick Fury. All the S.H.I.E.L.D. files on Winter Soldier went missing at the same time Fury did his disappearing act," Stark says.

The bruises on her face are beginning to discolor, which makes it harder for Stark to read her expressions.

"He told me he's not working for anybody, and I believe him. He wanted Captain America's shield because he doesn't trust *you* with it."

"He told you that? About the shield?"

"He didn't have to. I could see it in his eyes. It was personal."

"How well did you get to know him in those few weeks

you trained together? Is that why you lost? You couldn't go all out against…an old friend?"

Yes, that is the truth of it, but she can't reveal that.

"No, it's not like that. I know how he thinks. We were weapons forged by the same smith. We were both used in the same way."

Her memory dredges up the images from the awful night she followed up an informant's tip to break into the KGB weapons warehouse in *Chelobit'evo* near the asylum. It was there, in a dark corner behind racks of rocket launchers and crates of flamethrowers, that she found the most dangerous weapon in the warehouse. She had wiped away the condensation on the coffin-sized glass cylinder and seen him suspended in bubbling liquid, with pulsing tubes inserted in his nostrils and veins. Dormant: not dead but not quite alive either. The Winter Soldier between assignments.

Stark is not to be put off.

"If you know him so well, what do you think he'll do next?"

"He blames you for the death of Captain America."

"He'll have to get in line for that one, Natasha."

"He is capable of cutting to the head of the line. He is capable of defeating the best security S.H.I.E.L.D. can put up."

She slips off the exam table and pushes back her wild red hair.

"He's coming after *you*, Tony Stark."

INTERLUDE #6

SIN has dressed for the occasion in what she considers her fighting outfit: a red bustier, matching thigh-high boots and black tights and gloves. The occasion is a raid on a Wall Street data-processing firm that is the nerve center of the Asian stock market. The crew she has assembled for this incursion includes King Cobra, Eel, and a newcomer called Viper. Sin has collectively dubbed them the "Serpent Squad"   but in her own mind, she thinks of them as the "Slime Society."

This is not a stealth operation but a brutal break-in during (late) working hours with guns blazing, venom spitting, and electrical bolts zapping. It is also a test of sorts to determine whether the Serpent Squad is worthy of serving the Red Skull.

The on-site security at the firm is heavy due to terrorist threats, corporate espionage, and the anger of American workers over outsourcing. Sin's father has supplied her with detailed intelligence on the deployment of armed guards and the location of the central alarm system. Before the head of security can activate the red-alert warning, Sin sends him sprawling with a salvo from her .44-magnum pistols.

"Let's see what you've got, boys!" Sin yells as she guns down another guard.

King Cobra wraps his elastic legs around the throat of a guard, crushing the life out of him while firing venom projectiles from his wrist-shooters at two others. His resentment of Sin's leadership is apparent.

"Be mindful of your *tone*, Sin. There is only one of us here who has yet to prove himself."

Sin calls to Viper as she holsters her guns and uses her thumbs to gouge out eyeballs.

"You heard the man, Viper. You have to prove yourself by inflicting terror, pain, and agonizing death if you want to be part of this squad."

Viper raises his fists and projects contained force fields that pulverize the bones of a security agent, turning his internal organs to mush. His voice is low, and all but expressionless.

"You are definitely your father's darling little girl, Sin."

Viper's fists are still smoking as he uses them to pulp and flatten the face of a guard who is begging for his life.

Red Skull's daughter is happily kicking out the teeth of a female data administrator while giving Eel the order to fry the servers and mainframes. Eel complies by inducing a flash overload that bypasses the surge-protectors and turns every chip in the facility to smoldering silicon scrap.

Sin leads her cohorts out through the shattered doors while Viper mops up the survivors. King Cobra has the audacity to ask what the place they just trashed was.

"All the data from the Chinese, Japanese, and Korean stock markets gets processed here for the morning bell on Wall Street."

"So we just crashed the stock market?"

"Not entirely, but enough to warm the cockles of father's heart. Nothing like a little anarchy mixed in with your capitalism, right?"

Viper and Eel find Sin's joke hilarious. King Cobra asks, "What's next, Avengers Mansion?"

Sin's reply stops the laughter dead.

"Not quite. We're going to go kick some S.H.I.E.L.D. butt."

ELEVEN

IN the East Village—on the roof of what used to be called a flophouse but is now termed "transient accommodations"— Bucky Barnes breathes in the night air and escapes from the dingy claustrophobia of his room. He has been modulating his rage and rethinking his strategy. He knows better than to act rashly, and he is a patient man. But he also knows his foes are not resting, and his window for action is closing fast.

The Red Skull is behind it all. That is the one thing Bucky is sure of. Even though, in Lukin's employ as the Winter Soldier, he himself shot Red Skull, Bucky knows that the evil mastermind has cheated death before. A single bullet might not have done the trick. Being dead is the best cover there is. Red Skull's footprint has been evident in too many of the terrible things that have happened, including the killing of Steve Rogers.

Crossbones, the shooter he turned over to S.H.I.E.L.D. by way of Falcon, is just a puppet being manipulated by some intermediary for the Red Skull's benefit. The old *Roter Totenkopf* is too clever to soil his own hands handling thugs and assassins. Winter Soldier is now a ghost *ronin*, a wraith with no master, and as such has no access to the intelligence channels that might help in his search for Red Skull.

The cloud cover breaks, and Bucky catches a glimpse of the Helicarrier as it circles in a racetrack pattern over

Manhattan, Brooklyn, and Queens. He notices it is flanked by a pair of subcarriers, which function like the destroyer screens on conventional seagoing aircraft carriers. The smaller, faster airships are added security and can intercept any perceived threats to the mother ship.

He regrets blowing the cover of Fury's hijacked L.M.D. while searching for the shield. There might have been another way to accomplish that. The fake Nick Fury could have been put to better use affording him access to the Helicarrier. There are two people up there he would like to get his hands on: Tony Stark, of course. The second is Crossbones—who can at least lead him to the intermediary, and then possibly to the Red Skull himself.

There's no way to know how much Black Widow told them during her debriefing, but it was certainly enough for them to be expecting Winter Soldier to come calling. Bucky has no idea how he's going to get into the Helicarrier, but he knows what Steve Rogers would have said.

"There's always a way."

But until he finds a way, he's going to keep up his search for the Red Skull by any means at his disposal.

In the secure holding area on Level Seven of the Helicarrier, Brock Rumlow sits in the interrogation room across the table from Professor Charles Xavier, the founder of the X-Men and the most powerful psi-talent on the planet. The purported assassin of Captain America has not answered a single question. But that is to be expected, since Professor X has not asked any. The only sound in the room for the past half hour has been the rattle of the chain that secures Crossbones' wrists to the table and an occasional electronic hum from Xavier's wheelchair. At last, Rumlow breaks the silence.

"I can feel you in there, rummaging around, you know. In my mind."

Xavier waves at the two-way mirror to signal he wants to leave. The locking lugs on the steel door retract as he wheels himself away from the table.

"That is a sensory illusion. Your memories, hopes, and fears are egregious, but no more so than the usual homicidal sociopath. I'm done here."

Crossbones grins and shakes his shackles.

"Come on, don't you want to dig into all that stuff I suppressed about my childhood?"

Professor X rolls to the door. He doesn't bother to face Crossbones when he replies.

"If I were a vindictive man, I'd drag the memory your subconscious has totally blocked into the light of day: what your mother's boyfriend did to you with the socket wrench when you were seven, and what you did to your mother's kitten in revenge."

Tony Stark is waiting for Xavier on the other side of the door.

"Did you get anything out of him, Charles? He's been stonewalling us for days."

"I probed as deeply as possible, Tony. Someone has erased entire sections of that man's memory. He doesn't even know for sure the Red Skull is supposedly alive, let alone what his plans or his whereabouts."

Through the two-way mirror, they can both see Brock Rumlow making faces at them. A shadow passes over his face, as if a bad memory has bubbled to the surface.

"Was it another telepath who did the erasing? Can you tell something like that?"

"A telepath would have been more selective and removed only what was necessary. This was a brutal excision of whole swaths of memory. He's lucky he's not having blackouts. I'm sorry— retrieval by any means is impossible if the neural pathways are no longer there."

In the interrogation room, Crossbones beats his forehead against the steel tabletop.

Xavier touches the two-way glass.

"You can't keep him in the Helicarrier brig indefinitely, Tony."

Tony Stark thinks for a second that his mind has been read. But he knows the Professor respects his privacy. He averts his eyes from the sight of Crossbones punishing himself.

"We're transferring him to the maximum-security level of the Raft."

Professor Xavier has always been dubious about special facilities built to contain and control superhuman and mutant criminals. But Crossbones is nothing much more than an extraordinarily strong human with a high pain threshold. The high-security prison off Rykers Island in the East River should be more than enough to contain him. It occurs to Xavier that the vulnerable link in the chain of custody is the means of transfer between the Helicarrier and the Raft, but he doesn't voice his opinion.

The next day finds Falcon on the roof of the *Daily Bugle* building in Midtown Manhattan. He has opened a small, secret compartment in the back of the iconic sign's fifteen-foot-high "B." At head level, Falcon faces a tiny lens and an even tinier microphone. This is one of eleven communication hubs Nick Fury has hidden in scattered sites around the city. Falcon has had to memorize the locations and the logic behind the rotating access codes. It's as secure as anything can possibly be, since the signals are encrypted and piggyback on legitimate communications channels, but Falcon and Fury choose their words with the possibility of interception in mind.

"The main office is going to hell in a handcart, and that new kid decided to turn off his damn phone. We need to get him back on the program, and fast."

"He's a maverick, boss—just like you in your younger days. Could be he's cooking up a deal of his own?"

"If he has his way, heads will roll in a few corner offices."

"I think we may be glad to see one of those offices vacated."

"But the other exec is a good egg in a lousy situation who may be derailed for now but has a chance of getting back on track."

"You're more forgiving than I thought, boss."

"No, just practical. More like a sergeant in the field than an officer in headquarters. You have to find that maverick and get him back into the herd."

"I hear you, but if he's off the grid—"

"Keep in touch. I have a couple of options I'm looking into that might flush the kid out of the woodwork."

Falcon turns off the unit, reseals the compartment, and turns to see Sharon Carter step out from behind the big air-conditioning condenser, where she has been keeping out of the camera frame. Falcon shrugs.

"Fury's just as much in the dark as we are about where Bucky is."

"I knew he'd have contacted you first if he had any leads."

"It sounds like Nick is setting out bait traps or casting lures, but even a wily old campaigner like him might have a hard time out-double-thinking the Winter Soldier. I have serious doubts—"

"Where's this going, Sam?"

"I'm thinking maybe we should give S.H.I.E.L.D. the heads-up—let Tony Stark know Bucky is gunning for him."

A huge flock of pigeons circles the *Bugle* sign and settles on top of the giant letters. Sharon is distracted as it enters her mind that the birds are the Falcon's eyes and ears. They all seem to be looking at her. She snaps her attention back to the conversation at hand.

"Tony already knows. They suspected as soon as Bucky took down Natasha, and they knew for sure after they debriefed her. Winter Soldier doesn't operate haphazardly. He has a plan, and Steve's shield is part of that plan."

All the pigeons turn to bob their heads in Falcon's direction.

"Don't you think you need to share that insight with Stark?"

"I'm not communicating with them, Sam. I don't trust them right now. Lord knows, they've got enough resources to work it out from their side of the street. If we want to find Bucky, then we should concentrate on finding the Red Skull. Bucky will wait for the opportunity to go after Stark, but he's got to have Skull on his hit list, too. In Bucky's view, Stark may take a lot of blame, but Red Skull had to be the one who set all the wheels in motion."

Falcon steps up on the ledge and spreads his wings. The pigeons take off from their perches and swarm around him.

"Hop on, Sharon. I've got some leads on an A.I.M. base. Let's start shaking the tree. There's no telling what might fall out of it."

Sharon locks her arms around Falcon's shoulders, and he steps off into blue sky. It's a straight plummet, a hundred feet down before they catch a thermal to soar through the steel-and-glass canyons of the city.

"Finding the Red Skull will lead us to Bucky." Sharon has to shout above the wind. "And we can't forget it was the Red Skull who had Steve killed. Nothing's ever simple with that evil maniac. That was just the first act in a bigger scenario. He's planning something, and he needed Steve out of the way. The bad blood between them goes back too far. If it was just about killing Steve, Skull would have made a long, drawn-out production out of it and rubbed it in his face."

"Pretty heavy inductive reasoning there, Sharon. You sure you don't know something I don't?"

The silence from Sharon goes on too long. Falcon can feel her heart pounding. It's puzzling, but he lets it go. She's been through hell lately.

"Okay, so we steer clear of S.H.I.E.L.D. and go after the bad guys, instead. We've got us a *plan!*"

INTERLUDE #7

IT'S another routine psychological assessment at the S.H.I.E.L.D. Administration Building. Agent 776 has reported to the session on his lunch break, still in uniform. The psychiatrist's office is dimly lit and furnished in U.N. General Service Modern with no personal touches whatsoever. Agent 776 is eager to get his fitness rating approved, and he is trying hard to appear sincere and open. Although he knows he must have been talking for the last fifty minutes, he can't remember a single thing he said. That should alarm him. Somehow, it doesn't. It seems perfectly fine. Everything is perfectly fine. Perfect.

"Everything is perfectly fine," the psychiatrist says in an evenly modulated voice. "And you understand exactly what I am telling you to do, Patrick?"

"Completely, Doctor. I am to—"

"You are not to speak of this to anybody, and you are to forget I told you to do so. Isn't that just perfect, Patrick?"

"Yes. Perfect."

"Then you may report back to your duties at the resupply station. Be ready for the change tomorrow morning."

"Thank you, Doctor."

TWELVE

THIRTY-SEVEN floors above the psychiatrist's office in the executive suite, Agent 352—Lindley R. Hermann, a section leader of the 3rd Emergency Reaction Team—stands at attention before the director's desk.

"Sir, I believe the United States needs a Captain America now more than ever. As a combat veteran in top physical shape, with no living relatives, I am volunteering to be considered for the honor. Sir."

Unseen by Hermann, his service record, the report on his deep-background check, and his medical file are scrolling on a retinal-bounce display beaming into Tony Stark's right eye. Stark is dismissive but understanding.

"Thank you for your devotion to duty, Agent 352. There's no plan for a new Captain America. The shield and uniform are retired. This matter is not open for future discussion. Is there anything else you wish to speak to me about?"

"No, sir."

"Your offer is appreciated. You are dismissed."

The agent executes a smart about-face and exits the office wearing his dignity like a badge.

Stark waits until he is sure the agent has left the suite entirely before he buzzes his receptionist.

"Please screen my appointments more closely, Anna. I have

a ton of work I have to finish before I report back to the Helicarrier."

"Understood, sir. There is one more person waiting to see you. He says he has a letter for you from Steve Rogers. Shall I tell him you're too busy?"

"No. Send him in."

The middle-aged man who enters Stark's office is wearing an expensive but conservative gray suit and carrying a monogrammed Moroccan leather briefcase. He does not offer to shake hands but sits down with the case on his lap.

"How do you do, Director Stark. My name is Maurice Greely, and I am an attorney representing the interests of one Steve Rogers, currently deceased. I must say, you are a difficult man to see. I've been trying to get an appointment for a long time—"

"And what interests are you representing, Mr. Greely?"

The lawyer snaps open the locks on his briefcase.

"During what you called your 'Civil War,' I was given a letter to deliver to you under certain circumstances—one of those circumstances being the death of my client. Believe me, I never wanted this kind of burden, so it is with great relief that I pass it on to you."

A plain white business envelope is taken from the briefcase, placed on the desk, and moved a nominal three inches in Stark's direction. "For Tony Stark only" is written in a neat hand on the sealed envelope.

"All I know is that the envelope contains the last wishes of Captain America. You can verify his handwriting, and he has included things known only to you and him. He said that despite everything that had happened, you were the only one who was capable of doing what needed to be done if he fell."

"Why not just amend his will?"

"I suggested that. But he insisted this was private, and only between him and you. He said you would understand once you had read it."

Tony Stark opens the envelope, extracts the letter, and pauses to look at the attorney without unfolding it. Greely does not make a move to leave.

"My commission is not fulfilled until I witness you reading the contents. Those were my explicit instructions from Mr. Rogers, and—"

Stark unfolds the letter and reads it. He reads it again, and then a third time. He refolds the letter, reinserts it in the envelope, opens his desk drawer, places it inside, locks the drawer, and drums his fingers on the desktop before he raises his eyes to the lawyer.

"Thank you, Mr. Greely."

Mr. Maurice Greely, Esquire, closes his briefcase and leaves with no further comment.

Again, Tony Stark waits until the reception area is clear before he buzzes Anna.

"I need the Black Widow in my office ASAP."

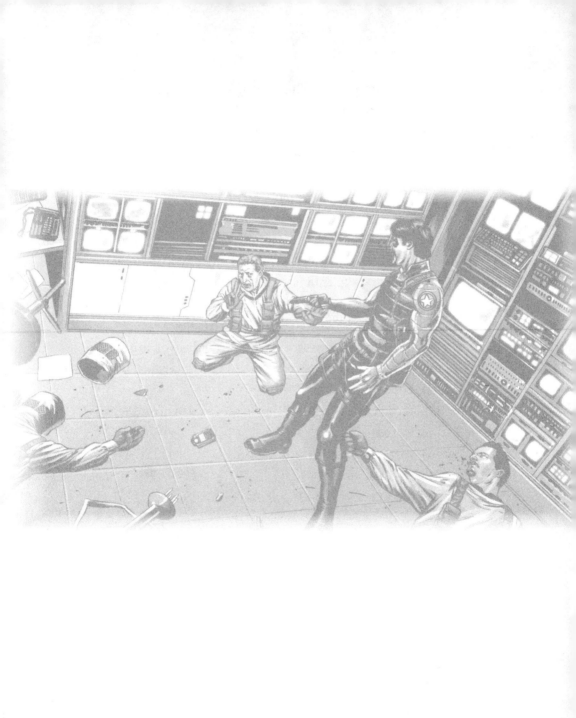

THIRTEEN

THERE is no subtlety to a direct frontal assault. You just bust in the door and take down everything that moves.

Bucky, in his exhaustive search for Red Skull, had gone through the list of dormant A.I.M. sites and checked them out one by one. On the second day, he got lucky. One of the roving listening posts that had a record of working with King Cobra was back in action and staffed with a full complement of techs and security specialists. The site's re-manning had been accomplished with unmarked vans, but a rooftop vantage point had allowed Bucky a glimpse of the yellow boiler suits and bucket-shaped yellow cowls of A.I.M. operatives as they debussed from the van directly through an alley door. He knew his targets would be clearly marked.

Bucky sheds his leather jacket on the fire escape as he descends to the alley and slips on his black domino mask. He ramps up the power capacitors in his EMP projector to maximum and fries the control circuits of the steel door so the locking lugs are frozen shut. He's not going in that way, but he doesn't want anybody sneaking out the back.

Walking around to the front of the building is a calculated risk, but it's the wee hours of the morning in a commercial neighborhood with no nightlife. The building is full of small businesses that supply trimmings, zippers, and buttons to the fashion industry, so the front door is more a barrier to prevent winos from sleeping in the lobby than it is a deterrent to burglary. A hard push with his prosthetic arm is enough to gain entry. The door to the A.I.M. listening post itself is reinforced steel like the alley door. A thermite charge burns through the lock; one blow from Winter Soldier's robotic arm sends the door flying inwards, crushing two operatives. Most A.I.M. members are disaffected tech geeks with no muscle tone or fighting skills, so mopping up is relatively easy. The few who are armed don't know enough to use their weapons from behind cover and suffer the ignominy of having their faces smashed in with the butt stocks of their own plasma-projector rifles. There are no M.O.D.O.C. (Military Organisms Designed Only for Combat) squads at this location, so Winter Soldier hardly breaks a sweat. He walks around the facility kicking the weapons out of reach of the marginally conscious before he approaches the first of the three yellow-clad misanthropes purposely left fully conscious for interrogation. Yanking off the hood reveals a sallow, bearded face, one eye wide with fear. The other eye is squeezed shut under the muzzle of a very big pistol.

"You've got one chance, stupid. Where's the Red Skull?"

"I don't know! I swear—"

Blood and broken teeth shower the other two potential intelligence sources as Winter Soldier rearranges the facial structure of their reticent cohort with the butt of his pistol. The more defiant of the two gets his kneecap shot off, and the smoking pistol traverses to the A.I.M. operative who has soiled his uniform and can't control his shaking. Winter Soldier is forced to shout to be heard above the screaming.

"Your buddies are going to be called 'Gummy' and

'Stumblebum.' Do you want to be 'Lefty,' or is your memory going to suddenly improve?"

"He wasn't lying. We haven't communicated directly with the Red Skull—just with his crazy daughter, and with King Cobra."

"Keep talking."

"She's way off her nut, but she's not stupid. She knows everybody is looking for them, especially after that Wall Street raid. We have no way to initiate contact with her. She calls us."

"For what? What job are you doing for her? What's the intel you're gathering and passing off to her?"

"S.H.I.E.L.D. resupply and maintenance stations—the ones on top of skyscrapers. They service the Helicarrier and subcarriers. She wanted the names of the agents at each location and their shift schedules, as well as the schedules for subcarrier supply shuttles. We weren't told what they wanted it for."

Sin had been right not to tell them, but that doesn't matter. Winter Soldier is certain he now knows what Sin plans to do. But how to find her? If he had twenty agents at his disposal, he could mount a surveillance operation on all the resupply stations. By himself, and unable to man a stakeout 24/7, his odds of being at the right place at the right time are minimally sixty-to-one. He's better off waiting for her to strike and trying to pick up the trail. He will not be goaded into acting prematurely.

He is the Winter Soldier.

He has all the time in the world.

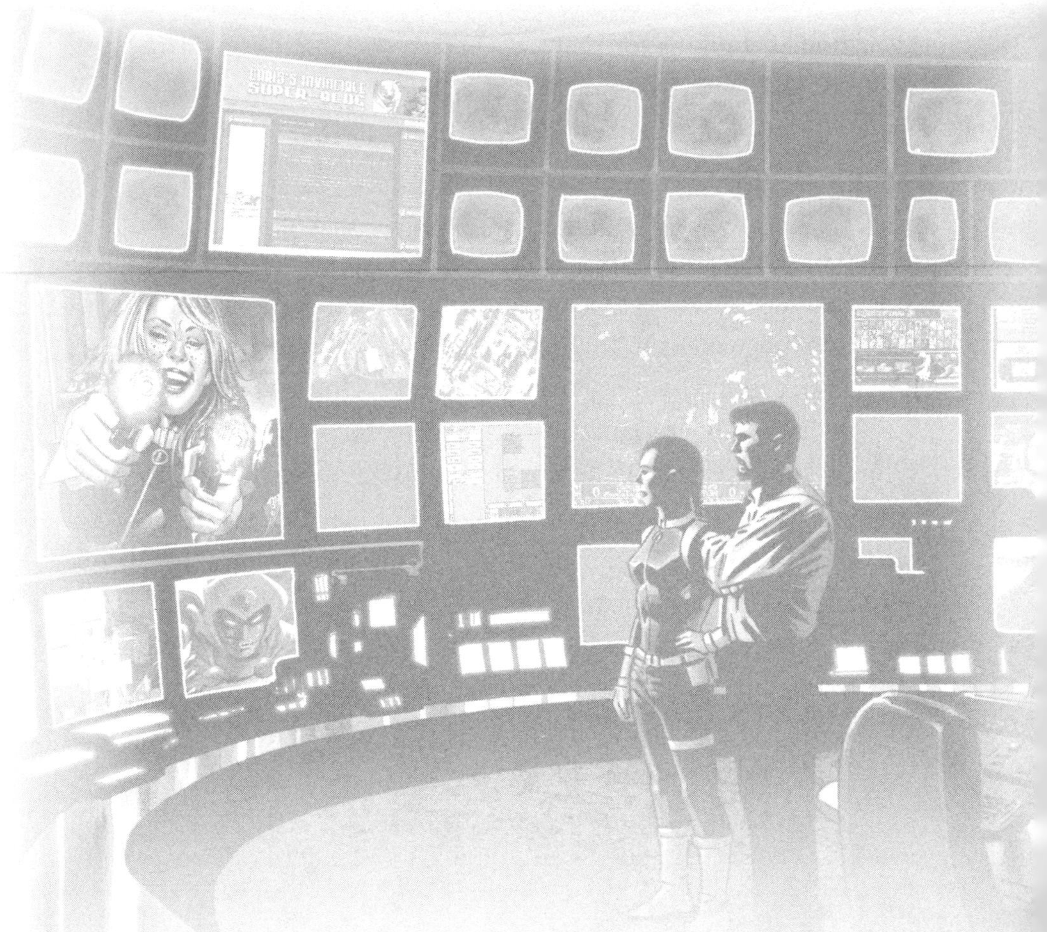

FOURTEEN

THE Helicarrier's Central Combat Information Center is a windowless room connected to the Command and Operations Bridge by a short catwalk. There are no light fixtures in this chamber. All the illumination comes from hundreds of monitors, multifunction situational displays, and holographic projectors. This is the central hub where all S.H.I.E.L.D. intelligence data is sorted, processed, and tagged for evaluation. There are backup sites in deep bunkers in widely dispersed locations around the world. But in combat, and during major operations, the CCIC is the main nerve center that feeds strategic and tactical information directly to the Command and Operations Bridge. Helicarrier crew members call it "The Hive," and they call the intelligence analysts who staff it "drones."

Deputy Director Maria Hill had ordered the CCIC cleared of all personnel for a private briefing with Director Tony Stark. S.H.I.E.L.D.'s two ranking officers face an array of monitors displaying multiple surveillance-camera shots of the same individual: a freckle-faced, red-haired girl in a S.H.I.E.L.D. uniform gleefully shooting similarly dressed agents with a pair of large-bore automatic pistols.

"Facial-recognition programs confirm her identity as Sinthea Schmidt, the Red Skull's daughter," the deputy director reports. "She calls herself Sin these days."

The images on the monitors shift to wider coverage. Sin and

her crew on a rampage through a subcarrier—shooting, smashing, strangling, and electrocuting all who stand in their way. Tony Stark is studying the faces of Sin's colleagues.

"I recognize King Cobra and Eel, but the third creep is a mystery to me."

"After we enhanced the audio, we could hear the others calling him 'Viper.'"

"Another one? Madam Hydra's going to love him."

"She shot the first one—maybe we'll get lucky, and she'll shoot this one, too."

On the screen, the carnage escalates. Sin has worked herself into an ecstatic berserker state. She howls with laughter as she shoots, stomps, and kicks her way through the subcarrier's corridors.

"They actually got aboard a subcarrier?" Stark asks, reaching for the remote. "They breached our security that easily?"

"They stepped on to the subcarrier wearing authentic uniforms and flashing actual security-access cards. They even had holographic-image generators that made their faces look exactly like the agents they were impersonating."

"Walk me through it, Maria. Details, please."

"The Helicarrier is only assigned a nominal number of prisoner-security specialists since we're not equipped to handle a lot of detainees on board. When we moved Crossbones to a subcarrier for transfer to the Raft, they had to make a stop at a resupply station to take on the secure-transfer team. That's where it went wrong."

Stark hands Hill the remote, playing Monday-morning quarterback with himself. How stupid had it been to not realize doubling the security on the Helicarrier and at the Raft meant nothing if the resupply station was left vulnerable? But how easy could it be to compromise any S.H.I.E.L.D. facility? He turns to Deputy Director Hill, who has anticipated his question and has already used the remote to bring up forensic-investigation footage of the resupply station on the roof of the Trans-Unilateral Telecom Tower in downtown Jersey City. Dead agents, stripped to their underwear, lay sprawled where they fell. Most had not drawn their weapons.

A S.H.I.E.L.D. ID card with a photo of a blond man with chiseled features fills the central screen.

"This man—Agent 776, Patrick Stansfield—turned off the surveillance cams, switched the security-data-transfer lines into a repeating loop, and put the alarm system on standby, then simply opened the door and let them in."

Tony Stark catches the illogic of Hill's statement immediately.

"All that was inferred by on-site examination after the fact? How is it possible to know all that?"

"Stansfield had some minor personal issues and had a yellow flag on his file. While that was being sorted out, Internal Security had assigned another agent on the site to surreptitiously record Stansfield on duty with a micro-corneal cam. The cam, which resembles a normal contact lens, went undetected by Sin and her crew."

The director of S.H.I.E.L.D. sits down at an empty console and rubs his eyes.

"And Agent Stansfield was killed along with everybody else at the station, as were security personnel on the subcarrier? I was the one who authorized the transfer, and I'm responsible for not spotting the weak link in our security. I'm going to write personal letters to the families of every agent that was killed."

The deputy director almost tells Stark it isn't really his fault but decides this might be read as sycophancy of the worst sort. She also feels strongly against assuaging any sense of guilt the director might have. *He* should *suffer*, she thinks. *As long as the psychic pain doesn't impinge on the efficacy of the organization, why not let him feel the full brunt of the hurt.* Maria Hill switches back to the surveillance videos from the subcarrier. In the heat of the battle, with alarm Klaxons blaring and emergency lights flashing, Sin shoots the restraints off Crossbones and takes the time to engage in a long tongue-wrestling clinch when they should have been running full-tilt to the escape pods.

"This is unconscionable," Stark says as he averts his eyes. "Crossbones was our only link to the plot that killed Steve Rogers, and we let him get spirited away from under our noses."

"There's more, Director Stark."

"Oh?"

"There were supposed to be a dozen more agents on duty for the transfer and hand-off. They all went off the grid right before the raid. No GPS signals, no commo responses, nothing missing from their living quarters. They just vanished."

Stark slumps at the console momentarily, then sits up alert and angry.

"We've got a mole—or a major penetration, at the very least. I want every field unit reprioritized to hunt down Sin and Crossbones. I want the entire Intelligence section vetted by Internal Security, and vice versa. After that, both sections are going to run deep-background investigations on the dead and missing agents, and account for every second of Agent Stansfield's activities for the past year."

"I'll upload all that to the file dump as soon as possible. Is there anything else you need, sir?"

"One other thing. I got in a preliminary field report from Black Widow, who I assigned to track down Winter Soldier. Also got in a whole file of NYPD incident reports that were tagged because our analysts think Widow was involved. It seems she's been rousting the dive bars and fleabag hotels Bucky has been known to frequent. Lacerations, soft-tissue damage, fractures, and concussions were listed in the police write-ups. But nobody wanted to file a complaint, and everybody involved developed convenient cases of amnesia about the appearance of the perp. Black Widow's report lists all the bars mentioned in the police write-ups."

Maria Hill carefully assesses her options in replying. She has definite opinions about Natalia Romanova, but will voicing them come off as being spiteful? She has ambitions, which have been sidelined by Tony Stark supplanting her as director. She also has a duty to give the director an honest assessment.

"You sent a former Russian spy and assassin to hunt down another former Russian spy and assassin. The techniques and methodologies they employ are neither subtle nor gentle. What did you expect?"

Stark gives a verbal command to the computer controlling the displays, and a digital copy of the report appears on the main screen.

"As you said before, Maria—there's more. She gives a detailed account of her inquiries into the underground-mercenary circuit, illegal-weapons suppliers, itinerant-intelligence purveyors, snitches, and the usual hard guys with something to sell. She came up with zilch. I also get the impression she's holding something back."

Deputy Director Hill is inwardly amazed at how little this man seems to understand about women. But her face does not betray her when she answers.

"Women always hold back something about men they've been involved with."

"She said they only trained together. And she told me Bucky blamed me for Cap's death, and that he was planning to come after me for that. Isn't that a major betrayal of his trust?"

"I doubt she used the adverb 'only.' That changes the meaning completely. And sometimes a small betrayal is the blind that covers a bigger one."

The words are out of her mouth before she has time to regret what she has said. But there is no retracting them. She has to let them lie on the table like little white worms.

"Thank you, Maria. You've given me a lot to think about."

INTERLUDE #8

"**THIS** isn't what we agreed upon, Skull. Our pact was highly specific in its details."

"So was the Molotov-Ribbentrop Pact between Hitler and Stalin, and we know how that one turned out, do we not?"

"Yes, with the death of your master and the rise of the Rodina, the Motherland."

"You call that rising, do you, Lukin? Five decades of expending resources in a losing arms race and exporting revolution to countries still mired in tribalism, and you still can't get a decent Schnitzel in Moscow."

"And how is your glorious Thousand Year Reich faring, then?"

"Who cares about the Reich? I am bigger than fascism now. I am my own force."

"No. You are an ignorant sadist, Johann. And you are taking far too much time out there because you are distracted by personal vendettas. You are losing track of the goal we agreed to work toward together. Don't make me fight you for dominance. This is my territory, and I will crush you if I have to."

"You will do nothing of the sort, Lukin."

"You don't want to put that to the test."

"There is no test. I know that what you stand to gain from this...alliance is too great for you to throw away. I know this because I have seen your most private and hidden thoughts."

"Damn you, Red Skull—"

"Yes, that is a given. And what could you have possibly been thinking? That I was asleep in here all this time?"

FIFTEEN

HE'S sitting in a bar. But it isn't a blue-collar neighborhood watering hole, dive bar, or biker hangout like the usual haunts of James "Bucky" Barnes. This is another all-male establishment but definitely catering to an upscale clientele more likely to order cosmopolitans than boilermakers. Changing his patterns was simply good tradecraft after he caught the first whiff of Black Widow on his trail. Forsaking the SROs of the Lower East Side in favor of trendy-but-pricey hostelries along the West Side Highway was also part of the evasion agenda. He has slipped the bartender a sizeable tip and let it be known that he's not looking for trouble, he's not a cop, and he just wants to be left alone to sip his imported Pilsner and watch the cable news.

When the news item finally comes on the TV, it is afforded less airtime than the spectacular public meltdown of a popular former child star. The report is based on a leak from an "anonymous inside source," and is couched in euphemisms and vague assumptions. The gist of it being that Brock Rumlow—a.k.a. Crossbones, the only suspect in custody for the murder of Captain America—has apparently escaped with the aid of unnamed accomplices. S.H.I.E.L.D. has not released an official statement, which leads news analysts to believe there were casualties whose families have yet to be notified. Unconfirmed rumor has it that the escape occurred during the transfer of the prisoner from the Helicarrier to the Raft. The reaction from the bar patrons is unanimous. "They should have let that creep take a walk off the Helicarrier flight deck." The bartender turns to comment on the news report to the brooding hunk in the leather jacket. But he's gone, and there's a pile of cash next to the empty glass on the beer mat.

His initial outrage percolates away as Winter Soldier makes his way across the rooftops heading uptown. Anger clouds judgment, and he needs all his faculties if he wants to get his revenge. The analytical part of his brain is parsing the input, rearranging the known facts, overlaying them with probabilities, and readjusting the curve. The known facts are: The Red Skull has all the best motives for breaking Crossbones out; the Red Skull's daughter, Sin, acquired data on S.H.I.E.L.D. resupply stations from A.I.M.; the resupply stations service the subcarriers, which are the most secure means of transferring a prisoner. Therefore, the most likely scenario is that Sin—acting on her father's orders— orchestrated a raid on a subcarrier to free Crossbones, and that the murderer of Captain America is now free to do more of Red Skull's bidding. The one sure lead Winter Soldier had for locating Red Skull is now gone, and the only option remaining is one that requires him to go where he never wished to go again: Kronas Tower in Midtown Manhattan.

The lair of Aleksander Lukin.

The train of Bucky's logic starts with his most treasured memory of recent times: the last time he fought side-by-side with Captain America, in London during the lead-up to the Civil War between the superhumans. The Red Skull had unleashed an upgraded version of his giant "Deathbot," which Captain America and Bucky had first encountered during the Second World War. It had been a classic tag-team maneuver with Cap providing the distraction that enabled Bucky to throw an explosive charge into a hole in the robot's armor. One of the buildings destroyed in the Deathbot's rampage had been the London headquarters of the Kronas Corporation. In retrospect, that was revealed to have been a brilliant sacrificial gambit that obscured the cold fact that the Deathbot had been constructed in a tunnel system owned by Lukin's company. The nagging question remains: Would Aleksander Lukin have put aside his abiding hatred for Red Skull to collude with him toward a mutual goal?

Bucky is on his way to find out by whatever means is at hand. Penetrating the security at Kronas Tower would be nearly impossible for anybody other than Winter Soldier. As the deadly instrument of Lukin's will, he had enjoyed complete access to the most secret and secure corners of the skyscraper. He had come and gone through hidden stairs and passageways, traveled vertically up and down internal air shafts, and crept through subterranean ducts from adjoining buildings. The passwords and security codes change daily, but he was privy to the algorithms that created them.

Winter Soldier had been a perfect weapon and zero security risk because his memory could be selectively wiped after every mission. But now he *remembers*, and that perfect weapon is running loose with no decent restraints—operating beyond the pale, with little mercy in his heart for the man who used him with no mercy at all.

SIXTEEN

YOU'D think an organization full of technical geniuses would learn from past mistakes. As many times as A.I.M. facilities have been taken down recently, all they've done is increase the complexity of their entry codes. It seems that tech geeks are very good at protecting themselves against other tech geeks, but pretty useless against the likes of Falcon and me.

I shoot out the lock, and Falcon punches down the door. A few of them have the wherewithal to mount a modest armed defense, but most of them just run around in a panic. Luckily, the armed ones are the type who look down their noses at conventional firearms in favor of pulse pistols and plasma projectors of their own design, which are too complex to be field-practical or dependable. Those of us who have to deal with the A.I.M. fanatics refer to them as "beekeepers" or "bucket-heads" because the cylindrical hazard-suit helmet they wear resembles the headgear of apiarists.

The fight stands in the balance when one of the A.I.M. members gives the order to call out the M.O.D.O.C. Squads. The last thing we need is well-armed armored goons with a hive mind showing up to rain on our parade. Falcon yells, "Stop that bucket-head!" One of the wounded beekeepers is staggering toward a big, red panic button mounted on the wall under a yellow-and-black-striped safety cover. He's got the cover half-lifted when I bring my elbow down hard on his spine just below where it meets his skull. No "Military Operatives Designed Only for Combat" are being summoned that way.

Team fighting involves watching your partner's back, but my preemptive foray leaves an opening for a bucket-head with a flamethrower to step out from behind a corner. He sets Falcon's costume alight with a stream of jellied gasoline. I drop to a knee and get off one supported and aimed shot with my pistol, rupturing the compressed fuel tank on the flamethrower operator's back. Sparks from the bullet entry ignite the contents; the operator runs down the hall, screaming, *en flambé*.

Falcon is pulling off his burning shirt with one hand and punching out bucket-heads with the other. He is a sight to dismay the remaining A.I.M. security goons, since his gloves and head are still on fire. I grab a fire extinguisher and start to douse him, but he is not having it.

"Don't waste time over me," he says as he sinks his fist into a yellow-clad midsection. "Get to the computer bank before they erase everything. We need that intel to find the Skull."

Nick Fury had provided us with a ground-penetrating radar scan of the A.I.M. facility, so I already knew which underground passage led to the computer suite. There's no resistance as I run through the maze of corridors with my pistol ready in a two-handed combat grip.

I enter the computer chamber to find a senior A.I.M. tech punching a long series of numbers into a keyboard while an armed goon urges him to speed things along. Again, the tech-geeks are undone by their addiction to complicated security measures. The armed goon lets loose at me with a shoulder-fired plasma cannon that singes my right shoulder and gouges a ten-foot furrow in the corridor wall behind me. I put three rounds of high-velocity, armor-piercing 9mm through his center of mass before I traverse my point of aim to the tech-geek who's taken off his helmet to read the LED numbers on the security lock. I tell him in no uncertain terms to get the hell away from the keyboard. He complies, raising his hands as if to protect his face. He is so scared that snot is running out of his nose and mixing with the blood splatter from his companion. He is pleading between the whimpering and sniffling.

"Please. Don't kill me."

I take my gun sights off his face. I start to say, "I'm not a—" But I am holding the same gun I used when—

Oh my god.

I blink, and I see Steve on the courthouse steps. I see the blood welling from the wound in his shoulder. I see the look in his eyes when I draw my—

I close my eyes, but the image will not go away. It just coalesces into sharper focus, and I hear the three pistol shots echoing over and over.

Nausea hits me like a punch in the gut. Turning away, I lose my lunch in a series of painful spasms. It brings no relief to the despair and self-disgust. In my peripheral vision, I see the tech-geek reaching for the plasma cannon in the hand of the goon I shot. All I have to do is pivot and shoot. I just watch him, instead. Let him do it for me, I think. Let him end my psychic pain forever. It's an odd relief I feel as the weapon rises, and I am staring directly into the muzzle. The tech no longer looks frightened. He looks jubilant. Triumphant. His finger tightens on the trigger.

A red boot smashes the tech's face to a pulp, and the plasma cannon clatters to the floor.

Falcon.

He's standing over me, asking whether I'm okay. He's bare-chested, and angry red burns cover his shoulders and back. He must be in terrible pain, but his concern is only for me.

I tell him I'm fine, and I just lost my equilibrium for a minute. I know it's a lame excuse. I can see he doesn't believe it, but he doesn't press the issue. I ask myself how I deserve a friend like this. I wonder whether he would still be my friend if he knew what I did.

"Let's just get what we need and get out of here, Sam."

SEVENTEEN

TRANSCRIPT of secure encrypted voice communication between agent Natalia Romanova (Black Widow) and Director Tony Stark.

NR: I ran out of other leads, so I started a rotating surveillance on the A.I.M. sites that the S.H.I.E.L.D. counterintelligence team believes are also known to Nick Fury.

TS: On the assumption that the data was provided to Bucky deliberately by Fury?

NR: We don't know that. Winter Soldier may have compromised Fury's security and accessed the files himself. He has the technical expertise to do so.

TS: You wouldn't be reporting in if you hadn't found something. Do you know where Bucky is now?

NR: No, but I found an A.I.M. listening post that had been sanitized recently—all hard surfaces wiped down with bleach, and all computers wiped. Some hardware at head level has been removed. That may be because of bullet damage. Soviet-era wet-work operatives were trained to go for head shots. There were traces of smokeless powder residue and blood inside one of the ventilator ducts. I snaked the floor drains, and I found a spent .45 ACP cartridge caught in one of the traps. The Winter Soldier was definitely there.

TS: There are a lot of operatives out there using .45 caliber—

NR: I had a gunsmith friend check the rifling markings on the shell. She said she'd never seen anything similar. I checked the OSS records from the Second World War. They had insisted the barrels in the .45-caliber automatic pistols supplied to the USSR as part of the Lend Lease program have a unique twist, so they could be identified in the future. The gun that ejected the shell I found was part of a shipment to Russia in 1942, and no specimen of that shipment has ever surfaced in the United States—until now.

TS: That's very convincing, Natasha, but where does that leave us?

NR: Nowhere. But when I concentrated my attentions on another A.I.M. site, I found it was in the midst of being raided by the former Agent 13, abetted by the Falcon.

TS: Sharon Carter and Sam Wilson were on the same trail?

NR: Exactly.

TS: That would mean...

NR: That they probably have the same source of intel?

TS: Is it stretching you too thin to keep an eye on Carter and Wilson as you search for Winter Soldier?

NR: Impossible to maintain covert surveillance on a subject who can fly and has every bird within a half-mile spying for him.

TS: Stay on Bucky, then. Give me the heads-up if you find anything, no matter how trivial.

NR: Understood.

With one hit of the "delete" key, Director Stark erases the only record of his communication with Black Widow. He is in his office on the top floor of the S.H.I.E.L.D. administration building, an armored sanctum that has more flat-screen monitors than a motion-picture editing suite. It is a functioning smaller version of the Combat Information Center in the Helicarrier, with the main difference being that all the monitors and retrieval systems can be controlled from Stark's desk.

The director leans back and slowly rotates his chair to scan the panoply of screens displaying diverse streams of information, edited blocks of surveillance footage, and scrolling columns of data. One large screen begins flashing, signaling a pre-flagged incoming alert. Stark grays down the other screens and expands the flashing one to cover half the wall. It's Agent 32—the leader of the investigation team that went to interview Dr. Benjamin, the psychiatrist who had been conducting the evaluations on all the missing agents. Although the burly agent fills most of the screen, other agents can be seen behind him pulling books from shelves and opening drawers.

"There's nobody here, sir. His house is deserted."

"Is that a preliminary assessment, or have you ripped up the floorboards yet?"

"Sir, we shut off power at the main trunk and made an armed forced entry covering all egress points. We then conducted a room-to-room in complete darkness with night-vision goggles and came up with *nada*. The power has been switched back on, and we've got the forensics unit going through now with dogs, sniffer packs, and metal detectors."

Tony Stark feels a migraine coming on. He wishes he had a drink. But he always wishes he had a drink. He is about to sign off when he sees a forensics tech in a white crime-scene coverall whispering to Agent 32.

"Sir, one of the dogs found something in the basement."

The camera wobbles as it follows the tech and Agent 32 down the stairs to the basement where a dog handler, a panting beagle, and two enforcement agents are standing next to an open chest freezer that has been partially emptied. The forensics tech is explaining as the camera approaches the freezer.

"Charmaine—that's the beagle, sir—she kept coming back to the freezer, so we started taking out the frozen dinners and bags of venison and pheasant, and I think we found Dr. Benjamin, sir."

The camera tilts down into the freezer to reveal the psychiatrist on his side in a fetal position, his head nestled between a package of pork chops and a family-sized bag of broccoli florets.

"He's got a bad case of freezer burn, sir. I'd say he's been in there a long time."

EIGHTEEN

THE man who used to be the Soviet's premier assassin and dirty-tricks specialist waits in the dark for the man who used to be his controller. The alarms and sensors have been deactivated, and a loop circuit has been wired into the control box at the door so the system appears to be functioning normally and will respond to the entry code. Three guards with Russian Mafia tattoos are unconscious and duct-taped in the pantry.

Aleksander Lukin's penthouse atop the Kronas Corporation Tower boasts picture windows with stunning views of the city in all directions, but the Winter Soldier's attention is focused on the door that provides entry from the private elevator.

When the elevator opens, two distinct voices can be heard arguing. Winter Soldier steps back into the shadows, behind a wall. Lukin had always been a very private individual, so the Winter Soldier had not even factored the idea of Lukin allowing even a close colleague into his sanctum into the plans. Now, those plans have to be rethought, to account for an unknown factor. Winter Soldier decides to wait until he can assess the new situation before he acts.

"Damn you, Red Skull—"

It's Lukin's voice, clear as a bell. Lukin is having Red Skull over for vodka and caviar? The two archenemies are now in league with each other? How can that be? Winter Soldier inches farther back. He can't see who has stepped out of the elevator into the foyer. Footsteps are approaching.

"Yes, that is a given. And what could you have possibly been thinking...?"

That's definitely the Red Skull replying. The inflections, the pronunciation of "given" as "giffen," the slight sibilance—but the timbre of the voice itself is all wrong. The pitch is too high.

"...that I was asleep in there all this time?"

The speaker steps into view, and it is Aleksander Lukin. There are no other passengers on the elevator. The man is having a conversation with himself in two different voices.

The thought enters Winter Soldier's mind that Lukin has gone over the edge into complete insanity, and then he decides he doesn't care. He slips out of the shadows and slams the Russian oligarch against the wall.

"Surprised to see me, Lukin?"

"I'm surprised you didn't kill me outright. You've lost your touch, Winter Soldier."

"No, I'm saving that for later."

"Then why are you here? Not looking for work, are you?"

"Not hardly. You disgust me, you know. You always made out how your worldview was so superior, that you had such lofty ideals and such loyalty to a higher cause—but now you're nothing but a sham."

Lukin attempts to hit Winter Soldier with a right hook, but a metallic hand catches the fist mid-strike.

"That was stupid, Aleksander. You, of all people, should know that isn't going to work on me. So, tell me—why are you working with the Red Skull? I overheard you rehearsing a conversation with him, talking to yourself. That's low, even for a mass murderer like you."

"Are you sure you want to be tossing that word around?"

Lukin can feel the grip tightening on his lapel. He doesn't seem concerned or worried in the slightest. Alarm bells that should have been going off in Winter Soldier's brain are muted by overwhelming anger.

"Don't push it. Just tell me where I can find Red Skull, and maybe I'll let you off with nothing more than a couple of broken arms."

"You want to find the Red Skull? Oh, that is quite amusing. *C'est très drôle*, as the French say. More so than you realize."

A hidden panel in the opposite wall slides open before Winter Soldier can answer, and the towering over-muscled mercenary known as Crossbones strides into the room followed by Sin. Both have pistols drawn and ready.

"Hands off the boss man, sidekick."

Sin giggles. She thinks her lover is *so* clever.

Lukin pulls his hand loose from Winter Soldier's grip.

"Do you see now?"

Crossbones holsters his gun and gets in the first punch before Winter Soldier can release Lukin's lapel and turn to face him. Several punches, kicks, and combinations batter the smaller man to the floor. Sin stands ready with pistol aimed in case Winter Soldier gets the edge on her boyfriend.

"You're going to hurt, but you won't die just yet," Lukin says as he pulls a red rubber mask from his pocket. "We need you for something very important."

As Lukin draws the skull mask over his head, the timbre of his voice changes. Red Skull is now completely in charge of Lukin's body.

"Would the Aleksander Lukin you knew ever cooperate with the Red Skull voluntarily? Weren't you trained to be on the watch for anomalies like that? Very sloppy pedagogy on Lukin's part."

Winter Soldier intercepts a vicious kick aimed at his head with his robotic arm and sends Crossbones staggering backward, trying to regain his balance. Before Bucky can follow up with a counterattack, Sin is on his back and pressing her pistol muzzle into his temple. Her finger takes up the slack on the trigger. Her father's voice growls, "I said we need him for later. Did you not hear me?"

Sin is lifted off her feet by Winter Soldier and flung across the room to bowl over Crossbones. Winter Soldier is on both Sin and Crossbones in a flash, smacking Sin out of the way with a powerful backhand. He hauls Crossbones to his feet, takes him up in a full body lift, and brings him down headfirst on a Le Corbusier mechanics desk, instantly turning it into very expensive kindling.

"Did that hurt? Probably not enough to suit me, but we can fix that."

Sin attempts a knife thrust from behind, but Winter Soldier deflects it with his prosthetic arm, shattering the blade. A knee in her gut and an elbow in her face puts her down on the floor in a dazed and bloody state.

"Haven't you ever fought anybody who knows what they're doing? Or do you specialize in innocent bystanders?"

It is not the Winter Soldier who turns to the man who has Red Skull living in his head. It is the grown-up boy who was once Captain America's fighting partner.

"Don't go away. I'll get to you next."

There is no expression to read on the mask. It is just the face of death molded in rubber and tinted red.

Captain America's grown-up boy-partner stands over the semiconscious Crossbones and kicks away the splintered pieces of the desk.

"You shot my friend, and I don't have many friends."

Mechanical fingers close around Crossbones' throat and lift him until his feet are dangling an inch off the floor. The fingers start tightening like a vise. The mercenary's boots kick, seeking traction that isn't there. Under the black-and-white skull mask, veins are popping. There is no exultation in Bucky's face, only determination. A shudder runs through Crossbones' body.

"Interesting," says the body of Aleksander Lukin speaking with Red Skull's voice. "Steve Rogers would never have thought of cold-blooded murder as an option."

It is the Winter Soldier—not Bucky—who drops Crossbones, then turns to address the man with the red mask.

"You do not have the right to speak his name."

"His name means nothing. He's dead."

The Winter Soldier's march across the room carries the Red Skull to the row of windows facing south until the back of the red rubber mask is touching the glass.

The steel fingers that had just been squeezing Crossbones' throat are now poised to crush the larynx of the man who is speaking with the Red Skull's voice.

"You're the one who deserves to be dead."

"For what? I give orders, and people die. Joan of Arc did

that, and she's a saint. *You're* the one with real blood on your hands, Winter Soldier."

"You go to hell."

"Then send me there. Do what Captain America could never accomplish. Of course, then you'll never find out who it was that betrayed him."

The steel fingers begin to loosen. A grin spreads across the red mask.

"Oh, and one more thing...*Sputnik.*"

The eyes roll up in Winter Soldier's head, his muscles relax, and he falls, senseless.

On the other side of the room, Crossbones drags himself out of the wreckage of the desk, gingerly touching the raw welts on his neck. Sin is still out cold. Crossbones limps to the crumpled figure at the feet of his boss and kicks him hard. There is no response.

"Damn. How'd you do that?"

"It's the old shutdown code implanted by his Soviet handlers. Unfortunately, it only works once."

"Why didn't you use that while he was, you know—"

"Giving you and Sin a thrashing? I needed to see if he was really willing to kill you. Because if he wasn't, he would be completely useless to me."

NINETEEN

NO.

This can't be happening, can it?

I'd been feeling crummy for a long time. But that could be chalked up to the circumstances of the past few months, right? I have very good reasons to feel bad, the least of which is my inability to shoot myself and get it all over with. Why shouldn't I have constant headaches and nausea? My rationalization is that I have to make good on what I did by going after the people who used me to do their dirty work, but how do I do that when they can exert control over me whenever they want?

So here I am standing in my bathroom again. But instead of my pistol, what I have in my hand is a damn white plastic dipstick with two solid bars showing in the results window.

"Positive."

What are you going to do, Sharon Carter? What are you going to do?

Denial is the first phase. A frantic search on the Internet tells me possible reasons for false positives include five types of cancer. Not an alternative that brightens my day.

Denial gives way to despair, but I'm already in that over my head. I'm already angry, too. Too angry to give in, too angry to let the bad guys win by default, too angry to wallow in self-pity.

I go for a five-mile run. That helps some. I sit at the bottom of my shower with the water spraying on me until my toes turn to prunes. But nothing shuts my brain off or stops the steady stream of memory. Nothing dampens the pain.

The baby has to be Steve's.

There was nobody else.

What should have been joy is turned to desolation by unremitting guilt. The more I think about, the worse it gets. Memories come back, clear and bright, when I want them to be fuzzy and indistinct.

Details.

The painful memories of details observed up close, taken for granted at the time, but treasured now. Treasured, yet stabbing my conscience with icy daggers. The gold flecks in the blue of his eyes, only visible from inches away. The heat of his breath on the back of my neck when he slept next to me. The scent of the aftershave he insisted on buying at discount drug stores, because it was the one he used to get at the PX during the war. All daggers through my heart.

And the worst memory of all, from the hospital after the shooting: Steve on the gurney in the ambulance with the EMTs plugging him into IVs and applying pressure bandages to his wounds—the way he looked at me, and said my name, and told me I took his breath away.

He knew.

Steve *knew* what I had done.

TWENTY

AFTER the salutation, the letter starts off, "If you are reading this, things have gone worse than either of us could have imagined..."

The letter sits on Tony Stark's desk, in his office in the S.H.I.E.L.D. Administration Building. He has read it ten times; each time he reads it, he is more perplexed and more confused. Each time he reads it, his mind races down new avenues of probabilities, cherry-picks the most likely, and extrapolates scenarios. Nothing is clicking into place. No eureka moments. No joy.

In an alcove in the wall opposite the big bank of monitor screens is a single framed black-and-white photograph. Not a pristine art print, but a creased and faded contact made from a large-format negative. It is a group shot depicting Captain America, Bucky Barnes, Sergeant Nick Fury, and Corporal Dum Dum Dugan standing in front of a bombed-out farmhouse somewhere in Europe during the Second World War. The ruins are still smoking, and there are bullet holes in what are left of the walls. The weapons in their hands are locked open on spent magazines, and their ammo pouches are empty. It is obvious they have been told to smile for the camera. Maybe the picture was intended to sell war bonds. It was important to put a good face on the war back then. But what soldier smiles after a firefight? The Duke of Wellington's comment on Waterloo was, "The only thing sadder than a battle lost, is a battle won." Can men such as these be turned from the beliefs for which they had been willing to lay down their lives?

Tony Stark has reviewed all the media and surveillance footage, all the phone-cam videos, and all the helmet- and lapel-mounted camera footage from U.S. Marshals, NYPD, Homeland Security and S.H.I.E.L.D. itself. He has read every written report by every witness. He has studied a dozen action assessments written by profilers, psychologists, ballistics experts, and image-manipulation specialists. He has done all he can do, and still he feels like he is missing something.

"Computer, upload file 'Fallen Son' on all screens."

A wall of monitors and various holographic projections spring to life, playing out the events on the Federal Courthouse steps the day Captain America died. There are hundreds of different POVs and angles, but not a single frame of Steve Rogers when the fatal three shots were fired seconds after the first shot from the sniper rifle. No satellite imagery, either, because they had all been diverted. The hand of Nick Fury is evident in that one, probably because he had more than one plan to free Cap he didn't want recorded.

Sharon Carter is the center of focus in many shots. That stands to reason. She's photogenic; she was prominently wearing a S.H.I.E.L.D. uniform and therefore easy to track in the crowd. The director watches the playback of Sharon rushing to Cap after the first shot is fired. She was one of the closest witnesses at the moment the three fatal shots were fired, but she claimed she didn't see anything—

"Computer, roll back to the sniper shot."

In an enhancement of news-camera footage, the dancing red dot of the laser spotter is clearly visible on the back of the marshal ahead of Steve Rogers. Steve yells, "Look out," and then shoulders the marshal out of the way. The shot rings out. Cap starts to fall, and somebody shouts "sniper."

"Computer, roll back before 'sniper' audio, go wide and slo-mo."

The wall fills with images of the crowd on the courthouse steps moving like they are swimming though molasses. A bearded man wearing a hoodie and dark glasses points across Foley Square. His lips are in synch with the slowed-down audio of "sniper." The entire crowd turns to look in the direction of the pointing finger, and so do most of the cameras. In the two shots where the camera doesn't turn, Sharon Carter can be seen as she continues to move toward the falling Steve Rogers until she is obscured by people in the crowd going up the steps to try to get a better view of the building where the sniper's bullet came from. At no time does Sharon Carter turn to look across the square.

"Computer, blow up man wearing hoodie and dark glasses."

"Invalid request. Subject wears nasal and maxillary prosthetics."

Tony Stark sits down hard and stares at the frozen image of Sharon Carter running up the steps toward Steve Rogers, and he lets out a long breath. He buzzes his personal assistant.

"Anna, that list of Dr. Benjamin's patients—did that include inactive agents, as well?"

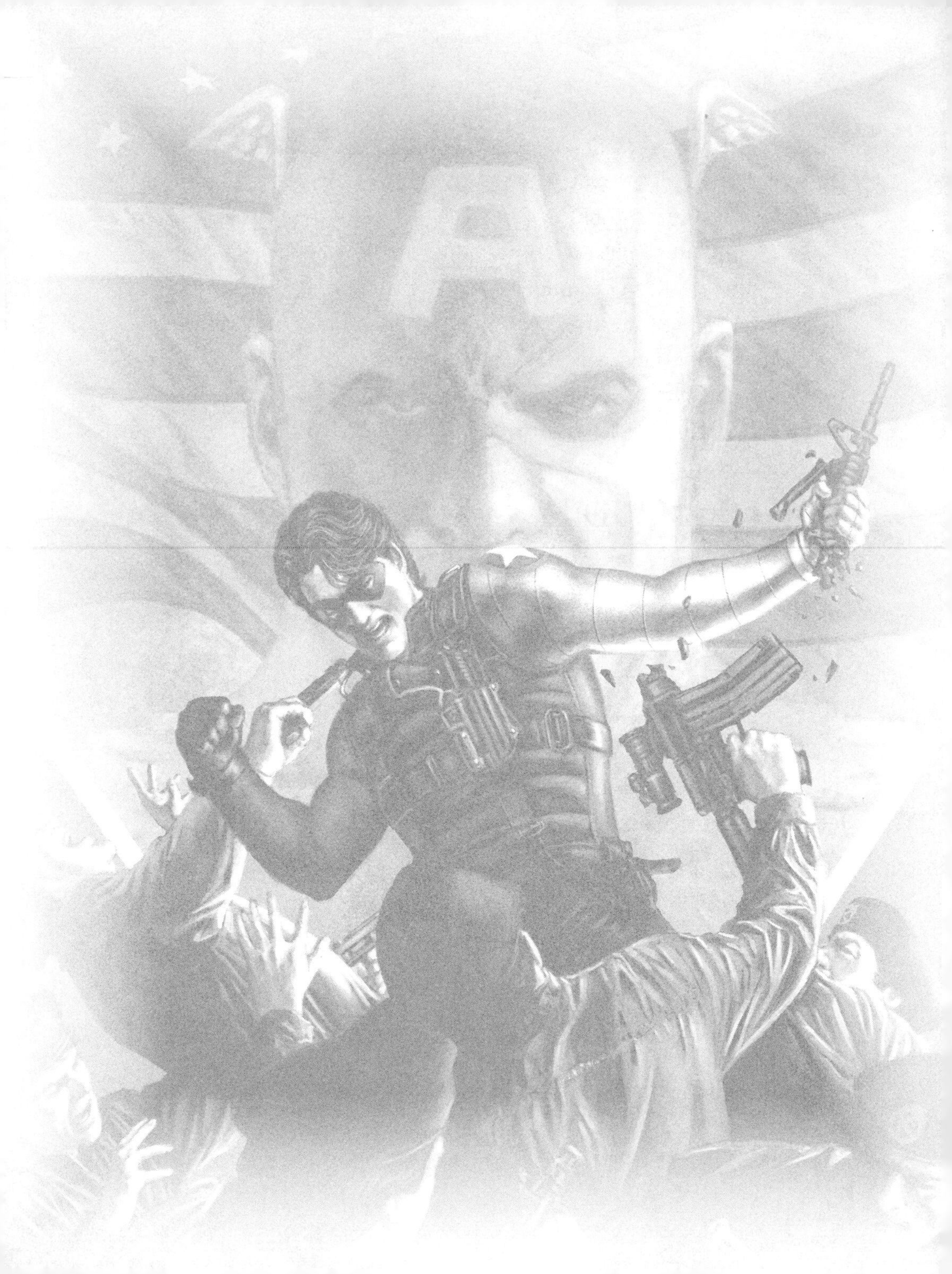

PART THREE

LEGACIES AND CULPABILITIES

INTERLUDE #9

THE superhuman containment device in Doctor Faustus' lab in the Kronas Tower had required six new high-voltage lines to be run up from the basement to power the dampers and suppressors. Workers on adjacent floors experienced extreme lethargy, nausea, and memory loss. Some of these effects could reasonably be attributed to one of the devices being tested in Arnim Zola's lab down the hall on the same floor. After one senior data analyst died from a pacemaker failure, the floors under and above the secret labs were vacated and sealed. When workers in the building across the street started complaining of headaches and nosebleeds, it was decided to dismantle the device and reassemble it in a highly armored R.A.I.D. facility deep under the city. Additional shielding was added so workers and attendants could see to the physical needs of those confined in the device without experiencing undue discomfort. The reassembly was completed just in time to clamp in the very first detainee.

The man spread-eagled on the cruciform containment device is James Buchanan Barnes—once known as "Bucky," later known in the rarified upper strata of intelligence agencies as the "Winter Soldier." He is writhing with psychic agony as selected images of the assassination of Captain America are fed into his brain through electrodes attached to his head.

Doctor Faustus enters the containment room to observe his

captive subject in greater detail. He is fascinated by the grimaces and gnashing teeth that are outward manifestations of the pain within. He inches closer, the better to appreciate the twitches and spasms. The subject's eyelids are fluttering so rapidly that Faustus readjusts his monocle and leans in even closer. The monocle drops from the doctor's face as the Winter Soldier's eyes open wide. Faustus instinctively jerks his head back as Bucky's teeth snap together at the space vacated by the doctor's nose.

"You're awake…"

"Maybe not. Come closer again and find out."

Faustus assumes a semblance of composure.

"I think not."

"Then you're smarter than you look, whoever you are."

"I am Doctor Faustus, and I've been waiting a long time to meet you. Indeed, I have heard so much about you over the years, I feel like I already know you."

Winter Soldier leans forward, straining at the containment device. His eyes narrow dangerously.

"Know me? You don't know *jack*, fatso."

"I will, Bucky. Very soon I will know you better than you know yourself."

TWENTY-ONE

CAN'T wear my black-and-white S.H.I.E.L.D. utility uniform anymore, so I slip into an all-white jumpsuit. It's tight but stretchy and allows complete freedom of movement—thank God for sports bras. On my feet go sensible boots with grippy soles and good ankle support. I'm going for practicality and comfort over style and camouflage. With the number of surveillance cams and sensors in the city, I'm not hiding from anybody once I commit myself out there. After I finish strapping on my personal sidearm, I'm ready. I'm a minimal-makeup person, but I like my hair to be sort-of presentable, so that's where I make my mistake—by going into the bathroom and looking in the mirror.

The bearded man with the monocle is in the reflection— standing behind me, peering past my ear, his hand on my shoulder. But there is no hand on my shoulder.

"Ah, that is better, Agent 13. Ready for action? Ready to go to work again?"

It's like a steel door slamming shut in my brain. There is a part of my consciousness running around in tight circles screaming, "Don't listen to him!" The part of me that lies beyond the steel door obeys like an automaton. It's like that feeling you get when you find yourself saying something you know will result in bad consequences, but you say it anyway—magnified a thousand times.

When I try to resist the soothing voice whispering in my

ear, the world goes into a spin, and I nearly black out. When I do exactly as the voice tells me, a tremendous sense of calm and well-being envelops me. Faustus's technique is extremely Pavlovian, and it works.

I am walking into my living room when I hear the flutter of wings outside my window. A flash of red and white appears on my fire escape, joined by a lithe figure all in black. I duck back into my bedroom before their eyes can adjust to the comparative dimness. Somehow, I know what the voice in my head is going to tell me to do. I don't like it, but I can't disobey.

"Hey, Sharon, you up yet?"

Falcon. I love the guy, but why does he always have to come through my window like Peter Pan?

"How do you know she's even here?"

I know that voice. It's Black Widow. What's she doing here with Sam?

"She was in a bad way when I dropped her off here last night. I don't think she'd have gone out. Hey, Sharon, it's Sam. I've got Natasha with me. Are you all right?"

I slide open my closet door and enter the combination on the safe that's hidden behind the shoe rack. I have to partition this action in my mind, not let it leak to the other side of the steel door.

"I'll be out in a minute, Sam. I'm still getting dressed. Just make yourselves comfortable."

Feathers rustle. Of course, Redwing is there with Falcon. Perched on Sam's wrist and preening, no doubt.

"Turns out Black Widow is searching for Bucky just like we are, Sharon—and she's got some issues *vis-à-vis* Maria Hill, too."

The weapon I take out of the safe needs thirty seconds to cycle up to full power. It won't work until the ready light comes on. I don't want to be doing this. Sam is my friend. Dizziness begins to overpower me. I want to tell them to run, but thinking this almost makes me pass out.

"Stand up and smile, Sharon. You can do this."

I lean against the wall to steady myself. I can hear myself speaking, but I'm not conscious of forming the words.

"Oh, Sam. You're the only person I know who uses *vis-à-vis* in normal conversation."

As I walk out into the living room, I hear the faint chirp of a S.H.I.E.L.D. communicator. Natasha answers her unit. She's got an invisible earpiece.

"What's up, Tony? I'm with the principals right now—"

"He knows! He's telling her! You have to act now!"

I raise the weapon and fire twice.

"That was easier than you thought, wasn't it? Don't you feel better now?"

"Yes. No. God, I want to die."

"No, that will not do, Sharon. Come to me. I can resolve these difficulties for you. Everything will be much better. As long as we do as we are told. It's time to join the revolution, my dear."

<u>EXCERPT FROM STEVE ROGERS' LETTER TO TONY STARK</u>

...I'm trusting you to do two things:

Don't let Bucky drift off into anger and confusion. He has a chance at a new life—help him find his way. <u>Save him for me.</u>

As for Captain America, the part of it that's bigger than me—that has always been bigger than me—don't let it die, Tony.

America <u>needs</u> a Captain America, maybe now more than ever. Don't let that dream die.

Yours,
Steve Rogers

TWENTY-TWO

SOMETIMES you are fully aware you are having a dream, but the wonder of it—or even the sheer terror of it—is so entrancing, you will yourself to keep dreaming and not wake up.

James Buchanan Barnes is having one of those dreams. The years he spent as Winter Soldier have been stripped away, and he is a teenage Bucky again. The blue-and-red uniform feels comfortably familiar on his skin. He is on a mission deep within the Third Reich's "Fortress Europe" with his best friend, Captain America. They are trudging across a smoking gray landscape of urban rubble that at times looks like St. Lo on D-day, London during the Blitz, and the World Trade Center site after 9/11.

In the dark sky, two fighter planes with swastikas on their tails bank to begin a strafing run. Cap and Bucky dive for cover as streams of bullets plow parallel furrows in the debris-strewn cobbles. In the lee of a shattered church wall, they observe the planes turn to set up for another pass. There are bombs attached to the belly racks. The next attack will be more deadly than a hail of lead.

Captain America points to an opening in the church floor where stairs lead down into darkness. Do they descend to vaulted catacombs? Is this the gate to Hades? Or the beginning of a fantastical trip down the rabbit hole?

Bucky takes the lead, plunging into the unknown. He's the

one carrying the Tommy gun, after all. The dark coalesces into a mine tunnel with rough-hewn timbers. Voices up ahead argue in German. Two soldiers in field gray with coal-scuttle helmets and stamped-metal submachine guns. Silent signals pass between the two heroes. A brief scuffle in the dark, and two Wermacht troopers lie in twisted heaps. The mine walls have somehow morphed to an open leaden sky. Artillery flashes on the horizon. Red tracer rounds flit across a blasted terrain. Bucky follows the glowing bullet stream to a mud-filled crater where a German machine gun stutters prolonged bursts of full-metal death. Captain America leaps into the crater in a red-white-and-blue blur, hammering the machine-gun crew with his shield.

Bucky watches in horror as his friend and mentor lifts the heavy belt-fed weapon from its tripod and turns it on the troops advancing through the haze. Troops wearing olive drab, carrying M1 Garand rifles.

American troops.

"Steve! What are you doing? Those are our guys!"

The face that turns to answer Bucky is distorted with unfamiliar hatred.

"Make way for the master race."

The muzzle of the machine gun turns toward Bucky, and the tracer rounds seem to float like expanding red balloons before the searing pain of their impact unleashes a scream that goes on and on.

When the screaming stops, the gray sky, the rubble, and the mud-filled crater are gone. Bucky is sagging in the restraints of the containment device. Doctor Faustus is stroking his beard with one hand and fiddling with his monocle with the other. A blonde nurse in green hospital scrubs hovers at his elbow. Something about her face looks familiar to Bucky. He is too groggy to place it, and his vision is blurry from the drugs.

"Very interesting, indeed. I expected you to break easily after what they told me had been done to you by the Russians, but you are giving me quite a challenge."

Bucky would love to bite the nose off Faustus' face more than ever.

"Get out of my head, fatso."

"I understand more about the workings of the human mind than anyone on the planet, boy. Do you imagine I truly care if one such as you disparages my ample girth?"

What passes across Bucky's face might be considered mirth if it weren't so frightening.

"Nobody likes to be called out for being a bubble-butt, you bloated bucket of blubber."

Doctor Faustus maintains his façade of equanimity, but his voice betrays his wounded vanity.

"Your asinine alliterations fail to goad me, but I like your spirit. It shows you have a mean streak, and that is something I can bend to my own purposes."

Faustus turns to the nurse who is assisting him. She holds a tray with an array of loaded hypodermics.

"Double the dosage this time."

"Yes, Doctor Faustus."

She jabs the needle into Bucky's arm and presses home the plunger. The face that glares at Faustus is pure Winter Soldier with no trace of Captain America's young sidekick in his merciless eyes. The glare fades to blankness, the eyelids droop, and the chin hits his chest.

Doctor Faustus pops out his monocle to clean it with his tie. "Excellent. Now, let's start again, shall we?"

TWENTY-THREE

SAM Wilson is in a REM dream state. He sees himself lying in a narrow infirmary bed with an IV tube stuck in his arm, and sensors taped to his head and chest. The POV is unusually high, and the focus remarkably clear. With a start, he realizes he is observing himself through Redwing's eyes, and he awakens to see Tony Stark standing over him. Over Tony's shoulder, a flash of dark feathers reveals the raptor perched atop a medical data monitor mounted high on the wall. Sam sits up, and pain shoots through his neck.

"Damn, Stark. How long have I been out?"

The answer comes from across the room, where Black Widow is leaning against a bank of centrifuges.

"Since yesterday morning when she zapped the pair of us with a S.H.I.E.L.D.-issue neural-neutralizer."

"She? Who are we talking about here, Natasha?"

Tony Stark answers.

"Agent 13. Sharon Carter. She's been compromised. To what extent, we are presently uncertain. But we are reasonably sure it was Carter who shot Steve Rogers three times at close range—and that it was her shots, not the sniper's bullet, that killed him."

Falcon springs off the bed and immediately regrets it. He is clutching his head and gritting his teeth when he says, "No way!"

"I didn't want to believe it either, Sam."

That's the last thing Falcon wants to hear.

"That's bull. Sharon *loved* Steve. She'd lay down her own life for him. You, of all people, do not get to accuse anyone else of—"

"Let me finish. It's highly likely that she's no longer in control of her own mind. And she's not the only one."

Natasha takes Sam Wilson by the arm and sits him down in a hard chair. Falcon's anger is still there but redirected now. Black Widow's voice is level but brittle.

"In the past few days, twenty S.H.I.E.L.D. agents have disappeared, and the one major link between all of them was that they were undergoing psychiatric review by the same psychologist in our administration building. We think Dr. Benjamin was working for Red Skull."

Falcon puts the pieces together.

"That's how they were able to free Crossbones."

"It would seem so, Sam. Half the security detail assigned to Crossbones failed to report and hasn't been heard from since."

"This shrink, Benjamin—he brainwashed Sharon?"

"And many others. We're still running a damage assessment."

"So you caught this guy?"

"A S.H.I.E.L.D. investigative team found Benjamin's frozen corpse in his own basement. He'd been there for months. Somebody had been successfully masquerading as Benjamin all that time: That somebody would have had to have been a trained psychologist as well as a master of holographic disguises."

Sam is putting it all together in his head.

"That would make a short list. Add a history with Captain America to the mix and the list gets even shorter. Doctor Faustus tried to brainwash Cap into committing suicide more than once.

The last time, he used holograms—in Red Skull's house, no less—but Faustus was shot dead in his cell while in Federal custody."

Black Widow resumes her tale.

"We sent a forensics team to exhume Doctor Faustus. The body in the coffin had head lice, bedbug bites, and a large quantity of cheap Muscatel in his stomach. The Doctor Faustus we know would turn up his nose at anything less than a Chateau Lafite Rothschild—let alone anything with a screw-top, sold from a cooler."

"Faustus and Red Skull working together?" Falcon says. "And Sharon's under their control? That is not good news, people."

Stark strokes his trimmed beard.

"True, but there is one other thing we should consider. Sharon could have killed the two of you. Neither Red Skull nor Faustus would have hesitated to order her to do so. But instead, she stunned you with a neural-neutralizer."

"Does it matter, Tony?"

"It might."

TWENTY-FOUR

THE Winter Soldier has faded away again, and Bucky is front and center. This time, the dream has a narrator. The boy-sidekick seems to remember that the voice belongs to somebody he called "Fatso," but he can't conjure up the face to match it. That's the way it is with dreams. Except this one seems better produced and edited than the disjointed ramblings the subconscious usually screens. The voice is supercilious and pedantic.

"Do you remember what it felt like, Bucky? To be part of a team? You were a member of the Invaders, the Allies' secret weapon against the Axis war machine."

Bucky finds himself in the gray, generic rubble of a battle long past. There are tanks rumbling past—big green Shermans with white stars daubed on their turrets. German 88s thunder in the distance. The slow, steady cyclic rate of Browning Automatic Rifles plays counterpoint to the buzz-saw rip of the MG-42s.

The Invaders are charging an entrenched wehrmacht position. Bucky is covering Cap's right flank. Sub-Mariner is taking point. Human Torch and Toro are blazing overhead. Bucky drops a spent magazine from his Thompson gun and slaps in a full clip, never missing a step.

"Of course, unlike the others, you had nothing special to offer. They soared above you. All of them. Can you remember that overwhelming jealousy? That sense of not being able to measure up?"

Even in his delirium, the boy-soldier knows what is being said is not right.

"That's nowhere close to the truth. You're projecting your own messed-up small-mindedness on to me. That's how you would have seen it, not me."

"There's no point arguing it. They were like unto gods, while you were a mere human stripling..."

The Tommy gun spits lead. A figure in field gray throws up his arms and tumbles head-over-heels.

"...a boy-murderer. A post-adolescent killer of men."

"Stop it! It was war. We all killed. We had to."

Across the cratered dreamscape, bedraggled German troops put up their hands and approach the Invaders under a white flag. They stumble through the mud and blood with the shambling gait of beaten men, their eyes downcast. Captain America is hefting a .30-caliber Browning water-cooled machine gun as if it were a child's toy. He begins to shout as he pulls the trigger.

"The only good Nazi is a dead Nazi!"

A steady stream of copper-jacketed lead cuts a swath through the surrendering enemy soldiers. Cap repeats the heinous mantra again and again. Human Torch and Toro rain fire down from the sky. Sub-Mariner strides imperiously through the German ranks, breaking necks with his bare hands.

No.

"That's not Cap. That's not the Invaders."

The past evaporates, leaving the Winter Soldier facing Doctor Faustus in the containment room. The blonde nurse in the white uniform is prepping another hypodermic. There is no more straining against the restraints. But there is no resignation, either—just calculation and patience. Better to conserve strength than expend energy wastefully.

"It's not working. You can't make me believe those guys were anything but heroes."

"Is that so? I think you need to be shown that in the real world, there are no true heroes."

The nurse has the next needle in Winter Soldier's arm already. The tang of salt air fills his nostrils. Sea birds are crying, and a supercharged engine is roaring. He's Cap's young sidekick again, and his fingers are numb from clinging to the fuselage of a top-secret American prototype aerial drone stolen by Baron Zemo. Captain America is hanging on to the wing. The two of them know the new weapon cannot be allowed to fall into Hitler's hands, but they also know that the one-of-a-kind aircraft can't be replaced. Bucky pries open the guidance-system hatch and makes a horrifying discovery.

"Steve, it's booby-trapped. It's going to explode! We have to drop off!"

"No, Bucky. We can't let it be destroyed. You have to defuse it."

Even with the wind fierce in his eyes, Bucky can see that the self-destruct unit is serially wired to two anti-tamper devices.

"Can't defuse it, Cap! We're both going to die!"

"You still have to try, Bucky. And since I'm the one who matters and can't be replaced, I'm the one who's going to survive. Do your duty, soldier."

Cap lets go of the wing and falls away toward the cold waters of the sea. It seems that even above the roar of the engine,

Bucky can still hear the relays on the detonator clicking into place.

"But you failed, didn't you? The device detonated, and all of Uncle Sam's investments were wasted: the drone prototype, Captain America, and you."

"I died. Cap never said that. He would never—"

"That's what was in his mind, Bucky. But you didn't stay dead, did you? You were brought back to life, and your blown-off arm was replaced, and you were turned against your own people. You were put in limbo between assignments, so you had no life apart from inflicting terror and death. What a horrible fate, and all because Steve Rogers considered you expendable."

"That's a lie. Steve told me to jump. It was my own decision."

"The facts are that he survived, and you died in the freezing waters—unwanted and unappreciated. Cast off like worthless junk."

"No."

"Can you deny any of the facts?"

"I'm confused—

"The only time you were ever appreciated was when you were the Winter Soldier."

"But—"

"So who would you rather be? Bucky or Winter Soldier?"

The man in the containment device falls silent and closes his eyes. Ten minutes pass without a stir. The nurse grows visibly nervous. Doctor Faustus waits patiently. He has waited through longer silences in his time. Faustus lets his attention wander for a moment, and he turns back to find an intense pair of brown eyes staring back at him.

"What am I doing in these restraints, and why the hell are you staring at me like that?"

"Do you know who you are?"

"I am the Winter Soldier."

"Do you know who I am?"

"You're Doctor Faustus. You work for my boss, Lukin."

"And whose command are you under, soldier?"

"I follow orders, and you are higher on the chain of command than I am."

"Excellent. I knew that all I had to do was lead you back to where you had already been."

The Winter Soldier rattles the restraints.

"You can unlock me now, Faustus."

Doctor Faustus presses a button, and the containment device releases the Winter Soldier.

"Now, you can return my weapons."

"Not yet. I don't take anything at face value. Are you prepared to follow my orders as you would those of General Lukin?"

"I thought we had already established that?"

Faustus extracts a large automatic pistol from the pocket of his tent-like jacket and extends it butt-first.

"I require a practical demonstration of your loyalty. I want you to take this gun and shoot my nurse. A clean head-shot, please. We are not sadists."

The nurse drops her tray. Hypodermics roll across the floor.

Doctor Faustus backs away to give the Winter Soldier a clear field of fire.

"You remember Agent 13, don't you? Sharon Carter, consort

of Steve Rogers, enemy of the Russian Motherland?"

    Winter Soldier raises the pistol and takes careful aim. The look in her eyes tells him all he needs to know, and he is quite resigned as he squeezes the trigger and feels the recoil.

INTERLUDE #10

KRONAS Corporation operates a training center at a remote location in the middle of a dense forest. It looks and functions like a military base, and that is exactly what it is. Tonight, most of the Kronas security forces are gathered at the center to hear an address from their leader: Aleksander Lukin, corporate oligarch and ex-general of the KGB. Lukin ascends to the podium wearing the mask of the Red Skull, but is it really the Red Skull wearing the form of Aleksander Lukin? Who can tell? Certainly not Lukin himself, who has had the Red Skull living in his brain for so long now he can no longer distinguish between what thoughts are his own and what thoughts are those of Johann Schmidt. For all intents and purposes, the man standing behind the microphone at the podium is the Red Skull wearing Lukin's form.

The security men have been prepped with a special gas concocted by Doctor Faustus to ensure their wholesale acceptance of what is about to be laid out for them. The former S.H.I.E.L.D. agents subverted by Faustus have been similarly treated and are watching an encrypted broadcast at a secure location. Red Skull has no need to tap the microphone to make sure it is live—the sound technicians know the consequences of failure.

"Soldiers of Kronas, I am the Red Skull, and I have made a pact with your leader, the great General Lukin. Together, Aleksander Lukin and I shall lead you down the path of greatness.

The days of glory for which you have all waited so long are nearly upon us."

The crowd murmurs with no great confidence, the gas notwithstanding. Why should they trust this stranger in the Halloween mask?

"Do not let this fearsome visage confuse you. It was meant to strike fear in the hearts of the weak and the inferior. It was meant to inspire the courageous and the strong-willed—like all of you."

The murmuring dwindles and stops. He has their attention now, and the gas is having its full effect.

"You, who are about to embark on a great adventure into the annals of history. You, who will never be forgotten because you will have dared to aspire to heights the lowly cannot comprehend. You, who will march with me and Lukin to unprecedented victory..."

He pauses for effect. The Kronas soldiers lean forward in anticipation, holding their breath.

"...when we write America's epitaph in its own blood!"

TWENTY-FIVE

I'M still alive.

I can hardly believe it. The pistol, with the slide locked open on an empty clip, is smoking in Winter Soldier's hand. The muzzle points directly at the tip of Doctor Faustus' nose. The heavier man's monocle and face are stippled with black, smokeless powder residue.

"One blank cartridge in the chamber."

The Winter Soldier says it so matter-of-factly I want to scream. Did he know that when he pointed the gun at me first, before he turned it on Faustus? But more importantly, does Doctor Faustus realize that the shock of thinking I was going to die has weakened his hypnotic hold on me? I don't have complete control of myself yet, but I can feel his power over me slipping. I have to bide my time, though. I have to work on taking back more control, but I can't let him know it's happening.

"The weight wasn't right."

What? The Winter Soldier said that. I have to concentrate. Have to stay sharp. The pistol rises. What's he doing? Is he about to pistol-whip Faustus?

Faustus issues a sharp command.

"Recalcitrance."

Two sharp electrodes pop out of the butt of the pistol in Winter Soldier's hand, piercing his palm and thumb. A "drive-stun" Taser on full power zaps him so hard he falls to the floor, writhing in pain as violent muscle contractions knot up his arm like a dozen cramps. Faustus looks at the twitching and thrashing with a revolting sneer on his face.

"I told you I take nothing for granted. You should have known I wouldn't trust you with a functional weapon. You could have at least tried to shoot Carter just for appearances."

Winter Soldier grunts through clenched teeth.

"Go to hell. Wasn't going to pass up taking a shot at your ugly mug, was I?"

A size-12 handmade English oxford comes smashing down on Winter Soldier's face with the considerable heft of Doctor Faustus behind it.

"Ah, James—you are becoming tiresome."

The stomping continues until the man on the floor is quite still and a pool of blood is spreading out from under his head.

"Nurse, I require a wipe."

There is a stack of gauze pads among the supplies on the stainless-steel medical trolley next to the containment device. I fold one and hand it to Faustus. He cleans the powder residue from his monocle, and then bends down to carefully daub the blood off his shoes with the same pad. I take advantage of the lull in the proceedings to shed the baggy hospital scrubs I'm wearing over my jumpsuit and combat rig.

A pair of R.A.I.D. troopers hauls away the unconscious Winter Soldier as Faustus leads me out of the containment room and into the corridor of the subterranean facility. Faustus expresses open disdain for the Red Skull's allies who are playing host to his containment device.

"Radically Advanced Ideas in Destruction. It's a particularly unwieldy name and smacks of hubris, as well. Don't you agree, Agent 13?"

"I'm no longer Agent 13, and I couldn't begin to understand the motivations of a group like R.A.I.D., let alone guess the reasoning behind what they call themselves. But I am curious, Doctor Faustus: How did you know you hadn't broken the Winter Soldier?"

I realize my mistake as soon as the words are out of my mouth. I shouldn't have expressed any curiosity. He's going to know his control is slipping.

"He was too compliant right away. A hostile subject is always more problematic. You have to break them over and over again to be sure."

He didn't notice. He's in full gloat mode, too full of himself. The R.A.I.D. troopers dump Winter Soldier on a grate that feeds into a drain and hose him down, washing off the worst of the blood. Faustus goes on.

"They're useless until they are fully broken, you know. They have to be willing to do anything for you—to die for you and especially, to kill for you. As well you know, my dear."

"Of course, Doctor."

"My mother would have done anything for me. She would have died for me and yes, even killed for me. She was very strong, my mother was. Just like you, Sharon."

Why is he telling me this? It's too creepy for words.

The R.A.I.D. troopers are dragging Winter Soldier face-down by his feet back to the containment device. His chin hits the irregularities in the floor. His teeth snap together like castanets.

Faustus natters on in his maddening, self-involved way. I imagine working over his face with a ball-peen hammer, smile, and nod at the appropriate times.

The dish that will be served cold will still be savory.

TWENTY-SIX

THE raptor circles high above the grimy alley where Falcon and Black Widow stand at an open manhole cover.

"Are you sure you're hearing him right, Sam?"

"It's not like hearing anything, 'Tasha. Redwing is showing me what he saw—sort of like projecting it in my head. And what he saw was Sharon going down into this manhole right after she zapped us in her apartment."

Redwing spirals down and takes up his perch on Falcon's arm. There's something about the bird's eyes that reminds Natasha of velociraptors in a dinosaur movie.

"Didn't your bird get zapped, too?"

"He caught the residual damage from me—same neural pathways that allow us to communicate. He recovered quicker and followed her. But he won't go down into a sewer, not even if I'm going."

Black Widow stares down into the foul-smelling darkness at her feet.

"I agree with Redwing. I do not relish the thought of going down into a sewer. Nothing good ever comes of it."

"We have to do this. We have to find Sharon."

"Then let's get on with it."

Redwing casts off from Falcon's arm and settles on a fire escape, where he drinks from a water bowl set out for a cat. He watches, unblinking, as Falcon and Black Widow descend on iron rungs into the New York City storm-drainage system.

"Sewer" is a misnomer of sorts. Most of the rainwater that falls on New York City runs off roofs, sidewalks, asphalt, and other impermeable surfaces instead of being absorbed into the ground. It must be redirected to the surrounding bodies of water by a series of conduits. The smaller conduits merge into larger tunnels, which is what Falcon and Black Widow are moving through. Falcon is brooding, keeping his thoughts to himself. Black Widow breaks the silence.

"Are you all right?"

"I just found out that my good friend shot and killed my best friend, and that she's out of her mind. Yeah, I'm just fine."

"Good to know, Sam."

A passageway just off the nexus of three major conduits is boarded over with plywood and affixed with an official-looking sign that reads, "CLOSED FOR CONSTRUCTION."

A drag mark curves away from one side of the plywood along the filth of the tunnel floor, in an arc indicating a hinge on the opposite side of the plywood. Falcon tugs at the board, and it swings open to reveal a narrow corridor that curves to the left. The corridor ends at a metal hatch. Sam reaches for the handle, but Black Widow stops him. She carefully examines the edges of the hatch.

"Just checking for alarms and booby traps. Can't ever be too careful these days."

A not-very-reassured Falcon tugs open the hatch.

The continuation of the corridor beyond the hatch is crisscrossed by a tight network of laser beams.

Falcon steps back.

"That's A.I.M. or R.A.I.D. technology for sure. I say we stand down, call it in, and let a S.H.I.E.L.D. assault team rain on their parade."

Black Widow takes a circuit-bypass unit from her belt pouch.

"That's about as subtle as a B-52 bunker-buster bomb strike. We want to get Sharon out of there alive, don't we?"

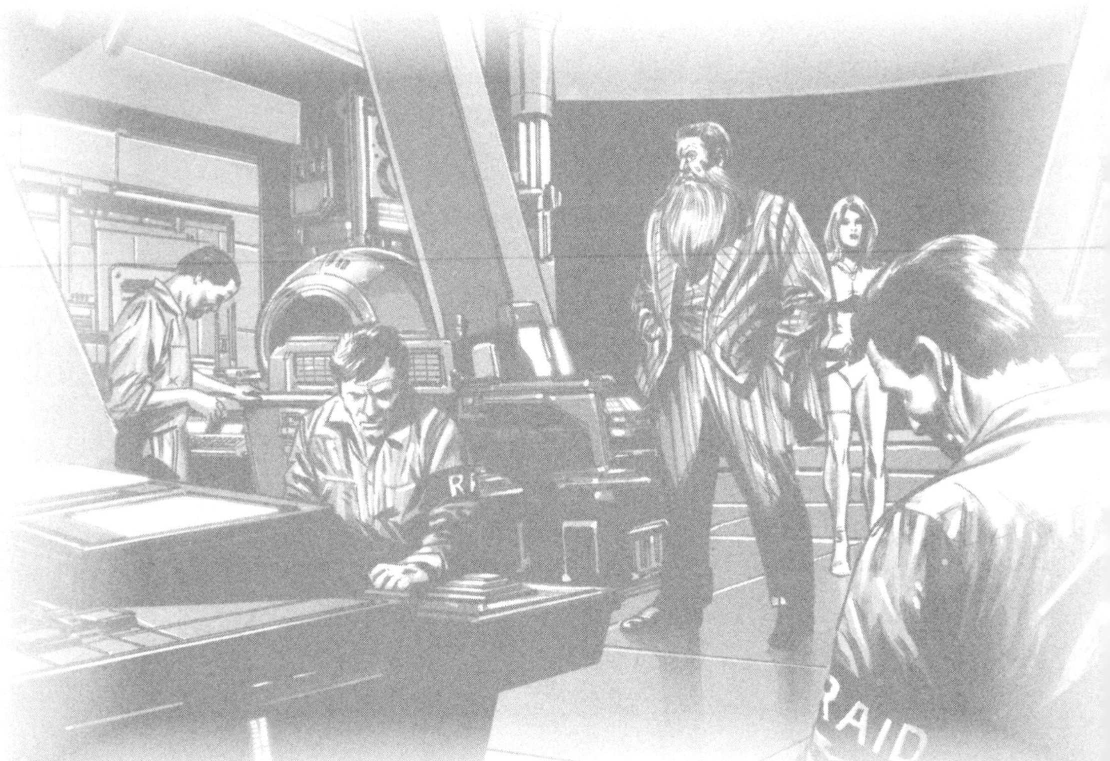
RAID

TWENTY-SEVEN

THE R.A.I.D. nerds are hunched over their consoles or tapping furiously on their tablets when I follow Doctor Faustus into the control center. They are tacitly ignoring the face of the Red Skull glowering from the main encrypted-communications monitor. I suppose Red Skull thinks as little of them as they do of him. They are just utilitarian items to each other. If that masked maniac were here in the R.A.I.D. facility with us, I would find a way to wipe that sneer off his face. The security nerds carry pistols. I have no doubt I could overpower one of them. But I have to put wishful thinking aside for now and plan carefully. I'll only get one chance, and I'll have to make the most of it. Skull is furious at being kept waiting.

"It's about time you showed up here, Faustus. Too good to answer your messages, are you?"

"I was taking care of business. Your business, Johann. Attending to our subject, as it were."

"Don't address me by that name, and stop dragging your feet. Your progress with the subject is unsatisfactory. I want the Winter Soldier back in operation, the way he used to be. Efficient, reliable—and, most of all, *compliant.*"

Faustus rocks back and forth in his expensive oxfords, hands deep in his pockets, showing no subservience at all.

"And if it can't be done in time?"

"Do not complicate my plans with your failures. If he cannot be useful again in life, I will extract value from his corpse."

Red Skull doesn't bother to sign off, he simply breaks the connection. The screen goes black.

I should have known that they meant to kill him all along. Nothing in my training prepared me for resisting mental takeover and manipulation, but I have to do it. I have to do it, and I have to make the Red Skull pay for what he's done.

Red lights start flashing on the control consoles. Somewhere, an alarm Klaxon blares. A security team runs through the control center and down a corridor toward the alarm. A R.A.I.D. tech turns to address Faustus.

"Security glitch, sir. There was a power fluctuation in one of our perimeter fields a few minutes ago, so I sent an armed maintenance team to check on it."

The blinking red light reflected in Doctor Faustus' monocle makes him look more diabolical than ever.

"Why wasn't I informed immediately?"

"These things happen. Rats gnaw on the cables, water damages the circuits—but the team never reported back, and their GPS units went dead."

"Is that when you initiated the alert and sounded the alarm?"

"No, sir. First I dispatched a security squad to investigate. I sounded the alert when they failed to report, and their locater units went off the grid."

Pushing aside the tech, Faustus looms over the console. He calls up all the surveillance-cam imagery and the facility map, which shows the security teams as green blinking lights converging on the perimeter breach. My heart flutters a bit as the surveillance cams start to go dead, and the green light closest to the breach goes out.

Faustus pulls himself erect and turns to face me directly.

"I don't believe we're done with you yet, Agent 13."

What?

I've heard that exact phrasing before—

Oh my god, it's a *trigger*. It's reinstalling and reinforcing all the controls I've managed to dismantle so far. I try to resist. I must partition my mind so the real me is still intact and safe, if not fully in charge.

Another green light winks out on the facility map. A tech at another console shouts in panic.

"We have visual confirmation, Doctor. It's the Avengers."

The tech holds up his tablet, which is being fed a helmet-cam image from one of the security squads. The picture is shaky and blurred, but seems to show one figure in black and another figure in red pummeling and kicking their way through completely overmatched R.A.I.D. troopers.

Faustus is now visibly shaken.

"That's ridiculous. Impossible. How could they—?"

"It's just two of them. Black Widow and Falcon. Should I close and lock all the blast and containment doors?"

I am dazed and numb. It's almost like I'm seeing everything as a disembodied spirit—a ghost of myself, disinterested and observing at a distance. Faustus is stroking his beard obsessively, thinking hard.

"Complete lockdown. Deny access at containment doors for all security cards except for mine. Erase all the hard drives, dump printouts in the burn box, and start evacuation procedures. And bring me my damned prisoner."

He turns to me, grips my jumpsuit collar with his sausage-like fingers, and pulls my face close to his. His breath stinks of jellied pig knuckles and smoked eel, shreds of which are still caught between his teeth from lunch.

"I don't believe we're done with you yet, Agent 13."

Doctor Faustus transforms from an odious man with halitosis to a venerable mentor. Everything he has ever said makes perfect sense to me. I know that whatever he asks me to do is in my own best interest. It makes me very happy to please him in every way.

But then, why do I have this nagging sensation of unease?

He draws a familiar-looking weapon from his jacket pocket and tucks it into the empty holster on my belt.

"You're a soldier, Agent 13. You will do your duty without fail, won't you?"

"Of course, Doctor. I will always make the choice that will benefit our cause."

"Good."

He has not released my collar. He is dragging me down the corridor with him. More lights are flashing, and security teams are jogging past us with heavy weapons. I can hear gunfire now, bursts of full-automatic, and the high-pitched hum of advanced energy weapons. I try to keep pace with Faustus' clumsy run, but I'm just stumbling along. Why won't he let go? I only want to serve him.

Even though he possesses a number of duplicate security cards, he has to search through his pockets until he finds one that lets us enter the escape suite. This is actually a hangar for a R.A.I.D. stealth transport—a clunky squat thing with stubby wings, all flat planes joined in angles to best deflect radar. It sits on a launch rail that slopes upward through a tunnel that probably passes through a derelict building in the industrial neighborhood above. The ramp door on the tail of the aircraft is open, and techs are loading last-minute security items as the launch turbines rev up to speed. The pilot is standing on the ramp, checking the chronograph on his wrist. The window for escape is less than five minutes, at this point. I see it all, crystal clear, and I couldn't care less. That's how it is when somebody else is in charge of your mind.

A communications tech runs up to Faustus.

"Doctor, your prisoner has escaped. We dosed him with a sedative, got him out of the containment device, and locked him in an Adamantium-laced straitjacket. But he took down two whole security squads with just his feet."

Luckily for the tech, Faustus isn't holding a gun, or the tech would have a smoking hole in his forehead. I'm glad Faustus isn't angry with me. All I want to do is please him. Faustus hands me one of his security cards.

"Agent 13, you have three minutes to subdue the Winter Soldier and deliver him here. We will not wait a second longer. Now go."

I don't waste time answering him. I run full tilt toward the source of the commotion in the corridors, against the stream of fleeing R.A.I.D. techs.

"*Faster, Sharon. You have less than ninety seconds to find him and—*"

"Save him. Yes, I must save him."

"*No, that is not part of the protocol. Subdue him and bring him to me.*"

"But you'll kill him."

"Obey your orders, Sharon. Remember, you killed Steve Rogers, who meant a lot more to you than this one. You can kill him, too, if I ask you to, correct?"

Somehow, I'm down on my knees on the corridor floor. Muscle spasms and nausea sweep over me in waves. I need to follow orders. But I need to save Bucky. It's like my brain is trying to rip itself in two. I can't let Faustus down, but Bucky was—is—oh, lord…Bucky. Am I saying his name out loud?

"I'm right here, Sharon. And it's okay."

And there he is, standing over me. His face all bruised and battered. His arms still locked in Adamantium restraints. Blood all over his boots.

Bucky.

"We're getting out of here. You and me. I let Cap down on the courthouse steps, and I'm going to make it right."

Oh, Bucky. It's all too wrong to ever be made right again. But I don't say that aloud. He gives me that boyish, earnest look of his.

"Come on, Sharon. Get it together, and let's blow this pop stand. I know there's a part of you still in charge in there."

I'm in here, but not in charge.

I pull out the neural neutralizer that Faustus returned to me, thumb the power switch up to "full," and squeeze the trigger. Bucky is still twitching uncontrollably on the floor as two R.A.I.D. security troopers arrive to help carry him back to the escape transport.

Security teams cover our retreat, keeping up a steady suppressive fire. Falcon and Black Widow are less than fifty yards behind us. I force myself not to think about them. It keeps away the vertigo.

Bucky is dumped roughly into the transport. The hydraulic pistons close the ramp, and we accelerate up the launch rail. Explosive charges blast open the building covering the escape silo, and fragments of brick and timber bounce off the fuselage as we zoom skyward. I strap in as best I can, watching Bucky bounce and roll as we hit thermals and wind shear between the buildings. The pilot shouts over the din of the engines.

"One of them is coming after us, and he's gaining!"

Somebody who can fly fast enough to catch up to a R.A.I.D. mini-jet? That has to be Falcon. He's my friend—wait, he's my *friend*—pain stabs through my brain. The pilot is maneuvering wildly to shake the pursuit. Bucky goes weightless as we flip over to roll into a dive, and he slams back to the deck as we level out. We go nose-up, and Bucky rolls all the way back to the ramp.

The ramp.

Steady, Sharon. Compartmentalizing my thoughts, I unbuckle my seat belt and stand. I take a secured-cargo harness strap and clip the snap hook to the D-ring on my combat harness.

"What are you doing? Sharon, stop. What are you—?"

"Shut up."

"What did you say?"

"I said, 'Shut up.' I know how to get rid of the Falcon."

Faustus knows what I'm doing before I grab the handle to the emergency ramp. Unfortunately, he's too smart to unbuckle his seat belt.

Bucky, the only one in the compartment who isn't strapped in, is sucked out before the ramp opens completely.

Before I close the ramp, I see Falcon change his flight path to intercept Bucky's plummeting body. It's not much, but it's the best I can do under the circumstances.

The pilot announces that we are at sufficient altitude for full passive-cloaking stealth mode. We are now invisible to S.H.I.E.L.D. radars and sensors. Doctor Faustus is not what you would call mollified.

"What's going on in the rest of your mind, Agent 13? Hmmm? Why would you release our prisoner?"

Keep it simple and straightforward, Sharon. Don't elaborate, and don't allow any leakage of your real thoughts.

"Because it worked. Falcon didn't stop us, did he? And weren't you going to kill the prisoner, anyway?"

I force myself to think about Swedish furniture and ironing—anything but the truth. Faustus stares at me, unblinking. Minutes tick by before he says anything.

"Yes, well—I have reviewed the permutations and extrapolations; all the alternative outcomes are highly unsatisfactory, and quite terminal. Your actions may have doomed us in Red Skull's eyes, but that net result is possible to negotiate." Keeping the relief off my face takes considerable will.

INTERLUDE #11

THE Red Skull is quite to the point.

"You're right, Faustus. I should have you taken out into the alley and shot you behind the ear."

"But long-term practicality trumps short-term emotionality?"

They are walking through a corridor of a secure private level in Kronas Tower. The techs and security men who pass the man with the monocle and the man in the skull mask in the hall ignore them with good reason: the desire to stay among the living.

"But failure, like losing the Winter Soldier..." the Red Skull hisses. "Most would have fled rather than bring me such news."

"A man must be responsible for his mistakes. How many grand plans have come to ashes because subordinates failed to pass negative results up the chain of command?"

Red Skull tilts his head sideways to examine Doctor Faustus, much like a predator sizing up a competitor in a territorial dispute.

"Your mind is a Machiavellian maze of double-thinking and triple-dealing. Your motives are hidden in veils of deceit. But I need you to finish your work, so I'll suspend judgment for now. The woman is another matter. I want her punished."

"She is confined to a cell, Herr Skull. I shall deal with her soon enough. As for my work, I need to know if the body is ready."

"Arnim Zola assures me that it will be soon. But I am forced to move up the timeline. Our sources have informed us that the damned boy-soldier was saved by the Falcon and is now a prisoner in the Helicarrier. He knows our secrets and is now in the hands of our enemies."

TWENTY-EIGHT

FALCON'S voice crackles over the speakerphone in Tony Stark's office aboard the Helicarrier.

"Is he conscious yet, Tony? Have you talked to him?"

Stark pinches the bridge of his nose, wishing his headache would go away.

"Sam, he's awake and manacled to the steel desk in the same room where we interrogated Crossbones. I put a twenty-four-hour watch on him, and Natasha is in charge of the surveillance team. And no, I haven't spoken to him yet. The techs disconnected his prosthetic arm and took it to the engineering lab."

"Sounds like you're avoiding the interrogation."

"Natasha thinks it might be better if she makes the first move, with their history and all. She's letting him stew for a bit."

The director imagines what it would be like to glide on the thermals and fly outside the claustrophobic confines of a metal suit. He can hear the wind behind Falcon's voice, even with the filters on.

"Best be careful. We don't know what those sick freaks did to him. And listen, Bucky was important to Steve, so now he's important to *me*. Real important."

"I hear you, Sam. I hope you don't think I have to be reminded of that. Look, just focus on tracking down Faustus and finding Sharon. I'll do right by Bucky. I promise you that."

"I'm holding you to that, Tony."

A red priority call light is flashing furiously in Stark's peripheral vision.

"Have to sign off. Emergency call coming in from the engineering lab."

"Later."

"Director Stark here."

The voice on the secure internal line is familiar, and labored, gasping out information in desperate spurts.

"Sir, this is Milt Shapiro...senior engineer at Lab 3...sir, the *arm*...Winter Soldier's powered prosthetic...most of its design and components...sir, it's one of *ours*."

"It was built by S.H.I.E.L.D.? That would mean we had a Russian mole at one point."

Shapiro expresses an alternative opinion.

"Or the prisoner we removed the arm from...was working directly for Director Nick Fury—I mean, ex-Director Fury."

Pacing back and forth in front of his desk, Tony Stark mentally runs through a hundred scenarios and extrapolations.

"Listen up, Shapiro. Disconnect that arm's internal power source right now and lock it down in an Adamantium security locker—"

"Sir...it activated itself ten minutes ago. It utilized some sort of electrical-discharge weapon. Everybody else in the lab is still unconscious...it was gone when I came to, and a ventilation grill was torn open."

Stark stops dead still as the implications sink in.

"You didn't sound a class-A security alert immediately? That thing has been on the loose in the Helicarrier for almost ten minutes now?"

"Sir, authorization for that alert is above my pay grade, and—"

The line goes dead, the lights go out, and the background hum of mechanical activity on the Helicarrier goes silent.

The lights come back on, and a computer-generated voice announces, "Power-grid fluctuation—levels two, three, and seven."

Level seven is where the secure holding area is.

On a direct line to the secure holding area, Tony Stark gives the verbal password to the agents monitoring the prisoners in the confinement cells.

"Natasha, what the hell is going on down there?"

The video feed from the surveillance booth is fifty percent static. Black Widow responds while checking the loads on her Widow's Bite wristlets and cycling up a third-generation neural neutralizer.

"We lost power for a few seconds. All the cams in the confinement cells were dead when it came back on, along with the IR sensors and motion detectors."

Stepping into his suit-up module, Stark sends the voice command to put the entire Helicarrier on a 227 red alert as he gives Black Widow her orders.

"Lock down the whole level, Natasha. I'm on my way. And I want your eyes on Bucky right now. His arm went AWOL from the lab."

Stark is fully encased in his Iron Man armor before he finishes giving the lockdown order to Black Widow. The suit's internal systems are already powering up repulsors. He transfers communications to his helmet, and Black Widow's voice comes through his earpieces.

"I was looking right at him on the monitors just before they went black. That was less than a minute ago."

There are two seconds of white noise as she steps through the double blast doors and force-field disruptors into the containment area.

"Tony, I'm in the vestibule to the interrogation suite, and we've got six agents down. Everyone's breathing, but their weapons and ammo are gone."

"And the interrogation room?"

"The door's open. I can see inside from out here. The air grate is smashed out, and the manacle's been ripped off the steel staple in the desk. Bucky's loose, Tony. And he has his arm back."

A 227 red alert on the Helicarrier means that all corridors and passageways are cleared, and all personnel except for roving security teams are at their duty stations with hatches sealed. The big ship seems almost deserted as Iron Man flies through it. He comes to the massive elevators that move aircraft up from the hangar decks to the flight deck. This is the weak point in security lockdowns because the huge vertical shafts allow open access between the decks. If Winter Soldier is coming to Deck Two to take his revenge on Tony Stark, this is how he will get there.

Iron Man's faceplate is in the up position. He needs to talk to Bucky face-to-face. His suit gives him the latest situational updates from the Helicarrier Operations Room and from his armor's own systems.

"Level Two power fluctuation registered. Communications links and intruder-detection sensors severely compromised."

The repulsor-tech node implanted in his chest tells Iron Man that there is no active energy-field weapon nearby, thereby functioning as a built-in Winter-Soldier-detection system.

On the PA channel, Iron Man issues a fugitive-apprehension order for Winter Soldier with the proviso that security teams are not authorized to use lethal force. He is barely finished reiterating that the fugitive must be taken alive when he is attacked from above and behind.

The blow from Winter Soldier's powered arm sends Iron Man flying across the hangar deck. Gyro-stabilizers and quick reflexes land the red-and-gold Avenger on his feet, facing an adversary bristling with submachine guns, pistols, and ammo clips lifted from the security team in the holding area.

"Smart move, Bucky—putting the power source for your arm on standby and shielding it until right before your strike."

"Smarter than your moves, Stark. Pretty damn stupid bringing me right up here."

The suit's threat-analysis system issues its warning and response confirmation of presets Stark had logged in on his way to the hangar deck: *"Precision EMP attack imminent. Armor powering off. Power source shielded."*

Winter Soldier's EMP, which could have fried half the power grid of downtown Manhattan, has no apparent effect on Iron Man. Tony Stark snaps down the faceplate on his helmet and locks it.

"Not so stupid, am I, kid?"

"Armor power on. Repulsors fully charged."

The double blast from both palm repulsors smashes Winter Soldier against a hangar wall. Iron Man's voice reverberates off the metal bulkheads and floor grates.

"You're wasting your time, and you're wasting mine. There's no way you can take me down, so let's deal with this like adults and—"

The punches delivered by the prosthetic arm resound off Iron Man's armored chest like a jackhammer, driving him back toward the giant aircraft elevators. The punches are followed by magazine-emptying bursts from two submachine guns, a fusillade from two pistols, and concussions from stun grenades that leave Iron Man with his back against a hangar bulkhead. The wall panels on the bulkhead hang dented and askew. Acrid smoke billows from the open bulkhead, and a shower of sparks rains down. The armored suit doesn't show a single scratch.

"This is futile. You can't win, Bucky."

"*Warning. Helicarrier onboard data-storage unit compromised. Schematic wiring diagrams accessed by unauthorized user.*"

Wiring diagrams.

Shower of sparks.

High-voltage cables for elevator power.

The prosthetic fist is already in motion when Tony Stark understands the implications, and he is propelled into exposed, arcing cables.

Iron Man immediately powers down and goes into shield mode to avoid shorting out completely. In the two seconds of complete shutdown, Stark exerts every bit of strength he has to push away from the bulkhead and break contact with the cables. He can feel his heart going into arrhythmia. He can feel the dark closing in as blood flow to his brain becomes erratic.

"*Danger of energy-field overload elapsed. Armor recharging. Power at 57 percent.*"

The Winter Soldier's arm is already around Stark's neck.

The arm built with S.H.I.E.L.D. technology. Technology supplied by Stark Enterprises.

"Helmet integrity compromised."

The helmet is more than compromised—it is halfway across the hangar, and Stark feels the muzzle of a S.H.I.E.L.D.-issue pistol pressed against his exposed forehead.

"Who's winning now, Stark?"

Tony Stark doesn't blink as he answers.

"I am."

Stark wiggles his fingers. Winter Soldier's eyes dart back and forth between Iron Man's two palms. The repulsor-beam emitters are glowing pale blue.

"I could have liquefied your brain inside your skull right from the start of our little brouhaha, and I can do it right now if you so much as flinch. But I really don't want to do that."

"Why not?"

"Because Steve Rogers asked me to save you from yourself."

"What?"

"Can we talk in my office?"

Winter Solder sits at Tony Stark's desk holding the letter from Steve Rogers. He has read it a dozen times. He doesn't look up from the letter as Black Widow enters the executive suite with a reinforced squad of S.H.I.E.L.D. security specialists armed with large shoulder-fired "elephant-gun" neural-neutralizers.

Stark, still sans helmet, dismisses the security team but tells Natasha to stay. The troops file out. The door self-locks behind them, and the area sound-damper turns itself on.

The man who looks up from the letter is more Bucky than Winter Soldier. You can almost hear the boy who followed Captain America to war in his voice as he reads the message out loud.

Silence, followed by Black Widow's curt "oh."

Bucky asks, "This is the real deal?"

Stark crosses his arms.

"The lawyer who delivered it has got Matt Murdock vouching for him, and our best graphologists swear it's Steve's handwriting. What say you and I put aside our personal differences here and find the man who's really responsible for Steve's death: the Red Skull."

Bucky pushes the chair away from the desk, leans back, and grasps the armrests. He speaks to the space between Stark and Black Widow.

"I know where he is. He's been right in front of your eyes the whole time—wait, don't get yourselves in an uproar. I didn't know until I was in his hands." The pause is less for effect than it is for gathering his thoughts. "He's Aleksander Lukin. Or somehow, he's inside Lukin's head. The Cosmic Cube is involved, so anything is possible."

Very little can stun Tony Stark. His reaction always involves his mind racing to find a solution, and he doesn't make his calculations public. Black Widow, just as methodical in a different way, recounts data at her disposal.

"I know Lukin. He's ex-KGB, a protégé of Vasily Karpov who turned himself into a corporate oligarch after the deconstruction of the U.S.S.R. He heads the Kronas Corporation and is rumored to have a private army. If he's now Red Skull, that means—"

With a wave of his hand, Stark turns on the multiple-monitor display on his wall.

"Computer, give me news-channel feeds and online press. Search subject: Aleksander Lukin, prioritized by date and importance."

The screens and holo-projections process through hundreds of video clips and articles until every one is playing the same news report time-stamped less than an hour before. The visual is a shaky live-cam image of an Ilyushin Il-96 airliner fuselage half-awash in choppy waters. The banner crawl at screen bottom reads, "KRONAS CORP CEO LUKIN DEAD IN PLANE CRASH."

The clipped narration is in BBC-standard "received pronunciation."

"...among the bodies recovered at the crash site was reclusive CEO Aleksander Lukin, who founded Kronas Corporation after his self-imposed exile from his native Russia. Details at eleven."

Bucky is first to speak. "It's a trick. He's not dead—not if Red Skull is still lurking inside his head. As Lukin, Skull could move around openly. He knew he had to cover his trail as soon as I fell into your hands. Lukin had to go because you have the power and resources to go after him."

"It's a sure bet that whatever the Red Skull's been planning, he's got to be moving the timetable up." Stark leans down on the desk to get his head level to Bucky's. "So are you going to step up to the plate, or not?"

"Plate? You're reading a lot into this letter if you think Steve was nominating me to take his place."

"The list is so short, it's only got your name on it."

The letter sits rock still in Bucky's hands.

"He's got Steve's girl. Your Agent 13."

Black Widow makes a move as if to touch Bucky's shoulder but stops short. "We know that. Sharon Carter is who Falcon and I were trying to save when we found you."

Bucky's head is shaking back and forth as if he could make denial real by making it physical. "Still, Steve doesn't say it in the letter. He doesn't spell it out."

"I know exactly what he wrote." Stark flicks the top of the letter with a forefinger that ends up pointing at Bucky's nose. "But it's not as if you're going to let anyone else be that guy. Right? You read the letter ten times? I've read it over a hundred times. Do you want to be the one to let him down? I know what that feels like. And believe me, you don't want to go there."

The letter is shaking in Bucky's hand as he reads it one more time. He slaps it down on the desk and stands.

"All right. I'll do it. But only on two conditions."

The former boy-soldier runs his real hand through his hair.

"First, you have your techs go inside my head and fix it so no one can ever control me again. Take out any remaining Winter Soldier fail-safe code words or implants."

"Done. What's the second condition?"

"I don't answer to you, or to anyone else. Steve didn't. And if I'm Captain America, neither will I."

Tony Stark has to think about it. But not for very long.

"I can live with that."

PART FOUR

BEST LAID PLANS OF MICE AND MEN

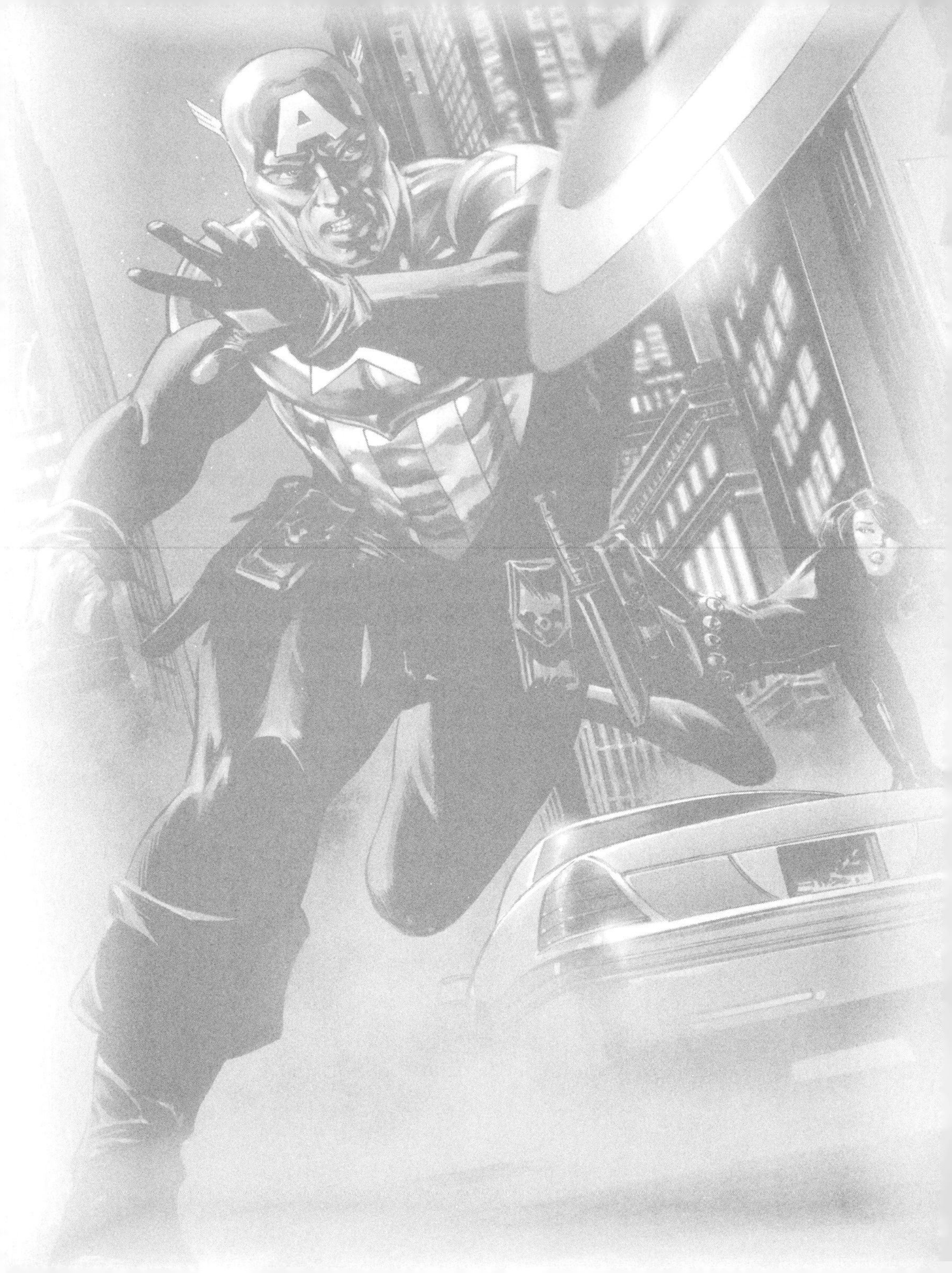

TWENTY-NINE

PART of the deal was that Bucky got a nicer place to live, a laptop with Wi-Fi, a smartphone, and a cable-TV connection with all the news channels.

Bucky had been slightly annoyed that after he and Stark had shaken hands, the present director of S.H.I.E.L.D. inquired obliquely about the former director, Nick Fury. Without letting go of Stark's hand, Bucky said, "Captain America doesn't sell out his friends."

The major trade-off he'd had to make was hanging up his guns, his knives, and the rest of his assassin's kit. Bucky had always used guns, even as a kid sidekick during the war. The Thompson gun had been an onerous weight for a slight adolescent to lug around, but he'd been thankful for its knockdown power when the Waffen SS had played dirty. Disarming was not too high a price to pay for the privilege and honor of wearing the Captain America suit. Not *the* Captain America suit: one he had redesigned with Tony Stark. Bucky had said, "I'm not Steve Rogers, and I won't pretend to be him."

From Bucky's point of view, he came out ahead on the deal. Guns, knives, and grenades had nothing on the *shield*. It was the real deal, an icon—like Excalibur but better, because the shield was symbolic of defending liberty. Wielded by a skilled hand, it could strike the enemies of freedom harder than any "terrible swift sword."

He has trouble thinking of himself as the new Captain

America. Not when he's wearing sweatpants and a T-shirt in a hotel room while watching three different news programs on his shiny new electronic toys. He hasn't thought of himself as James Buchanan Barnes in more than half a century. Much of what made him identify as Winter Soldier had been excised from his brain by S.H.I.E.L.D. neurological techs over three days that are now permanently gone from his memory. Bucky is who he is now, until he puts on the new suit.

Others have worn the suit and gone by the name of Captain America. Bucky knows this from reading Fury's secret files. None of them were the equal of Steve Rogers. During the 1950s, one went completely insane and had to be cryogenically frozen: William Burnside. Plastic surgery had even made Burnside look like Rogers. Not living up to the ideal was Bucky's main worry. But could anybody?

Bucky isn't lounging in an easy chair or lying on his bed as he absorbs the news from the Internet, cable feed, and data link. He's working out, practicing his moves, and honing his skills. Four to six hours a day, every day. It's his *job.*

The news is grim. If it wasn't grim, it wouldn't be news. School bake sales and lost puppies with happy endings can only sell so many toasters and cheap car-insurance policies. The financial crisis is the big story, and every other story is just another falling domino.

"...*shocking increases in world oil prices in the wake of energy giant Kronas Corporation's loss of CEO Aleksander Lukin*—"

"...*new Kronas CEO Vladimir Morovin set to double price of oil per barrel*—"

"...*Peggy Day Finance, a subsidiary of Kronas, announces it will foreclose on thirty thousand mortgages across the United States—"*

    "...very few of the Peggy Day foreclosures are linked to the subprime meltdown, but instead are the result of homeowners failing to read the fine print—"

    "...outraged citizens take to the streets in demonstrations—"

    "...hundreds arrested in cities across the nation—"

    "...huge police presence as thousands protest at Kronas Tower in Midtown—"

The images freeze on the screens, and the same banner rolls across all of them: "Your country needs you."

He had been wondering when his first assignment was going to come through. It takes Bucky two minutes to don pants and boots, grab the shield, and climb the stairs to the roof with the rest of the new uniform rolled in a bundle. The shield is housed in an anonymous black case that might pass for an artist's portfolio.

A blacked-out S.H.I.E.L.D. light troop transport is hovering above the ventilator units with Black Widow in the pilot's seat. Bucky respectfully straps the shield into an equipment rack, then slides into the copilot's chair and buckles up. He refrains from speaking until Natasha lifts off and is at altitude.

"I can't help noticing that on my first sanctioned mission as Captain America, they send *you* to nursemaid me."

Too much maneuvering around buildings is happening for her to look him in the eye, yet there is a hint of a smile there that almost goes unnoticed.

"I'm giving you a ride and providing backup, period. S.H.I.E.L.D. has no record of your existence. Total security wipe. Director Stark's deal with you was strictly personal. Officially, he can't publicly advocate an unregistered hero."

Bucky squirms into his uniform shirt and pulls on the gloves.

"But here you are. An Avenger. How's he going to answer that one if it gets out?"

"I am the Black Widow. I live among shades of gray."

Bucky snorts.

"That sounds like a catchphrase from an old radio melodrama: 'Evil-doers beware my sting!,' music up, insert Wilhelm scream."

"So you have a sense of humor, Mr. Barnes."

Bucky pulls on the mask as well as a whole new demeanor.

"Not when I'm on the job as Captain America."

The trace of a smile disappears from Black Widow's face.

"You've been practicing with the shield, I take it?"

"Yes, but I didn't really have to. Stark's tech people gave my arm some tweaks, programmed in trajectory codes, and rigged up a direct-targeting link with my right eye." He adjusts the eyeholes and tugs the mask taut. "I may never have Steve's integrity and selfless honor, but my aim and throwing arm may come close to his."

The Kronas Tower looms ahead. The avenue below is packed with protesters for three blocks in every direction.

"Damn, Natasha. The Red Skull has his *agents provocateurs* out in force tonight—wait a minute. I'm not expected to address the protesters, am I?"

But the S.H.I.E.L.D. transport has already passed the demonstration and is heading south down Park Avenue. Black Widow calls up an infrared surveillance image on the control panel's multifunction display. It shows two A.I.M. heavy transports alighting in vertical-take-off-and-landing-mode in front of the

Federal Reserve Bank in the Financial District. She taps the screen.

"We received a tip that R.A.I.D and A.I.M. were going after the gold reserves in the vault on Liberty Street. Of course, all the police are tied up miles uptown at Kronas Tower."

The new Captain America retrieves his shield, takes it out of its case, and stands bracing himself at the hatch. He automatically reaches for where his pistol should be and touches an empty belt. But the weight of the shield on his arm feels comforting. It feels *right.*

"I'm glad that the first time I go into action carrying Steve's shield, I'll be battling minions of his old foe. It looks like Red Skull wants to hit our economy from all sides until we're ripping ourselves apart from the inside. All these years, he's wanted to see our cities burn, and he's finally getting all his ducks in a row to make it happen."

"Apparently."

"All right, then. Let's go stop him."

The "bucket-head" A.I.M. techs have secured the twenty-kilogram shaped breaching charge to the bank wall, with R.A.I.D. troopers providing cover with assault rifles and rocket launchers. There are no firing cables to be compromised or radio detonators to be jammed. A simple, mechanical timer set for thirty seconds and protected by an anti-tamper device has been activated. The countdown cannot be stopped.

"Fire in the hole!"

Yellow-suited terrorists duck for cover. They have their heads down when the man in the red-white-and-blue costume races past them to pluck the explosive device from the wall with one hand.

A.I.M. techs are quick to assess the situation and order the deployment of their two Turbo Walkers. The articulated-leg armored fighting machines that resemble twelve-foot-tall steel ostriches lumber down the cargo ramps of the A.I.M. transports, their dual electric Gatling guns sweeping the street in targeting mode. But their intended target refuses to cooperate by presenting a clear shot. The star-spangled figure is in among the A.I.M. techs and R.A.I.D. troopers, swinging the heavy-shaped charge into their heads and deflecting bullets with his shield.

At twenty seconds from detonation, the techs rescind the firing order for the Turbo Walkers to preclude friendly fire devastation. It also dawns on them who they are fighting.

"It can't be him—he's dead!"

The shield ricochets off a terrorist's head and returns to the red-gloved hand that threw it.

"You can't kill what he stood for."

Said with utter conviction by the new embodiment of that idea: the *new* Captain America.

At twelve seconds from detonation, the techs have no choice but to reinstate the firing order to the Turbo Walkers. Two sets of laser dots begin to converge on the target with the star at its center. A voice rings clear over the gunfire: "Widow—cover me. I have to take down those machines."

The woman in black steps out from between parked cars with her MP5K submachine gun blasting accurately grouped three-shot bursts.

"Stop talking and do it."

Five seconds left.

The R.A.I.D. troopers who aren't hit by Black Widow's covering fire are mowed down by the Turbo Walker Gatling guns as they traverse horizontally following their locked-on target. The techs had inserted an "identify friend-or-foe" override when they reinstated the firing order, so the guns do not cease fire when the target passes *between* the two fighting machines.

The Walker that put its predicted-target-point "pipper" on the other first by a microsecond is the one that survives. The remaining Walker's targeting computer makes the error of traversing 180 degrees to track its "lock-on" as the new Captain America leaps above and over the turret.

There is one second left on the timer when the surviving Walker's threat sensor detects the shaped-charge clamped to its back. One second later, the adjective "surviving" no longer applies.

Black Widow slings her empty MP5K and takes down the last two A.I.M. techs with her Widow's Bite wristlets, but not before the yellow-suited fanatics activate the self-destruct charges within the two heavy transports. She uses a remote to summon the S.H.I.E.L.D. light troop transport as the newly battle-tested Captain America joins her. Fragments of still-smoking A.I.M. technology and shards of window glass rain down on the street.

"Did you know what you were going to do with that shaped-charge when you yanked it off the wall?" she asks. "Wait—don't tell me. Nothing matters as long as it works out. We should clear out. We're needed elsewhere already. You kept them so busy that none of these creeps was able to get a message out. Red Skull is going to be perplexed, and I like that."

The Captain America who isn't Steve Rogers lifts his gaze

to the buildings facing the Federal Reserve Bank.

"All those windows. All those people with phone cams. It'll be all over the news."

Black Widow lifts one perfect eyebrow.

"New Yorkers don't go to the window when they hear shots and explosions. I thought you knew that by now."

INTERLUDE #12

AS a precautionary measure, the Red Skull has transplanted Arnim Zola's lab yet again, this time to another remote location in upstate New York. He finds it amusing to stand in the doorway and watch Zola work: the relentless robot movements, the tireless plodding. Zola is sometimes indistinguishable from the machines and devices he operates, being more akin to them than to human beings. Red Skull finds that aspect of Zola alien and disturbing, but he also has an affinity for Zola: They are both trapped in bodies they weren't born in.

Red Skull clears Aleksander Lukin's throat. Zola pretends he doesn't hear. Red Skull speaks to him nonetheless.

"What news is there from your field operatives in the city? Have they secured the gold reserves like they were supposed to?"

As usual, Arnim Zola continues the task he was involved in before being spoken to. He acknowledges the Red Skull by turning the psychotronic box that sits where his head should be slightly in the speaker's direction.

"They are not my operatives. I had nothing to do with training or outfitting them."

"You're not passing the blame, are you, Zola?"

Moving to where he can see Zola's "face" in the holographic screen in his chest does not result in eye contact.

"Hardly. They have not reported in yet. Their GPS and

communications signals have stopped. This could possibly mean they are being pursued and have gone into stealth mode or activated passive cloaking devices. Unable to extrapolate their current situation with available data. Next question."

"When will you finish your work for me?"

"Later than when I projected if you continue to distract me. Do you want the chamber completed in a timely fashion or not? And what about the upgrades on the schematics for Faustus' contraption?"

Arguing with Arnim Zola is like arguing with a refrigerator. Red Skull turns back to the door.

"Very well, Zola. Continue with your work. You should know that we have succeeded in knocking them to their knees. I am merely concerned with keeping them there until we are ready to strike the final blow." He stops and turns at the door. "And it's nearly time for Faustus to launch the first wave of his psychological assault. You should come watch this with me, Zola. I am certain you will appreciate the irony of it."

Zola sets his machines on "automatic" and follows the Red Skull.

"Irony is at the core of the joke life has played on me—and you as well. Yes, this should be amusing."

THIRTY

THE meeting between Director Stark and the Secretary of the Treasury takes place on the commander's catwalk in the operations center of the Helicarrier. Localized sound dampers provide a bubble of sonic security. There is no provision to safeguard against lip-readers, but all personnel in the operations center have an ultra-ultra clearance.

To Stark, the *tête-à-tête* is progressing as expected, appointed bureaucrats of the secretary's ilk having not changed noticeably since the Sumerians invented double-entry bookkeeping.

"Mr. Secretary, the sources for the reports you're acting on are questionable at the very least and deliberate fabrications at the worst. I have highly reliable intel that the body found in the wreckage of the Kronas jet was not Aleksander Lukin at all. We've been telling your people this for days, and everybody up the chain is ignoring it."

The secretary seethes. He is eager to exert his authority.

"Don't take that tone with me, Stark. I won't stand for it. We are in the midst of a national crisis, and your unsupported allegations about dead men are going to have to go on the back burner until we can stop our economic free fall."

Tony Stark calls up a recent photo of Kronas CEO Vladimir Morovin on the center's biggest multifunction monitor.

"It won't be resolved unless you take action against the one who's actually perpetrating the collapse. Lukin is not dead, and this Morovin is no more real than the honest man Diogenes was searching for. This whole crisis is an orchestrated assault on the U.S. economy by the Kronas Corporation, which is now a front for the Red Skull."

There is no table for the secretary to slam his fist down upon, so he settles for clenching and unclenching his hands at his sides.

"That's a load of paranoid conspiracy malarkey based on hearsay, circumstantial half-truths, and actionable libel."

The picture of Morovin on the monitor is replaced by live news coverage of the large demonstrations in New York. Other monitors light up with scenes of similar discontent in Chicago, San Francisco, and Washington, D.C.

"Somebody is clearly organizing all this, Mr. Secretary. The stock market is near collapse, there's fear of a run on the banks, and ordinary citizens are hoarding food and gasoline." Stark has all monitors switch to different angles of the protest in front of the White House. "I had to take the precaution of assigning S.H.I.E.L.D. agents to keep the mob in check outside the White House."

"Where's the hard proof, Stark? Where is the documentation, the sworn testimony, the smoking gun?"

"The proof I have would compromise...ongoing investigations. Ask yourself this, Mr. Secretary: If someone wanted to cripple this country, what would be the first steps they would take?"

From his own point of view, the Secretary of the Treasury has already won the argument.

"No. Kronas Corporation is simply playing business hardball, trying to raise first-quarter profits or—"

"And how much has Kronas Corporation donated to your pals and cronies in the Senate? Particularly to the campaign fund of Senator Wright?"

The secretary's umbrage is preempted by the head of the S.H.I.E.L.D. intelligence-analysis department: "Director Stark, we just got a fix on our missing agents. All their GPS units just went active. They're in Washington, D.C., sir. Embedded in our crowd-control unit outside the White House."

The screens now show varying views of the S.H.I.E.L.D. crowd-control unit, its agents wearing distinctive black uniforms and armed with assault rifles.

Stark shoves the secretary aside to lean over the catwalk rail and shout to his operations staff.

"Jam all commo modes and frequencies around the White House, effective immediately. Shut down all signals going into that area. Dispatch the nearest cleared security team to seal the vicinity, and tell them to double-check all S.H.I.E.L.D. personnel they encounter against our list of missing agents."

A very irate Secretary of the Treasury is demanding to know what is going on. The director replies bluntly. "I'm trying to prevent a bloodbath."

Stark turns to his staff.

"Suspend that commo blackout for one second and transmit a compressed burst message. Contents of message: Stand down and clear weapons."

The entire operations room is riveted to the screens, watching the reactions of the twelve once-missing S.H.I.E.L.D. agents in front of the White House. One by one, they each repeat the director's order.

"Stand down and clear weapons."

The repetitions seem robotic, and the agents' eyes go blank. Instead of clearing their weapons, they snap back the bolts to lock and load.

Before the first shots are fired into the crowd, Tony Stark's stomach gives a lurch as he realizes what he has been tricked into doing. "Stand down and clear weapons" is a standard order. It is now clear that it is also the code phrase that triggers a pre-programmed action in the mind-controlled agents.

INTERLUDE #13

TRANSCRIPT of National Cable News Affiliates' interview with Senator Gordon Wright, chairman of the Appropriations Committee. Interview conducted by Roseanne McCarthy.

McCarthy:	May we have your reaction to last night's brutal and tragic incident when S.H.I.E.L.D. agents opened fire on protesters outside the White House?
Wright:	Appalling. Absolutely appalling on so many levels. As you know, I am a big one for accountability, which is why I supported the Registration Act. We are in need of tighter controls on how organizations like S.H.I.E.L.D. operate on American soil. And we need to protect our cities from rampaging mobs of mindless protesters who want nothing better than to tear down our way of life.
McCarthy:	S.H.I.E.L.D. has yet to make an official statement, but there has been a leak indicating that Director Stark will claim that last night's shooters were not active agents.
Wright:	Whether they were active or not is a quibble. What a pile of evasive hokum! They are not an American agency but an arm of the United Nations. We need our cities protected by real Americans.

McCarthy:	But who will do that, Senator? With cutbacks on municipal police forces, deep budget slashes in federal military spending, and the deployment overseas of so many National Guard units, who is there to do that protecting?
Wright:	I am diligently working on that, Roseanne. My committee is proposing an emergency bill—which I am sure will meet with bi-partisan support, and pass both the House and Senate. We propose to enter into a contract with an American company, Kane-Meyer Security, to restore order to the streets of our great cities and especially right here in Washington, D.C.
McCarthy:	I understand that Kane-Meyer provides security for many American holdings overseas and has contracts with our Departments of Defense and State protecting installations, bases, and embassy personnel.
Wright:	It's a company operated by Americans, and it employs Americans. And this will be putting tax dollars to work, protecting Americans while providing new jobs for Americans. How much more win-win can you get?

"...How much more win-win can you get?"

Extremely pleased with himself, Senator Wright hits the pause button on his DVR remote so the screen freezes on his smiling face. He turns to the man with the beard and monocle sitting on the GSA-approved leather couch in the Senator's office.

"Brilliant line for something I improvised on the spot, don't you think? I might use it as my campaign slogan when I run for the presidency—of course, that's going to take a lot more money..."

Doctor Faustus likes dealing with politicians. They are so reliably truc to form.

"We shall do more than fill your campaign chest, Senator. We have the means to smooth your way to higher office by persuading your opponents to relent. And if they are resistant to persuasion, they can suffer a fatal fall in the bathroom, or fail to survive a crash on the interstate. You do understand these unfortunate accidents can also curtail the lives of those who fail to deliver what they have promised us?"

The temptation for the Senator to ask, "Is that a threat?" is strong, but he wisely resists it. Faustus senses this and is gratified. He breathes on his monocle and wipes it clean.

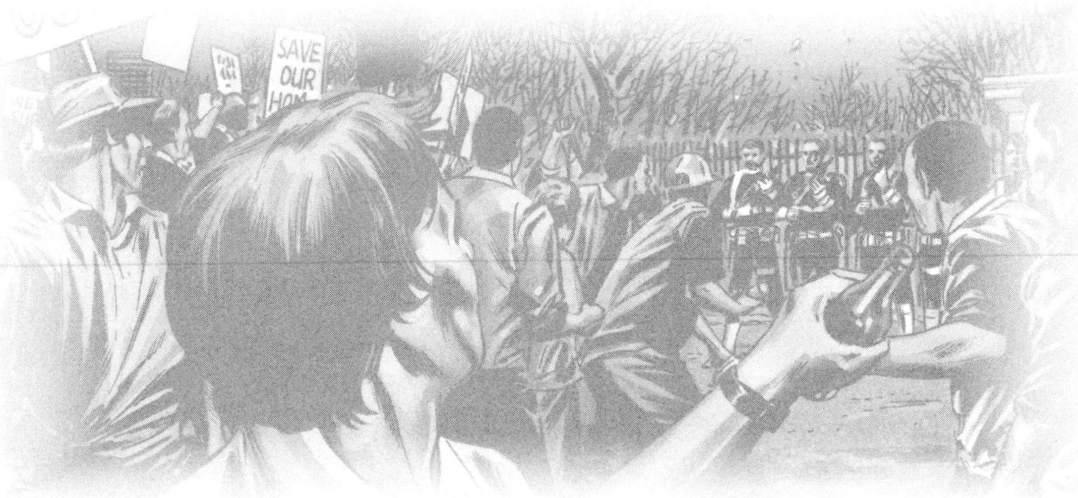

SAVE
OUR

THIRTY-ONE

THE bloodshed that marred the protest at 1600 Pennsylvania Avenue only days earlier did not diminish the turnout for the demonstration at First Street SW and Independence. It is Bucky, in jeans and broken-in leather, and not his costumed alter ego, who mingles at the edge of the crowd picketing the Capitol Building. To his way of thinking, a demonstration protesting violence that occurred at a previous demonstration seems nothing less than an invitation for more of the same. He shakes his head at the way righteous indignation can blind so many people to the obvious and override the instinct for survival.

"Where are your people, Natasha? What's the plan?"

Black Widow's voice is clear and crisp in his micro-earpiece. "You are the plan, Bucky."

"That's insane. This mob scene is a potential incubator for a riot."

"S.H.I.E.L.D. is mostly in lockdown due to the investigation launched by Senator Wright—which is why I'm your only backup, and why I'm idling buttoned-up in an alley two blocks away."

"Gotta sign off, 'Tasha. I'm getting the old hairy eyeball from a security goon."

The Kane-Meyer "rent-a-cop" in the quasi-paramilitary uniform pokes Bucky in the chest with a twenty-four-inch polycarbonate control baton, while keeping one hand on his pistol butt.

"You packin', Junior? Got any sharps in your pockets?"

"No on both counts. They sure didn't waste any time passing that emergency bill so they could approve the contract with you guys, did they?"

"Shut up and assume the position against that van."

The parked van has an alarm that starts whooping as soon as Bucky leans against it, palms flat and feet spread. The alarm irritates the security officer. The irritation grows when his body frisk produces nothing.

"Beat it. I see your mug again, I'm running you in."

Moving away from the edge of the crowd, Bucky reestablishes contact with Black Widow.

"So what are you doing for me besides watching my back?"

"Yesterday, Tony Stark called me into his office for a briefing about our suspension of activities and left the back-door access code for our spy satellites showing on his monitor. He doesn't make mistakes like that. I'm patching in right now. I've been running searches for Kane-Meyer on the data links for the last hour."

Something pokes Bucky in the back, and he almost reacts with a spinning kick. Instead, he turns around slowly. A kid in thrift-shop clothes hauling a cooler on a toy wagon is holding out a bottle of water to him: "Only a buck, mister."

It's a reasonable price; glancing around, Bucky can see that the kid has at least ten competitors who are doing a brisk business with protesters thirsty from shouting slogans and chants. The bottle in the kid's hand is exchanged for a crisp twenty-dollar bill.

"I'm treating the next nineteen."

Twisting off the plastic cap, Bucky looks for a trash can. Black Widow's next update stops him from taking a gulp.

"The search is paying off. Kane-Meyer is owned by a company that's owned by a company that's twenty steps up the chain owned by Kronas Corporation."

"Kronas causes widespread panic and unrest, and then pulls strings to have their own security force put in place to counter it all? That's a short-term business model, and the Red Skull is more of a long-game sort of player."

"Right now, on the ground, we can only deal with the short game. What did you say about a riot? Maybe this is all a *diversion*."

Bucky's thirst is getting to him. He raises the bottle again.

"Skull doesn't back long shots. How do you guarantee a riot?"

The fine print at the bottom of the water label comes into focus.

"...A division of KRONOS INTERNATIONAL."

An angry roar goes up from the crowd at the demonstration. Later, some witnesses will state that a man in a hoodie with a bandanna covering his lower face, threw a bottle of water at the Kane-Meyer security forces. Others will swear the security men started swinging their batons against the protesters with no provocation.

Bullhorns blare across the space between Peace Circle and the Garfield Monument, ordering the crowd to move away and disperse. More bottles fly through the air. A solid phalanx of Kane-Meyer security guards advances into the throng.

In less than a minute, Bucky is in an alley two blocks from the demonstration.

Black Widow deactivates the cloaking device, and the

S.H.I.E.L.D. Flying Car becomes visible hovering behind a Dumpster. She does not divert her eyes as Bucky strips off his street clothes and throws them into the car.

"Nothing I haven't seen before."

"Skull had it all planned," Bucky says as he dons the shirt and reaches for the shield stashed into the luggage space behind the seats. "The water was spiked, and it's probably stuff that dissipates without traces in the bloodstream."

Black Widow starts to open her door.

"Let's get out there. I'll cover you—"

Pulling on the mask, Bucky becomes Captain America. "No. I need you to be my eyes on the big picture. Plug into the sat-cams and the local surveillance networks. Update me on the roll. I have to go out there and do what Steve would have done. I have to save those people from being sacrificed as pawns in the Red Skull's insane game."

The Kane-Meyer security teams had entered the fray fully confident that what appeared to be chaos to the media was essentially under their control from the beginning. Now, that notion begins to dissipate as a red-white-and-blue shield mows down an entire rank of their vanguard, bounces off a lamppost, and is caught in midair by a man in a familiar-looking costume who bowls over three more Kane-Meyer stooges before his boots hit the ground.

The shield smashes another face, a red-gloved fist fractures a clavicle, and a boot with a rolled-over top dislocates a jaw.

The baton-wielding, helmeted ranks waver. "What the hell?"

The man with the shield shouts, "Get out of here, now!"

Some do, but most don't. The security forces regroup and

focus on a single target. Guns are drawn, escalating the fight to an unplanned-for level. Bullets flying true to their marks are deflected by a flashing disk of Vibranium, and then the man with the big white "A" on the forehead of his mask is among the shooters. Those who aren't *hors de combat* by way of thrashing shield or pummeling fist fall victim to friendly fire in the panicked melee.

Flashing red lights are converging on the scene along the Northwest and Southwest Drives: police and Kane-Meyer reinforcements. Phone-cam videos on social networks draw protest supporters and the morbidly curious to the area by the thousands. The man who would be Captain America begins to see the futility of his actions, as well as the consequences. The cognitive dissonance does not disable him. He is too strong for that.

"Bucky, I have something."

"It had better be good, Natasha."

"A stealth helicopter just landed on the roof of the Dirksen Senate Office Building. No clearance. And the IFF code doesn't match up to anything the military, police or Department of Defense has—"

"That's it. That's the main event that this riot is just the diversion for. I'm on my way over there. Hack the building's CCTV cams and see what intel you can hustle up so I don't bust in there totally blind."

The Dirksen Senate Office Building's common-area surveillance-camera system has already been hacked and is showing a continuous loop of benign images. The hallways and foyers covered by the cams are actually littered with the bodies of staffers and security personnel. The members of the crew that debussed from the helicopter on the roof, and who are responsible for the mayhem, are alerted to another intruder who has entered the building by crashing through a third-story window. They wait for him at the top of the stairs on the fourth floor.

"Are you there yet, Bucky? I think the cams are being spoofed."

"They are, Natasha. Lots of bodies here."

"Any clue to who did it? Do you want me to back you up?"

"I see the perps—nothing I can't handle."

Sin and her associates, the Serpent Squad, spread out across the top of the stairs. As she aims her pistol at the new Captain America ascending the steps, she laughs, "This is too good to be true."

INTERLUDE #14

THE Secretary of the Treasury is quite upset. He checked into a motel on the outskirts of Alexandria under a false name, and he has placed his video call to the new CEO of Kronas with his room Wi-Fi and a stolen laptop obtained from an intern who has socially unacceptable proclivities about which the secretary has agreed to keep quiet.

"Mr. Morovin, there are suggestions that your predecessor, Aleksander Lukin, is in reality still among the living."

"Mr. Secretary, it should be noted that S.H.I.E.L.D. has a history of making unsubstantiated statements about us. And at present, they themselves have been discredited and are under investigation."

There is no trace of emotion on Morovin's face on the laptop screen. The secretary wonders whether his own face is betraying him as he answers.

"It is still worrisome. There could be awkwardness if it came out that Lukin isn't dead."

"There could be awkwardness about your wife and family becoming aware of what you do on Saturday afternoons when they think you're playing golf. And how awkward would it be for you if the existence of certain numbered accounts in Switzerland and the Caymans came to light? These are not threats, Mr. Secretary. To paraphrase Dickens, 'These are not the shadows of things that will be, they are the shadows of things that may be, only.' Didn't we agree that America's long-term best interests are entwined with the continued rise in Kronas share prices? Is it not entirely beside the point if you should accrue some small net gain for your selfless patriotism? I certainly hope you are not contemplating backing out of our gentlemen's agreement, Mr. Secretary. That would be unforunate."

"Nothing of the sort, Mr. Morovin."

"Business as usual, then?"

"Do I have a choice?"

"Good night, Mr. Secretary."

The connection is broken, and the holographic projection the Secretary had been conversing with flickers and disappears.

In the Kronas Tower, the corporeal body of Aleksander Lukin crosses the office from beyond the edge of the webcam and sits behind the desk in the chair that had been "occupied" by the projection. It is the Red Skull who drums Lukin's fingers on the desktop, and it is the Red Skull who closes the webcam window and quits the video-call app.

Lukin, who has been reduced to janitorial duties in his own body, asserts himself.

"This is wrong, Skull. You've altered my plans beyond recognition."

"Don't be ridiculous, Lukin. It's for our mutual benefit."

"We were supposed to cripple them and show them the errors of their capitalist ways. Not negotiate with them."

"Negotiation is almost always a charade to save the dignity of those who have already crawled under your heel. And are their people not living in fear? Is there not uncontrolled violence on their streets? Will their cities not be burning by the end of the week?

Are they not well on their way to being crippled? They might never learn the errors of their ways, Aleksander, but they will surely suffer."

THIRTY-TWO

IN the Dirksen Senate Office Building, Bucky in his new Captain America suit faces off with Sin and her Serpent Squad of Eel, Viper, and King Cobra. He knows that Sin is the Red Skull's daughter, but the others are just strangers in costumes to him. None of them know that Bucky is the Winter Soldier.

He has no idea of their capabilities, but he is about to find out.

Eel attacks first with a massive electro-zap. Bucky pretends to shrug it off as if it were the static discharge from a fuzzy sweater. In reality, he is fighting to keep from blacking out. Bucky's muscles are wracked by painful galvanic spasms, and he is struggling to regain control of numbed nerve endings. But he isn't about to give Eel the pleasure of knowing his attack was effective.

Maneuvering to keep Sin between himself and Eel to prevent getting zapped again, Bucky uses his shield to deflect the bullets from Sin's pistol as he ducks under the spray from King Cobra's venomous wrist-shooters. The pain isn't going away. Bucky knows he has no choice but to fight through it.

Viper joins the fight, overconfident about the potency of his poison darts. He gets a shield smashed in his face and a knee in his groin for his trouble.

"Who is this guy?" Eel snarls. "Isn't Captain America supposed to be dead?"

Reloading and emptying her gun multiple times, Sin

screeches, "He *is* dead, you morons! This is just some two-bit ringer they brought in to look good in the suit!"

The shield bounces off two walls, knocks King Cobra's feet out from under him, and cracks three of Viper's teeth before returning to the red-gloved hand that threw it.

Eel voices what the rest of the Serpent Squad thinks: "For a two-bit ringer, this guy has all the moves *down!*"

Sin struggles to clear a jam in her pistol.

"When I'm ready, we'll all attack him together. He's not the real thing. We can put him down easy if we pull out all the stops."

As the Serpent Squad regroups, Bucky catches movement at the far end of the hall in his peripheral vision. A graying head is peeking out of one of the senatorial offices. *Is that Senator Wright?* The door slams shut.

Black Widow's voice crackles in Bucky's earpiece: "Full-scale riot engulfing the whole area. I had to move across the Potomac. How are you doing?"

"I'm a little busy right now."

"On my way."

"I can handle this."

"Not your call, soldier."

The Serpent Squad spreads out and charges Bucky from three sides—Eel on the left, Viper on the right, and both Sin and King Cobra in the middle. The necessity of all of them having to track the shield's flight as it ricochets around the hall erodes this tactic's effective advantage.

Before Eel can release another electro-zap, Bucky's flying kick connects solidly with his forehead and knocks him nearly senseless.

Viper is looking the wrong way as the shield hits his head from behind. The convulsions triggered by the blow are so severe that he has to grab his own tongue to keep from swallowing it.

After another carom off walls and ceiling, the shield still maintains enough inertia to give Sin a good crack on the head and break her collarbone. Concussed and reeling from the pain, she screams until she passes out.

The shield is back in Bucky's hand before Sin hits the floor.

Bucky allows himself a tight smile. *I can do it, Steve.*

King Cobra clutches his chest and collapses on the floor as if he were having a heart attack. Bucky is not fooled, but he gives King Cobra points for a wise tactical decision. After a quick glance at each to determine that Eel, Viper, and Sin are effectively out of action, Bucky switches his full concentration back to King Cobra.

Six shots from a high-powered pistol ring out in quick succession.

Bucky finds himself staring into the pile of a maroon Government Service Agency carpet and understands that he has been rendered momentarily unconscious and is now facedown on the floor. Pain radiates from his back like seismic waves. He fights it down and thinks hard. *Where is the shield?* If he dropped it when he fell, where would it be? He recognizes the swagger in the heavy footsteps behind him before he hears the voice.

"Nobody gets away with hurting my girlfriend, you star-spangled loser."

Crossbones.

The scene reconstruction runs through Bucky's head as per his KGB training: Crossbones slipping out of an office along the corridor and coming up behind him. Crossbones raising the revolver and firing. All six shots tightly grouped in the center of Bucky's mass.

A hard kick from Crossbones rolls Bucky over on his back.

Crossbones steps back to deliver another kick, and his boot crunches down on something hard on the carpet. Bucky watches though slitted eyes as Crossbones raises his foot to examine what is trapped in the tread. Bucky knows it's a deformed magnum bullet. It's deformed because it was *deflected.*

"Bulletproof inner layer under the shirt, bone head," Bucky grunts as he kicks upward into Crossbones crotch so hard that the big man's feet leave the floor.

A fast tactical assessment tells Bucky that Viper and Eel are out of the game, King Cobra is still playing possum, and Sin has recovered her wits and sassy lip—if not her tactical effectiveness.

"Don't just stand there like a dumb ox, Brock. KILL him!"

Crossbones shrugs and draws his fist back for a punch that never gets delivered because Bucky's iron-hard fingers have penetrated the intercostal space between the eleventh and twelfth ribs on Crossbones' right side. The fingers grasp the eleventh rib and crack it outward through the skin.

Most people would be screaming. Crossbones won't lower himself to such a display of weakness. He snaps orders instead.

"Quit your faking, Cobra—get Sin out of here. This situation is going to hell."

Bucky extracts his fingers from the rib cage, closes them into a fist and snaps Crossbones' jaw shut with a hard uppercut.

"It's already there, stupid."

At the other end of the hall, two burly Kane-Meyer enforcement troopers have kicked down Senator Wright's door and are firmly escorting the legislator down five flights of fire stairs to the basement tunnel that leads to the Capitol building. The Senator is protesting: "Faustus' plan won't work now—"

The larger of the two troopers tightens his grip on the Senator's arm.

"Not to worry, sir. We'll edit the footage. Keep moving."

The buzzing sound Bucky hears is hard to distinguish from the ringing in his ears that is the result of a fresh onslaught of right and left hooks from Crossbones. Between wondering how Crossbones can keep punching with a rib sticking out of him and how he is going to counter the relentless counterattack, it dawns on Bucky that his earpiece has been knocked loose.

A series of pile-driver jabs from his prosthetic arm gives Bucky the leeway to reseat the earpiece. Black Widow sounds as worried as it is possible for her to sound.

"—where are you?"

"Fourth-floor foyer, Natasha. I'm—"

Taking advantage of Bucky's diverted attention, Crossbones grabs him with both hands, lifts him above his head, and runs full-tilt at the window. With no purchase on the floor, Bucky doesn't have the leverage to inflict further damage. The last thing Bucky sees as he gets thrown through the closed window is King Cobra carrying a semi-conscious Sin toward the fire stairs.

The window explodes outward in a welter of splintered glass and molding. The best that Bucky can do for himself is to twist his body so he doesn't impact the pavement face-first. He has passed the second floor and is bracing himself when he hits—

—the hood of Black Widow's S.H.I.E.L.D. flying car.

Bucky grabs the windshield frame as the car slews 90 degrees with the rear fender scraping sparks off the building façade. Crossbones is poised in the shattered window above, ready to leap into the car.

Black Widow points her fist back over her shoulder over the trunk and unleashes a full-power 30,000-volt electrostatic bolt from her Widow's Bite into Crossbones' chest, toppling him back.

As the flying car circles to return to the Dirksen Building, Bucky flips into the shotgun seat, pulls off the Captain America mask, and takes a deep breath. He looks at Black Widow; for a moment, he sees a look in her eyes that he hasn't since their training days in Moscow a lifetime ago. He knows the mood is fragile, but he can't help himself.

"Damn, Natasha—you took your sweet time getting here."

"D.C. traffic is a bitch."

He would laugh if he didn't hurt so much. She avoids his gaze as she parks the flying car in hover mode outside the broken fourth-floor window.

Inside, they find Crossbones stretched out on his back with his feet still twitching and the burnt spot on his chest still smoking.

"Good. He's alive," Black Widow says, checking the big man's pulse. "But he won't be answering questions for a while."

"Nice one, Natasha. I bet lightning shot out of his butt."

Bucky picks up a bloody bicuspid from the floor and drops it on the unconscious Eel.

Viper's eyes have rolled up inside his head, but he is still grunting rhythmically.

"The interrogators will have plenty of fodder here before they have to worry about Crossbones," Bucky says as Black Widow calls in the Evacuation and Sanitation Team on her communicator.

The shield is where Bucky dropped it when Crossbones shot him. Picking it up, he can sense its iconic power even through his red gloves. *This must be what Excalibur felt like in Arthur's hand.* The analogy is a stretch, but it works. When Arthur died, the sword was thrown back into the lake to wait for the next deserving wielder. Bucky runs his fingers along the rim. *Am I the one?*

Nobody else is stepping up to the plate.

Stretching the blue mask back over his face, Bucky—for all it's worth—becomes Captain America again. Every step he takes toward the stairs reinforces that conviction in his heart. Black Widow is yelling at him to stop, but she won't follow. She has to be on-site when the E & S crew arrives. Besides, she's calling the wrong name. She's calling Bucky.

The drug-induced anger that had triggered the riot has faded, only to be replaced by older and uglier instincts: the urge to run with a pack, howl, and break things—the urge to burn.

This crowd's first instinct is to ignore the man shouting at them from atop a looted news van. More and more of them start to see the man is wearing what seems to be a Captain America uniform—and, yes, he's carrying a shield. The noise and hubbub lessens to the extent that a widening circle around him can actually discern his words.

"You are not solving any problems here. This is not the way to air your grievances so that they will be taken seriously. This is not the time to band together to tear down. This is the time to band together to build up. Go home and take care of each other. Once fear and anger rule our actions—"

A half-empty water bottle arcs over the throng and bounces off the shield.

"Shut up, you faker!"

"You're not Captain America!"

"Damn right! He's dead!"

The exhortations of the single man on top of the van become meaningless as Kane-Meyer Security reinforcements open fire on the crowd with tear gas and high-pressure water hoses. The melee is swept away in clouds of stinging gas until the plaza is empty except for the litter of broken protest signs and squashed plastic bottles. The man left standing on top of the van has tears running down his face, but he is not sagging in defeat. He is still proud and defiant. When the blacked-out flying car stops, hovering level with the top of the van, he gets in, and the car shoots north.

Bucky watches numbly as Black Widow climbs to cruising altitude, turns on the passive stealth gear, and sets the navigation system to follow I-95 north to New York. She adjusts the throttle to low cruising. She's not in a hurry. Bucky relaxes completely and lets his head rest on Natasha's shoulder. He only means to keep it there for a moment. He doesn't mean to fall asleep, but he does.

The lights of Philadelphia are passing beneath them when Bucky wakes up to the sound of a cable news station on the dashboard multifunction display monitor. He sees grainy phone-cam footage of himself on the van. The banner at the bottom of the screen reads, "Have you seen the new Cap?" A news anchor with too-perfect hair is reading from a teleprompter: "...multiple reports of a man in what appears to be a Captain America uniform attempting to defuse the riot." The banner changes to show a telephone number and a request to call in with new information.

The image shifts to indistinct security-cam imagery that appears to show Kane-Meyer troopers firing on Viper and Eel as Senator Wright is whisked to safety down a flight of fire stairs.

"Other shocking news from last night's riot was the attempted abduction of Senator Gordon Wright by super-powered terrorists, and his dramatic rescue by heroic Kane-Meyer Security agents. The Senator has praised those agents for going above and beyond the call of duty to rescue him—"

Black Widow clicks off the monitor.

"Thanks, Natasha. That was giving me a headache. Any interrogation updates from S.H.I.E.L.D. yet?"

"Crossbones is still unconscious in the ICU, and the other two were too small potatoes to be let in on the big picture. King Cobra might've actually known something, but he flew Sin out in the same helicopter they came in on. We did get the location of their bolt-hole safe house in New York out of Viper. A forensics team is tearing it apart inch-by-inch right now."

Near Newark, the flying car readjusts course to skim right over the Atlantic at wave-top level to avoid air traffic. Manhattan is a glow on the horizon. A red light blinks on the dashboard, indicating the autopilot is engaged. Bucky pulls on a plain gray hoodie to cover his Captain America shirt, stuffing the gloves into the hoodie's pockets. He turns toward Black Widow but says nothing.

Bucky wonders whether Natasha is conscious of him looking at her. She turns to face him, with one of those looks that seems to strip away years and overlay old memories. He finds it disconcerting. He breaks the gaze and looks out to sea.

"And what about Steve's girl? Have they got any leads yet?"

"Sharon. Her name is Sharon Carter. Falcon may have found something that will help track her. As soon as Tony makes all the red tape go away, S.H.I.E.L.D. can operate in the open again. How did we say it long ago? Like cooking with gas."

"But for now...?"

"For now, our credibility is still damaged, and all our ops on U.S. soil are under the microscope."

"Which means what, Natasha?"

"It means now that you are front-page news, you and I won't be seeing as much of each other."

"Oh. Okay."

But it's not okay. He feels like a fumbling boy, unsure and awkward with a girl to whom he is hesitant to reveal his emotions. He is thinking that he can change this. He has changed harder things.

"Do you remember it all?" she asks. "Do you remember all our time together when I was young?"

The Statue of Liberty is visible through the windshield.

Bucky can remember seeing it from the deck of a troop ship. His thoughts wander before he answers.

"I remember every second of it, *Natasha Alianovna*. You were the one good thing. The one good thing in all of it."

The rooftops of Manhattan flash by beneath the flying car. Bucky reaches back for the shield, encased again in its anonymous wrapper. The car slows and hovers over the roof of Bucky's hotel.

They are both aware of the awkwardness of the moment. Bucky has his door open already. All he has to do is step out and walk away. She says, "I have not forgotten either, *Zeemneey Soldat.*"

The kiss is brief, but more than friendly.

"Again." She breathes.

And a moment later: "One more time."

She is the one who breaks the last kiss and searches the depths of his eyes with their foreheads touching. Pulling his hood over his head, she shoves him out the door with a smile.

"Until we face the enemy together again."

He stands on the roof and watches the car rise and veer off toward the glow behind the clouds that marks the Helicarrier's location.

As he trudges down the fire stairs to his dreary room, he reflects that it really is okay—and that sometimes, it's possible to earn yourself a little peace.

INTERLUDE #15

"**YOUR** daughter has a compound fracture of the left clavicle. The bone was protruding through the skin. We've reset it, sutured everything back up, and put her in an immobilizing cast. The head injury is another matter. She may experience cognitive difficulties."

The doctor is aware of the oddness of explaining cranial injuries to a man who wears a skull on the outside of his head, but he would not think of saying anything out loud. Not to the Red Skull.

"I probably won't be able to tell the difference."

It is difficult to tell whether the Red Skull is joking. There are photographs of Hitler and Stalin laughing. There are none of the Red Skull.

"Tell me this: Will she be able to function? Will she be able to perform simple tasks? Like walking down into a basement and shooting somebody in the back of the head?"

The doctor gulps before answering: "I don't see why not."

"Inform me if her situation changes."

Red Skull asks one last question before walking out the door: "You don't have any qualms about terminating futile cases, do you?"

"No, sir. Not at all."

Sin's eyes are closed. She has not shown any outward signs that she has overheard anything that has been said. She is smarter than that. The apple does not fall far from the tree.

Her father is aware that everything he has said has

registered on Sin's consciousness, but he doesn't care. What else would she expect from him? He thinks she should count herself lucky that he had handed her over to Mother Night for a ruthlessly pragmatic upbringing instead of wringing her neck.

Red Skull steps out of the medical bay to find King Cobra waiting in the hallway. He seems intent on smiling, showing sympathy, and appearing obeisant at the same time.

"I hope your daughter's prognosis is favorable. I took it upon myself to prioritize getting her to medical treatment, and left dealing with the new Captain America to Crossbones and the—"

"Don't call him that."

"I'm sorry—?"

"He's not the *new* Captain America. He's the old Bucky playing dress-up with his dead mentor's suit."

King Cobra attempts to follow the Red Skull down the corridor inside the secret complex in upstate New York but is stopped at a blast door by a pair of R.A.I.D. security guards.

"Restricted area, Cobra," Red Skull says over his shoulder. "And Sin's prognosis is good. If it wasn't, there would have been the distinct possibility of *two* wet patches of concrete in the basement down among the bric-a-brac and failed projects."

With the blast doors shut behind him, Red Skull strolls down the steel-reinforced-concrete corridor that is as bomb-proof as the old German U-boat pens at Saint-Nazaire. He stops to peek into Arnim Zola's lab and backs out when he sees the dead water bugs littering the floor. Whatever emanates from Zola's devices is not conducive to living tissue.

Another set of blast doors protects Red Skull's private suite at the end of the corridor. Fully occupying a settee intended for two, Doctor Faustus is cycling through all the cable news channels on the big wall monitor. Senator Wright's florid face fills the screen on every channel.

Tamping down his fury at the invasion of his private space, Red Skull enunciates evenly, "How did you get in here?"

Faustus is sipping a passable *Saint-Émilion* as he munches on wasabi peas.

"When you moved operations from Kronas Tower and the compromised R.A.I.D. facility in Manhattan, you transferred the security codes, and my old card still works. Have my privileges been revoked?"

The Red Skull makes a mental note to have the codes upgraded as soon as time permits. He nods at the monitor screen: "What does our pet politico have to say?"

"He's announced his split from his old party, the formation of the Third Wing Party, and his candidacy for president. All three at the same time guaranteed him prime coverage. Very good peas, these, Herr Skull."

"Tangy, *nicht war?* Is he at least sticking to the script?"

"Very much so. Although his rhetoric is recycled and his delivery a bit hackneyed, it's what the electorate wants to hear and see. His press releases are getting good traction, as well."

Red Skull peruses the security-cam footage of the Senator's rescue from the "terrorists" on the screen.

"Such a simple plan: to stage a fake terrorist kidnapping of the senator and have him rescued by Kane-Meyer troopers; how easily it went awry because of one self-righteous meddler. I've noticed all the stations replay that doctored video constantly. I am amazed the fakery wasn't caught."

"Nothing to catch, since it's not doctored. We duplicated the stairwell, got two actors to play Eel and Viper, and made the Senator reenact it with the actual Kane-Meyer troopers. The two actors had fatal accidents."

"Brilliant, Faustus. And everybody is parroting the Senator's contention that Kane-Meyer saved the major American cities from burning to the ground."

Doctor Faustus turns up the volume with the remote. "This is the master stroke, though."

Stock footage of oil fields with seesawing pumps appears on the screen. The newscaster's voice projects bias in the form of reverent awe: "...And just yesterday, Senator Wright negotiated a deal with Kronas Energy to lower the price of oil back to pre-crisis levels, this on the heels of brokering the settlement that halted the foreclosure of thousands of homes across the country."

Red Skull picks up the remote, turns off the TV, and—taking the bottle from the sideboard—refills Doctor Faustus' glass. Faustus inhales the bouquet, not minding that he alone is drinking.

"Having your own minions publicly attack the senator should dispel any notions that he is actually our man, or that the Red Skull is running Kronas from behind the scenes."

"I suppose Lukin deserves some of the credit." The Skull settles in behind his desk. "Admittedly, the germ of the plan was his, although I find it tiresome that he complains about the means to the end. Who cares how we get to the result as long as we get there, and America lies in shambles."

A moment later, his own excitement at his impending victory propels Red Skull out of his seat to pace and rant. "And soon, our man Wright can campaign for the presidency as the savior of American prosperity—the shining knight who pulled the country from the brink of ruin and made the streets safe for old ladies and little kids. Slowly, the sheep will accept that hiring wolves to protect them is the only way, and they will come to understand that a police state is the only answer to the chaos of democracy."

It takes an exertion of considerable will for Faustus to suppress a yawn. He pretends there's cork on his tongue while Red Skull continues his harangue.

"Soon, Kane-Meyer Security will be a jackbooted, baton-wielding presence in every major city in this nation. My hand will wrap around the throat of the entire United States of America—"

"You mean *our* hands, I believe, Herr Skull?"

Dangerous seconds tick by while the Red Skull examines the possible reasons for Faustus' remark, their implications and extrapolated outcomes. He opts to change the subject. "Don't you have something else to do? A woman who has concealed her pregnancy from you, perhaps?"

The questions are rhetorical; to underscore that point, the Red Skull turns the TV back on and opens the blast door—indicating the meeting is over, and the guest is required to leave.

However, the opening doors reveal Arnim Zola, who glides into the room with his psychotronic ESP box swiveling to take in the wall monitor on which the footage of the new Captain America is being replayed. "An appropriate visual example of Jungian synchronicity at work. Yes. I am here to report that preliminary tests are positive and conclusive: Our new subject is perfectly viable, and resuscitation can proceed according to our revamped schedule."

Red Skull turns a triumphant sneer on Faustus, waving a hand in derision at the image on the screen.

"Very soon, it won't be just this stripling imposter wearing the flag. A Captain America with a much more authentic pedigree will emerge to inspire the pliable patriotic urges of the American people, and it will be a Captain America wholly under our control."

THIRTY-THREE

I may not have another chance.

There's a big fuss in the medical bay over Red Skull's daughter. And Zola's lab, or at least the periphery of it, is a hub of activity. Red Skull is more full of himself than ever. He sees his triumph within reach. And when people feel overconfident, they get careless. I hope his hubris strangles him.

Doctor Faustus is managing a political campaign while running a public-relations blitz, both of which are full-time jobs. He doesn't have a lot of time to spend inside my head making sure I toe the line. I'm also getting better at compartmentalizing and setting up barriers between the original "me" and the Sharon Carter under Faustus' control.

The prospect of motherhood is the most powerful motivator there is. My need to save my child—Steve's child—from these ruthless maniacs is what is driving me into the halls to search for a way out.

I'm certain there has to be at least one or two secret escape routes. That has been routine for every lab or facility that Arnim Zola and Red Skull have ever used, and I saw for myself the one Doctor Faustus utilized to beat a hasty retreat when Falcon and Black Widow attacked the R.A.I.D. site. That was when Faustus handed me one of his many security cards so I could get through locked containment doors to recapture Winter Soldier for him.

I never returned that card to him, and that now gives me a chance for freedom.

The most obvious escape route would be a tunnel, so I make my way down to the basement. There is free access to the utility rooms housing the furnaces and boilers. I give them a rudimentary search, but I don't think Red Skull would choose too obvious a location. At the back of a large storage area, I find a steel door marked "cleaning supplies" that requires security-card access. That's suspicious off the bat. I swipe and enter.

The room is too large for a supply closet. There are steel shelves full of sealed metal containers, stacks of large crates, and aisles between the shelves wide enough for a forklift. There is a hum that sounds like a refrigeration fan from the far end of the room.

The noise is from a freezer unit with two backup power sources. The thing is the size of a coffin and has a frosted-over glass inspection port. When I wipe away the frost, I see a face I know all too well.

It's Steve Rogers.

My knees are going rubbery, and my knees *never* go rubbery. Bile is rising toward my throat. I hear my forehead hitting the inspection port, but I don't feel it. Steve's face is inches away, but the details are getting fuzzy. It's my own breath fogging the glass again.

A thousand questions, and no answers. *Isn't he dead? Didn't I shoot him at Foley Square? Didn't I see his body at the morgue? Wasn't there a funeral and a burial? Is everything I know just a lie implanted by Doctor Faustus? Is my pregnancy even real?*

All those questions and more are cut off by the sound of the security door buzzing open.

In the darkest corner of the room, I slip behind the shelving and hunker down. It's not an ideal hiding place, but it affords me a view of the freezer unit. I watch a R.A.I.D. security team take up positions around the freezer as a crew of A.I.M. techs attaches a portable power unit to it. Another tech drives up a forklift. I hear Arnim Zola's robotic voice before I see him.

"Be very careful with that. If you damage him, and he can't be awakened, you will answer to the Red Skull."

I inch back as far as I can when Zola comes into view. The box that serves as his head turns in my direction, and the single red lens in the middle of it seems to be looking me right in the eye. I scrunch back farther and hold my breath.

The forklift backs out of the freezer room, followed by the A.I.M. techs and R.A.I.D. guards. The door closes, and the sound of footsteps fades down the basement corridor.

Zola's words ricochet around my brain. One word in particular stands out: "awakened."

Steve isn't dead.

They're going to revive him.

It feels like Christmas and the Fourth of July with opened presents and fireworks. But my escape plans are cancelled. I am not leaving Steve in their hands.

No way.

It won't be easy. They took away my gun again after I jettisoned Winter Soldier from the escape jet. Faustus didn't lock me up—but he forgot he gave me one of his security cards, so he assumes I can't move freely. Big deal. Getting through the containment gates and blast doors is one thing, but navigating the halls and corridors is something else again. I'm still wearing my white jumpsuit, which stands out among all the yellow and red here. It took me an hour to get down to the basement because I had to keep waiting for the next stretch of corridor to be empty.

I can't keep worrying about all the negatives. I have to get Steve away from here. There's nothing left but to start moving and make my way up to Zola's lab as best I can.

The security card is in my hand and I'm about to swipe the lock when the door opens and an A.I.M. tech steps into the room. I brazen it out with an authoritative, "What are you doing here?"

Confused, the tech blurts, "I came back to get the tetrachloromethane coupler—"

After I take him down with a roundhouse kick to his solar plexus, I strip him of his yellow beekeeper suit and helmet. He's also carrying a railgun, a pistol-sized weapon that uses an electric field to shoot hyper-velocity projectiles. I slip it into my empty holster.

A quick search of the empty spot where the freezer unit stood yields a stainless-steel fitting that could well be a refrigerant coupler. All I can remember of the name of the refrigerant is that it starts with a "T."

Ten minutes later, I'm at the door to Zola's lab, which unfortunately is guarded by a pair of very large R.A.I.D. troopers armed with kinetic-energy weapons. Holding up the stainless-steel device, I say, "I'm bringing the T-coupler."

They don't have any idea what I'm talking about, and I have no plan "B." I'd have to unzip the beekeeper suit to get at the railgun I took off the A.I.M. tech, so shooting them before they shoot me isn't an option. My choices ratchet down to zero as the guards level their weapons at me.

"That's the coupler for the tetrachloromethane hose."

Doctor Faustus has walked up behind me. He plucks the coupler from my hand.

"I'll take that."

He swipes one of the security cards he still has. The door opens to reveal Steve stretched out on an operating table, with Arnim Zola leaning over him, hypodermic jet injector in hand.

The box that serves as Zola's head stays motionless, but the lips move on the holographic projection in his chest.

"Good of you to join us, Faustus."

"Don't take that tone of voice with me, Zola. You wouldn't even have this specimen if it wasn't for me."

Faustus steps inside, and the doors slide shut.

I have no choice but to turn and walk away. But now I know where Steve is. And if they "awaken" him, I can walk him out of this place rather than wheel him out or carry him. I have to think positively. I have to keep my wits together. I have to do all of this because I am living for two people now.

Dawdling in the corridor is impossible, but I can make a circuit of the lab perimeter—passing back and forth on a cross passageway every five to ten minutes, changing my gait, alternating between slouching and a severely erect posture. I note that there is only one security cam, and it's pointing directly at the lab door.

On my fifth pass, the lab doors open. Zola and Faustus emerge side-by-side, pretending to tolerate each other.

"Complete success. Red Skull will be extremely pleased with me, Faustus."

"With *us*, Zola."

The next set of blast doors closes behind them before I can hear Zola's reply.

I unzip the yellow suit, take out the railgun, and step out of the passageway into the corridor to shoot out the security cam. My next two shots take down the R.A.I.D. guards. I swipe for entry into Zola's lab, drag the guards inside one-by-one, and close the door. I listen for any reaction, but there's none. The railgun is completely silent except for the small sonic boom from the projectile, which is nowhere near as loud as a conventional firearm.

I'm halfway to saving my man. Now all I have to do is get him out of here.

Steve is lying on the operating table with an IV glucose drip, and he's plugged into both cardio and brain-wave monitors. There's no respirator, so they've managed to get him up and running amazingly fast. Probably got pins and needles from head to foot, though. But none of these things would stop the Steve I know. I'm sure if I can get him to stand up, I can also get him to walk out of here. I glance back to the door and see that one of the R.A.I.D. guards is close to Steve's size. We can both breeze out under their noses with luck and some good, old-fashioned audacity.

I'm standing over Steve pulling the sticky EEG electrodes from his head, and his hands are stirring under the sheet that covers him to his neck. I'm so happy to see him breathing that the tears are rolling down my face and falling on his cheek.

"Steve? Can you hear me?"

His eyes open, and he looks directly at me with no recognition at all. When he speaks, it's not with Steve's voice or any trace of his faint Lower East Side accent. "Who are you?"

It becomes apparent as he sits up into the light that although he bears a facial resemblance to Steve, it's an artificial likeness—like it had been enhanced with plastic surgery. His gestures and body language are all *wrong.*

"You're not Steve," I gasp.

"That's my name. I am Steve Rogers."

The doppelganger shakes his head. The sheet slips off his upper body, and I see large areas of keloid scarring—healed burns covering one shoulder and much of his chest. That's what tells me who he really is.

"No. Your real name is William Burnside. You were part of an FBI program to create a new Captain America in the 1950s, but the Super-Soldier Serum they used was flawed. You were in and out of suspended animation for years until Doctor Faustus—"

The horror sitting up before me with Steve's face cuts me off.

"Doctor Faustus is helping me. I'm going to be Captain America again."

Faustus is the one who once tried to make Burnside over into a hate-mongering fascist super hero called "The Director." When Faustus had ordered Burnside to kill Steve Rogers, something inside him had snapped; he'd triggered a self-immolation device. Everyone thought Burnside had been dead all these years, but Faustus apparently had him stashed away. And Faustus has conveniently removed important parts of Burnside's memory. The doppelganger thinks he's Steve Rogers, but he's really a bad experiment gone worse—and a dangerous psychotic.

So Steve is really dead, and this lunatic is alive and wearing Steve's face. And now Red Skull and Faustus are going to set him up as the new Captain America. It's more than I can bear.

I'm not going to let that happen.

The railgun is in my hand and pointing at the imposter's head. He backs off, not comprehending why this is about to happen.

My finger tightens on the trigger—

INTERLUDE #16

"IT seems your patient isn't exactly your patient anymore, Doctor Faustus."

Aleksander Lukin, holding an A.I.M. knockoff of the S.H.I.E.L.D. neural neutralizer, stands over the limp body of Sharon Carter. The weapon isn't exactly smoking, but it is shedding stray ions.

"Your grasp of the obvious is impressive," Faustus says. "Am I addressing Lukin or Red Skull? It's hard to tell without the mask."

"Both. We are sharing today."

"This could have been a disaster if I hadn't brought you back to look at the results. Zola should have stayed here to monitor the subject."

"Zola had to go oversee the sterilization of the facility where you had previously stored the subject. We don't want any clues lying around that would bring the wrong people here, do we?"

Lukin/Skull pries the railgun from Sharon's hand and pockets it. "We really need to do something about her brain, you know. We can't have her running amok in her delicate state. In the meantime, she should be securely strapped down in the medical bay."

"Where your daughter, Sin, is recovering?" Faustus asks. "Such a lovely girl. Found her hacking into my personal files once. She said she was intending to help me organize them. Wasn't that sweet? I'll bet she's been helping you, as well, while you weren't looking."

Red Skull turns and walks out with no reply.

Faustus has to step over Sharon's inert form to lead Burnside back to the operation table.

"She was trying to kill me. Why would she do that?" Burnside seems genuinely puzzled. "She was very confused. She called me by my name, and then she said I was somebody else."

Faustus pulls the sheet back over the imposter's body. "Just the mutterings of a foolish girl. Everybody knows who you are. You're Captain America."

THIRTY-FOUR

THE motorcycle he's riding to upstate New York is still called "American Iron," even though it is only assembled in the United States from parts made all over the world. *But, heck*, Bucky figures, *if Captain America's riding it, that's all the brand recognition you need.* Its liquid-cooled dual-overhead cam 1,250cc V-twin engine may not get him places as fast as a flying car, but the scenery is better. The shield strapped to his back adds to the drag coefficient if he sits up straight, but he's not Easy Rider, is he?

A glance to the sky tells Bucky that Falcon is still flying high up there along with Redwing.

Last night, Bucky had the same nightmare he has had every night since he agreed to be the new Captain America. It makes no logical sense, but it makes a lot of emotional sense—which, he supposes, is what dreams are supposed to do. It's a pastiche from the war—some bridgehead in Holland. Tiger tanks and Panzer Grenadiers try to hold off the Allied advance, while Captain America and Bucky chip away at the German flank. Cap flings his shield and topples a Waffen SS officer. The shield is flying back, and Cap yells out, "Catch it, Bucky!"

And Bucky does.

But Bucky isn't Bucky anymore. He's wearing the new Captain America uniform, and he's holding the shield he just caught. The old Captain America is fading away like Alice's

Cheshire cat, with only the star on his chest remaining solid.

"Don't lose the shield, Bucky. I'm going to want it back."

"I won't lose it, Cap! Don't go—"

"Say it in Russian, Bucky."

"What? What does that mean?"

And then, even the star is gone.

Bucky feels like a little kid again, like the red-white-and–blue suit he's wearing is six sizes too big, and he'll never be able to fill it out. He's shouting, "That wasn't really me! That wasn't my fault!"

"What wasn't your fault?"

Bucky had sat bolt upright in his bed to see Falcon perched on the ledge of the cheap hotel window.

"Don't you ever come in through the door?"

"What, and walk up five flights of smelly stairs?"

"You're not here to throw down on me, are you?"

"Say *what?*"

"Sorry. What *do* you want, Sam?"

"Saw you on the news. I wasn't thrilled at first. But when I thought about it, I couldn't think of anybody who could do it better."

"Damning with faint praise, but go on."

"I got a lead on where Sharon Carter might be. I thought you might want to get in on trying to save Steve's lady."

"She's your friend, too, right?"

"She is that."

"Then let's do it."

That's all it took. Now, Bucky is wearing the suit and getting the wind and bugs in his face on the thruway heading north. It's a bright, beautiful day to be heading toward what might be a grim and nasty fight, but he remembers many days like this during the war. Most people alive today tend to think of World War II as a dreary black-and-white event. They don't realize that the push to Paris after D-Day took place between the beginning of July and the end of August 1944. Bucky saw some horrific carnage on days that were just as bright and sunny.

Falcon circles down and points to a road leading off the highway. Stopping on the side of that road, they have a short tactical briefing and planning session.

"Satellite imagery showed trucks going northwest on this road, departing from a suspected A.I.M. facility that we know was used by Doctor Faustus. The trucks stopped briefly at that complex there on the other side of the woods—an abandoned upscale mental-health clinic we now suspect was a front for Faustus. Who knows what went on there?"

Bucky can make out tall chimneys sticking up through the trees a quarter-mile away, reminding him of nightmarish places he saw in Germany and Poland.

"I've met Faustus. I can imagine."

"You have no idea, Bucky. Faustus tried to start a race war back in the day. He even brainwashed William Burnside, who the Feds had set up to be Captain America in the fifties. Can you imagine that? Using a guy who'd worn Cap's colors to lead a lynch mob of race-baiters and bigots?"

Just the idea of it infuriates Bucky, cementing his enmity toward Faustus.

Hiding the motorcycle in the bushes, the duo strikes off through the foliage toward the facility with Redwing flying ahead to reconnoiter. At the chain-link fence delineating the property's perimeter, they stop in the shadow of a tall pine as Falcon "sees" through Redwing's eyes.

"A.I.M. agents. The yellow-beekeeper-suit guys. Looks like they're shutting the place down, loading equipment on to one of their VTOL transports."

"Bucket-heads? Nerds with guns is all they are."

"One of Red Skull's top guns is there, playing head honcho on the job. Professor Arnim Zola himself. He's another psycho with roots in the Third Reich, like Skull and Faustus."

"I guess I don't have to ask which one us goes in high, and which one goes in low?"

Their combined attack from the ground and from the air catches the A.I.M. agents loading the transport completely by surprise. A third of them are laid low before the rest are even aware something is wrong. There is no loud discharge of firearms, shouting, or snappy repartee—just a methodically violent demonstration of team fighting elevated to an art form.

Falcon's economy of motion and combative efficiency remind Bucky of Steve Rogers. Not the style, exactly, but certainly the attitude. Watching Falcon in action makes Bucky think of the time he and Cap almost caught the Red Skull napping in Denmark. It makes Bucky smile—and care about not letting Falcon down, showing him he can do his job. Showing him he was right to place his trust in him.

When he's certain Falcon can mop up the remainder of the crew loading the transport, the man who was once a boy-soldier and now wears the uniform of Captain America rushes into a large structure that had once been the institutional laundry facility.

"I'm going after Zola, Falcon!"

Professor Arnim Zola is not a mere "nerd with a gun," but an armored cyborg wielding a Tesla-coil plasma pistol. The hydrogen bolt he fires would have blasted a hole through Bucky's chest if the shield hadn't deflected it. The back-blast fries the central nervous systems of four of Zola's A.I.M. stooges right through their protective suits.

A confused beekeeper stands directly between Zola and Bucky, but that doesn't prevent the deranged robotic professor from shooting, since meat and bone do little to diminish the energy of a hypervelocity hydrogen bolt. A smoking 10mm hole appears in the brick wall behind where Bucky had been.

Steve Rogers would have never played a defensive game. Bucky flings the shield, knowing full well he is defenseless until it returns to his hand. It's a seven-point carom shot, bouncing off steel support pillars, walls, and the concrete floor—making it impossible to predict the ultimate impact point.

Arnim Zola turns his plasma pistol on three support pillars, bringing down a large section of the second and third floors in the shield's flight path. Bucky has to make a lunging dive to save the shield from being buried in tons of rubble. Three of the remaining A.I.M. crew are not so lucky.

Zola has retreated up to a steel catwalk and is retraining his weapon on Bucky when Falcon crashes through the window and topples a twenty-foot-high heat-transfer unit on top of him. A flesh-and-blood human would have been crushed against the catwalk grates, but the cyborg Zola shrugs off the rusting metal and blasts a fusillade at Falcon that empties the charge in his weapon.

Climbing to what's left of the third floor, Zola dashes inside a windowless room and slams a steel door behind him. On the ground floor, the remainder of the A.I.M. agents have recovered a cache of plasma pistols and are punching more holes in the walls where Bucky used to be. As he throws the shield, Bucky calls out to Falcon, "I'll take care of these creeps—don't let Zola get away!"

Falcon rips open the steel door on the third floor to find Professor Arnim Zola plugged into a machine that takes up most of the room, vibrating at a frequency that threatens to loosen his molars. Six or seven monitors are flashing number sequences. Zola's voice booms from multiple speakers.

"You have accomplished nothing. I am taking everything of importance with me!"

It comes to Falcon in a flash that the number sequences are a countdown in seconds, and they have just passed 7.306.

At 3.963 Falcon zooms to the ground floor and grabs Bucky.

Falcon, carrying Bucky, barrels out of the facility at the 2.511 mark. They hit the ground, tumble, and roll. Bucky gets the shield up to cover both of them as the fireball engulfs the building and scorches a perimeter of fifty yards.

They stand, batting out live cinders while watching the devouring flames.

"What are you thinking, Bucky?"

"I'm wondering what Red Skull wants to hide this badly."

INTERLUDE #17

HE feels good to be back in the Captain America uniform because it is rightfully his. He knows this because Doctor Faustus told him so, and Doctor Faustus is right about everything.

He had been Captain America when it actually meant something to be Captain America. The uniform he wears is exactly the same as the one worn by the last real Captain America—not like the sleazy, redesigned rag worn by that ignoble imposter who went on a rampage in Washington and assaulted Kane-Meyer patriots who were just doing their duty.

Wearing the uniform is a hallowed trust of which one must be worthy. Bearing the title "Captain America" is the highest honor he can think of, and the idea of a pretender to that title besmirching the uniform is more than he can bear. It makes his burn scars itch maddeningly, but he forbears scratching through the sacred cloth.

The man at the podium in the plaza far below is another matter. Senator Gordon Wright embodies all the principles in which Captain America believes fervently. Another true patriot, Wright has come to Chicago on the first leg of a campaign tour that will hopefully wrest the White House from the traitor who defiles it.

A huge, enthusiastic crowd has gathered to hear the venerable legislator's earnest words. Wright invokes the Constitution but stresses the need for security. Wright uses the word "freedom" thirty-six times and "the people of this great nation" eleven times. Everything is going exactly as written in the script.

The man with the burn scars wearing the Captain America suit stands on the rooftop ledge adjacent to the plaza and adjusts the straps on the shield hanging from his left arm. It's not the original shield, of course. Not Vibranium, but a laminate of moly-steel, Kevlar, and carbon-fiber resin. It has a propulsion and guidance system created by an extremely patriotic organization called A.I.M., but that is a national secret. Doctor Faustus made him promise never to reveal it.

He is proud to be a part of this night. He understands the reasons for the careful scripting of this event. What does a little deception matter against advancement of the greater good? The fate of the nation hangs in the balance, and the enemies of liberty are truly ruthless.

The assassins rushing the podium are real enough. They are fanatical believers in a political stance diametrically opposed to what Senator Wright stands for. Does it matter that they were duped, prepped, and prodded toward this night's actions? Is it important that the weapons and opportunity were provided for them? Of course not. They are grace notes in a major orchestration.

He hears his cue and attacks as the would-be assassins draw their weapons and shout their slogans. Within seconds, they are lying at the foot of the podium, bloody and lacerated. The crowd is cheering. Captain America addresses the throng.

"My fellow Americans..."

THIRTY-FIVE

BUCKY had watched the newscast with growing anger and disgust. The man on the screen looked so much like Steve Rogers, but the words coming out of his mouth in support of Senator Wright were such twisted perversions of the ideals by which Steve Rogers had lived that Bucky wanted to smash the screen.

He had been in the downstairs gym in Falcon's loft, sparring and working out when Sam got the heads-up from Natasha to turn on the cable news.

Watching the address, and seeing replays of the assassination attempt and rescue, Bucky had been struck speechless. Falcon wasn't one to keep his opinions to himself.

"This is the Skull's work. It has to be. He's got the motive, the wherewithal, and the organization to make this happen. I just knew in my gut that Senator Wright wasn't on the level."

"And now Wright is linked with this new Captain America," Bucky mused. "Maybe both of these guys are a direct connection to Kronas, and to the Red Skull?"

A few days later, Bucky is standing in the crowd at another Wright rally, this time in Minneapolis. Falcon has begged off—he and Black Widow have to do a complete background investigation on the senator, his staff, and anybody he'd been in contact with for the past six months. Bucky wanted to get his boots on the ground and see Wright in action, especially if the other Cap was so tight with him.

The demographic that turns out to hear their demagogue is a cross-section of America that clearly deserves better. It disheartens Bucky to see Lincoln's quote about not being able to "fool all of the people all of the time" being trumped by the quote attributed to P.T. Barnum about how often a sucker is born.

Bucky has agreed to Falcon's request that he only be a passive observer. He is here to see whether the Steve Rogers stand-in makes another appearance and to try to track him. He's not supposed to take direct action. He is still an unregistered hero on a black op for Tony Stark, who is holding all the plausible deniability cards and will hang him out to dry if he drops the ball.

Seeing all the headlines on the newspapers littering the streets is what makes up his mind for him.

"IS CAP REALLY BACK?"

Damn straight he is.

But not the Cap bankrolled by the Red Skull.

At the motel where he stashed the motorcycle, Bucky dons the uniform and picks up the shield. Falcon won't be happy that he's going outside mission parameters, but seeing Wright work the crowd was an eye-opener. He can't let this lie.

The senator is staying at one of the most expensive hotels in town. He won't qualify for Secret Service protection unless he scores well in the primaries, so his security is being supplied by Kane-Meyer. A tough bunch of well-trained and well-armed pros. Just the kind that Winter Soldier would eat for breakfast. The one on the roof and the pair in the hall are unconscious before they hit the floor. The one on the balcony is problematic until he is fooled into opening the slider himself. Putting up a fight earns him extra bruises.

What Bucky sees in the bedroom and bathroom of the suite sets off all the alarm bells in his head—or rather, what he *doesn't* see. No luggage, no toiletries, nothing to indicate that Wright is actually staying in the room.

It's a trap.

The attack comes from the sitting room in a streak of red, white, and blue. The punches catch him unawares and send him crashing into a desk, splintering it. When he picks himself up, he is staring into the face of righteous indignation and it bears the features of Steve Rogers.

It speaks with Steve's voice, as well.

"I'm going to rip that fake suit off your back and make you eat it, imposter."

How surreal is this? Bucky thinks. Then he strikes back.

THIRTY-SIX

THE ICU in this facility's medical bay is tiny, so they had set me up next to Red Skull's daughter, Sin. I was on a security gurney in a four-point padded restraint when they brought me in, heavy canvas bands with thick leather straps on both ankles and wrists. They left me in the restraints and plugged me into the monitoring system while Sin screamed psychotic threats at me.

If she hadn't been in an upper-body cast and an immobilizing head brace, Sin would have been off her bed and strangling me. She had to make do with screeching the same expletive at me over and over. I offered to teach her some more imaginative invective, but that just increased the volume. Eventually she got hoarse and just lay there panting. She started screaming that the itching on her cast was so unbearable that she was going to have her father cut off their noses and other important body parts if they didn't take it off her. That particular harangue went on for three days.

So now one brave member of the medical staff has pushed in a cart loaded with a tray of scalpels and hemostats, an assortment of salves, and a battery-powered Stryker cast saw.

"Your collarbone has knitted enough for you to wear a flexible brace, so I'm going to remove your cast, Sin."

Sin isn't thankful at all. She starts yelling at the aide to hurry up, which I can see is annoying the guy. He unlocks the wheels on my gurney and pushes it flush with the wall so there's room between me and Sin for the medical cart to squeeze in.

I tell the aide very politely in my sweetest voice that my nose is itching and driving me crazy, and would he be so kind as to loosen the restraint cable on my right hand just enough for me to be able to reach it? Sin helps my cause by stepping up her nastiness and raising questions about the aide's parenthood. The aide loosens my right hand, making sure I can't reach the buckles and lock on my left hand. But I can now reach my nose, and the side of the gurney. I have a crazy outline of a plan, but the odds are stacked against me.

The saw is rotary, with a trigger and some sort of safety device. It's about the size of one of those giant pepper mills they use in restaurants and has a heavy power unit plugged into the bottom. It makes a dull whine as it cuts through Sin's cast. After sawing through the last section of cast, the aide engages the safety and lays the saw on the end of the cart farthest from me. He checks to make sure that I can't even reach the end of the closer cart. I have to bite my lip. My crazy plan might work.

The aide tells Sin that her flexibility looks good as he slathers her chapped skin with lotion. She is wiggling her torso as much as she can with her head still immobilized by the cranial restraints. The aide says that Doctor Faustus will be very pleased with her progress. That one really sets her off.

"Faustus can bite me! I've been through his secret files, and I know stuff that can get him lowered face-first into one of my father's acid vats!"

My hand may not be able to reach the medical cart, but I now have enough slack to reach the wall—and the gurney wheels are unlocked. I push off from the wall and roll until I can reach the close end of the medical cart. The aide sees the cart move and makes a grab for the saw, but I jerk on my end of the cart, causing the saw to slide across the top and into my hand.

The aide has to push aside the cart to get at me, but I have already cut through my right hand restraint by reversing the grip on the saw and activating the trigger with my nose. I cut up my forearm a bit but nothing arterial. When the aide tries to take the saw from me, I bash him in the temple with the heavy battery end.

He drops like a rock.

Sin is screaming her head off but talk about crying wolf. The medical staff probably keeps on playing online games or scraping their lottery cards. I'm a lot more careful about how I cut my other restraints.

"Keep it up, sweetheart," I say to Sin. "I'll be over there in a minute to settle up."

It must hurt like hell for Sin to be unscrewing her head restraint since any movement of her left arm has to be pushing and pulling on her broken collarbone. She does manage to free herself, but she isn't in what you might call fighting trim. Her attempt to brain me with the big stainless-steel cranial clamp she just unscrewed from her head goes ridiculously wild, which makes me underestimate her. I don't see the scalpel in her other hand until she's lunging at my throat with it.

My reflexes are still good enough to get my forearm up in time to stop the scalpel. It hurts like all blue blazes, but it's still better than getting an amateur tracheotomy. I bash her face so hard with the saw handle that the battery pack cracks off, making the saw completely useless.

I pull the scalpel out of my forearm, grab a fistful of Sin's hair, press the razor-sharp blade against her carotid artery, and frog-march her toward the door.

"We are walking out of here, you and me, and nobody's getting their panties in a knot, right?"

THIRTY-SEVEN

KARPOV, the Russian spymaster who turned Bucky into the Winter Soldier, had always said that hubris was the agent's biggest danger. It occurs to Bucky that a darkened hotel room in Minneapolis—during a knockdown-drag-out with a man who is not only dressed as Captain America but is also almost as strong and skilled—is not the time or place to be ruing a failure to remember life lessons.

Bucky's best moves get blocked, and he does not succeed in countering several punches and kicks that connect to bruising effect. By the time most of the furniture in the suite has been reduced to matchsticks, Bucky knows for certain that he is not facing any old ringer, but a product of some kind of Super-Soldier Serum. But that is categorically impossible, because there has only ever been one true Super-Soldier.

Impossible, because that Super-Soldier, Steve Rogers, is dead.

Impossible, because Steve Rogers would never have been capable of the unadulterated hate spewing from the imitation Cap's mouth.

"It hurts me to have to pound your despicable body to a pulp while it's draped in even a debased version of my uniform! I swear, I will remove it from your corpse and dispose of it with dignity!"

The real Cap could hate the idea and the deed. Never the man.

The real Cap wouldn't have the glint of pure insanity in his eyes.

A furious barrage of lightning punches propels Bucky through the plate-glass sliders and over the balcony rail. The senator's suite is in a setback—Bucky doesn't plummet the full thirty floors to the sidewalk but hits a part of the hotel roof three stories below. It's still enough to knock the wind out of him.

The man with burn scars covered by a Captain America suit lands nearby and faces the former Soviet assassin who is also wearing a Captain America suit.

"James Buchanan Barnes, you deserve to suffer more than this. You betrayed your country and killed loyal Americans to serve your masters in the Kremlin, and you *dare* to profane a uniform that stands for ideals you turned your cowardly back on?"

The words stagger Bucky more than any combination of punches and kicks ever could.

The words stab him through the heart, because they are *true.* There's nothing to deny. They are bald facts stripped of pretensions, and facing them is a soul-shriveling experience. But those horrible truths gloss over something very important. The truths totter atop a pyramid of lies and deceptions built by the Red Skull for his own evil purposes.

The man facing Bucky is not Steve Rogers but an insane puppet of the Red Skull. And he has to be taken down.

Bucky throws the shield—the *real* shield—and it shears through the edge of the pretender's shield as if it were cardboard.

The Skull's puppet Captain America is caught off-guard; he loses concentration long enough for the Vibranium shield to bounce off a vent pipe, ricochet from a chimney, and knock his feet out from under him.

Catching the shield in midair, Bucky brings it down hard on the other Cap's head before he hits the roof. Ripping off the man's mask is the ultimate shock—a stunned Bucky finds the face of Steve Rogers staring back at him.

"No way in hell. You're not Steve Rogers."

"Can't take it, can you, turncoat? I'm the real Steve Rogers."

The one man alive who has spent more time looking at the actual Steve Rogers than anybody else spots the little differences and the unfamiliar facial expressions and understands who is now in front of him.

"I know who you really are."

"I'm Steve Rogers."

"That's what Doctor Faustus told you, but he didn't tell you that he really reports to the Red Skull, did he?"

INTERLUDE #18

"WHAT is happening in Minneapolis, Faustus?"

In the command center of his secret facility in upstate New York, the Red Skull and Doctor Faustus are watching live, hijacked security-cam views of the confrontation between the two Captain Americas. A.I.M. techs are working furiously to suppress the feeds from the cams to security firms and local police.

"He's cracking," Faustus replies. "I told you he wasn't ready yet. The reality I set up for him isn't embedded securely enough. I needed at least ten more sessions—"

"Get him out of there before we lose him, too. Send the recall signal immediately."

"That may take a minute or two."

An A.I.M. security specialist enters the command center and rushes up to the Red Skull. "There's a situation down at the medical bay. Your daughter and Sharon Carter..."

THIRTY-EIGHT

"**...YOU** remember the Red Skull, don't you? Do you seriously believe that a psychotic ex-Nazi has our country's best interests at heart?"

The man with Steve Rogers' face is trying desperately to make all his conflicting memories add up to something that makes sense.

"No, that's not..."

Bucky backs off and lets the man stand.

"I can prove it. If you take off your shirt, there are keloid scars all over your chest, right? You're William Burnside, and you were really Captain America in the 1950s, but you...had *problems*, and Doctor Faustus—"

"This is not right. You're a traitor and a murderer..."

The glazing of Burnside's eyes lasts two seconds. There is a subtle change when they refocus, as if a switch had just been thrown. Bucky continues, not noticing the difference.

"I was those things, and I'm sorry. But I can help you—"

The movement is so fast that Bucky never sees it. Burnside may have gone insane, but he had actually been dosed with an imperfect version of a Super-Soldier Serum, that made him incredibly strong and swift.

Bucky finds himself plunging off the roof toward the pavement twenty-five stories below. Burnside screams from the parapet.

"You're *sorry?* You should be dead!"

Falcon slams into Bucky fifty feet from the pavement, changing downward inertia into a lateral glide path that has them both tumbling on the sidewalk two blocks from the impact point.

They both roll to their feet amid shocked shoppers entering and exiting the Nicollet Mall.

"Just smile and keep walking," Falcon says, striding nonchalantly. "And don't count on me catching you next time."

"I don't know how to thank you, Sam—but shouldn't we be trying to pick up Burnside's trail?"

Falcon shakes his head; "We have to spin our wheels and wait for Redwing to get a bead on where Burnside is going."

"Your bird is following him? You knew who he was all along?"

"I had my suspicions. But I didn't tell you because I thought you might fly off the handle and go after him yourself."

Falcon stops Bucky before he can say anything.

"If it makes you feel any better, I think Steve would have gone the same route."

INTERLUDE #19

"HOW did this happen?"

The Red Skull is barely able to contain his fury. Sharon Carter is lying in the corridor outside the medical bay with a scalpel embedded in her abdomen. A.I.M. medical techs and Doctor Faustus are kneeling to attend to Carter as Sin stands nearby, immensely pleased with herself.

"She was trying to escape," Sin smirks. "Trying to use me as a hostage, but I knew the code phrase Faustus used on her: 'I don't believe we're done with you yet, Agent 13.' She went all blank-faced and compliant after I said it, so I grabbed the scalpel and stuck her."

The slap sends Sin reeling.

"You stupid, stupid girl. You have no idea what you have done. Agent 13 and the gobbet of living tissue in her womb are vitally important to me in several ways. I should never have let you live."

The medical techs lift Sharon Carter onto a gurney and wheel her back into the ICU. Faustus peels off a pair of bloody latex gloves and lets them fall to the floor. There are specks of blood on his monocle and in his beard. He is speaking to Red Skull but looking at Sin.

"She will live. Whether we can save the baby is another matter. The coupling of the wound trauma with an arbitrary and capricious use of the code phrase may have undone months of work."

Neither Red Skull nor Faustus harbor expectations of contrition from Sin, and they get none.

On his way back to his private suite, the Red Skull notices the hum of electronic activity from Arnim Zola's lab. Inside, as usual, the robotic professor is plumbing the unknowable with the inexplicable.

"Nice of you to let us know you're back, Zola."

Zola ignores him, of course.

THIRTY-NINE

FALCON lays down a full house, nines high, and rakes in the pot. Bucky totals up his losses.

"I'm into you for a hundred and ninety-eight. Is the mook still in the diner?"

The two of them had been holed up in a motel room on the outskirts of Toledo, Ohio, for four days. William Burnside's room is three doors down. Burnside has done nothing but stay in his room and eat his meals at the diner across the street.

Sam gets up and peeks through the blinds with auto-ranging binoculars.

"He's having the liver and onions, with potatoes O'Brien on the side again. A creature of habit is our lad Burnside. Oh, and Natasha called while I was out filling the ice bucket. S.H.I.E.L.D. techs pulled the charred pieces of Arnim Zola's android body out of the rubble; they say he was plugged into some sort of transference device."

"I read Zola's file when I downloaded the A.I.M. dossier through Fury's backdoor link to the S.H.I.E.L.D. database. He's a body-switcher from way back, Sam. Nothing but a brain-wave pattern in temporary residence. But why isn't our Cap doppelganger going home to roost? It's like he's hiding out, avoiding his own crew."

Falcon pulls back from the window and shuts the blinds tight.

"An A.I.M. enforcement team just surrounded the diner. If Mr. Burnside isn't reporting back to Red Skull on his own, the beekeepers will drag him in feet-first. Redwing will have eyes on him either way, and we win."

Bucky looks through the peephole in the door.

"Maybe we should be helping him, instead of—"

"Using him?"

"I'm not big on stuff like that, Sam."

"Bottom line: I care less about him than I care about Sharon."

Bucky pulls back from the peephole.

"He's onto them."

Sam yanks open the blinds. Across the street, they see Burnside get up from his booth and run to the back door of the diner. Two squads of A.I.M. troopers with heavy-energy weapons cut off the alley behind the diner from both ends. There are flashes of bright light, and an unmarked van backs into the alley. One minute later, the van pulls out and proceeds down a side street.

Above, a circling hawk suddenly banks and follows the van.

INTERLUDE #20

RED Skull lets himself into Arnim Zola's lab. He notes that there is one less "spare" in the row of robotic bodies since the explosion at the abandoned mental-health facility. The absence of a replacement makes Red Skull wonder if Zola is slipping, or whether he is preoccupied with his work on Doctor Doom's device.

The most recent incarnation of Zola is mechanically transferring vials of a glowing pale-blue liquid from a cooler box to a machine that is leaking noxious vapors.

"You might be interested to know that we have our errant Captain America substitute back in custody, if not in willing spirit."

Unexpectedly, Zola stops what he is doing and regards the Red Skull.

"That makes another of Doctor Faustus' mistakes cleared up. In the old days, you would not have stood for such incompetence."

"The old days are over, Professor Zola. And despite his overblown ego, it was Faustus' control over Sharon Carter that made my overall plan possible. If she were only still of use to us."

Zola holds up a glowing vial with steel tongs. Proximity to the vial makes the sinuses contract in the body Red Skull shares with Lukin.

"We need her for one more thing, Herr Skull. That is, if you are still serious about proceeding. And I hope you are not. I am still constructing the platform, and I remind you that we can make only a single attempt—"

"My insolent daughter has left us no choice."

The Red Skull tugs the mask from his head, and Aleksander Lukin continues with his distinctive Russian accent, "Would you have us stuck like this forever?"

"If that is not a rhetorical question, the answer is 'no.'"

"Then whatever part of Doctor Doom's device still eludes your grasp, find it and complete the machine before your leader and I both go insane from our forced proximity."

FORTY

IN the medical bay, Sharon Carter watches Doctor Faustus enter the ICU through a haze of painkillers.

"You've lost your baby, my dear. I am truly sorry."

Not even the powerful medications can staunch the fierceness of the anger she feels toward Faustus, Red Skull, and all the rest. She strains at her bonds. She struggles to find words vitriolic enough to express what is inside her.

"The Red Skull is incensed. You realize there will be repercussions? Surely, you do. And you know, as well, that they never intended for you to keep the baby. They wanted it for their ends. Did you intend to die, to keep the child from their hands?"

"Yes, yes, yes," she snarls.

Doctor Faustus places an oddly cool hand on her forehead. Her anger and pain subsides, replaced by an artificial calm.

"That's better. Did you know that even the worst monsters may harbor the delusion of caring and may develop a real affection that overrides certain, shall we say, fixations?"

A horror is growing in the back of Sharon's brain, but something is telling her not to care about it.

"You are an amazing specimen, Agent 13. I sincerely hope you make it through the coming days. Do not be afraid of retribution from the Red Skull. He and Zola still need you. You are the *constant*, after all."

None of what Faustus is saying makes any sense to Sharon.

"I am absenting myself from the finale of this drama, but I am leaving you with two gifts."

He places a small blinking device in Sharon's hand. She knows what it is. It's her own S.H.I.E.L.D. GPS locater, and it's been switched back on.

"And this is my most valuable gift, my dear: I don't believe we're done with you yet, Agent 13." Her eyes go blank, and he continues, "Forget your grief. You were never really pregnant. It was all a bad dream. When I am gone, you will have complete control of your own mind again. Be strong, Sharon—and good-bye."

PART FIVE

UNRAVEL AND
RE-KNIT

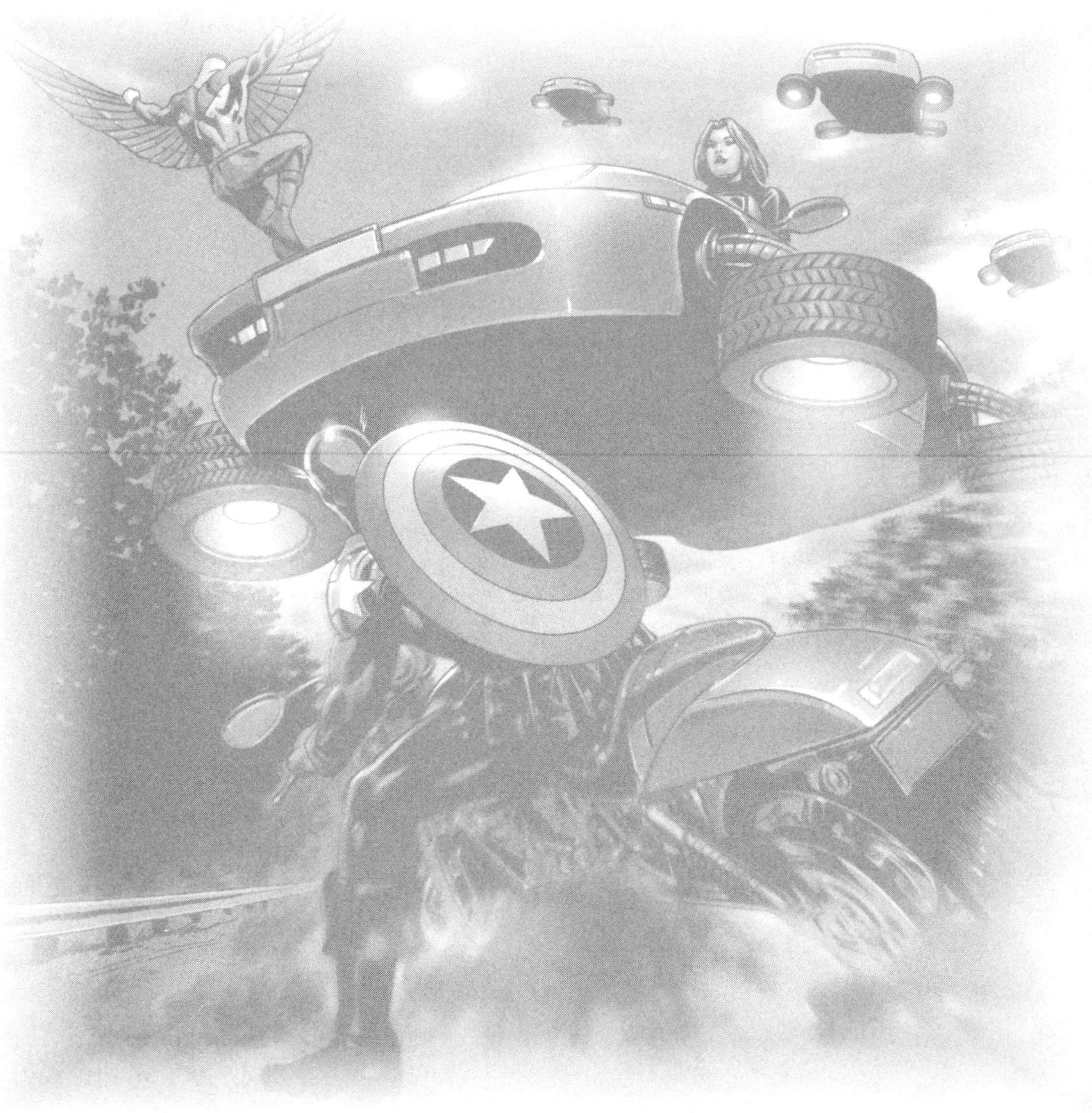

FORTY-ONE

BUCKY has been heading east toward Albany on I-90 for eight bug-eating hours. Above, Falcon rides the air currents, keeping track of the incoming intel from Redwing and other birds.

Redwing's endurance is limited by his need to kill and eat, so other birds along the route have been recruited to maintain a leapfrog relay of avian surveillance on the A.I.M. van transporting William Burnside. Eagles, barn owls, crows, sparrows, robins, finches, and yellow-bellied sapsuckers all have done their turns.

It was Redwing, taking over from a yellow warbler, that spotted the van descending a camouflaged ramp in a densely wooded area due east of Albany.

The two heroes stop to consult on the east side of the Hudson River, where I-90 turns south.

"The birds spotted air and heat vents sticking out of the ground around that ramp covering an area bigger than two football fields. Disguising them as trees might fool a hiker, but birds sure know the difference. I'd say there's a sizeable underground A.I.M. base in the woods there."

"More than the two of us can handle?"

"Does that matter?"

"Not if Sharon is in there."

As Bucky climbs back on his bike and Falcon spreads his wings, a small armada of S.H.I.E.L.D. flying cars, light transports, and heavy troop carriers descends and settles around them. Black Widow hops out of the lead car. Sam is ticked off.

"Damn, Natasha. Did you put a trace on me when you called while we were staking out the diner in Toledo?"

"Actually, we were tipped off by a disgruntled former associate of the Red Skull, who also informed us that you two might be on your way."

"And just who might this 'disgruntled former associate' be?" Bucky asks.

"Doctor Faustus decided to terminate his partnership with Red Skull and has neglected to inform him of the fact. As a gesture of good faith, Faustus turned on Sharon Carter's GPS transmitter last night. She's in—"

"An underground A.I.M. facility east of here?"

"We confirmed that. And it's not a trap. We've cased the place all day and tapped into their internal communications. We've compromised their radar, infrared detectors, and alarm systems. A bunker-buster strike will blast open entrances and escape tunnels in about two hours."

"Sounds like S.H.I.E.L.D. has this all covered, Natasha. Are we being uninvited to the party?"

"*Nyet, Zeemneey Soldat.* Faustus also told us that another part of Red Skull's plan is going into effect in Albany at the presidential debate. Captain America needs to be there to stop it."

"Captain America will be there," Bucky says. "What time?"

Black Widow hands him an earpiece.

"You have less than ninety minutes. Stark will monitor and update you as you go. Better move."

INTERLUDE #21

SENATOR Wright is perturbed. Doctor Faustus is in the bathroom of the Senator's suite in the best hotel in Albany, shaving off his voluminous beard.

"You can't leave me on my own at this stage, Doctor. Without your advice, and without your help rewriting my speeches, I don't believe I could have come this far."

Faustus pats his smooth cheeks dry and helps himself to a brisk splash of Wright's expensive aftershave.

"You need to relax, Senator. Everything will work out fine. I have to be elsewhere, but I will see you again someday. You can be sure of that."

Donning a suit jacket of much more modern cut than he usually wears, Doctor Faustus goes to the door with Wright at his heels. The Senator is fighting back a rising panic.

"But what about the debate? It starts in less than half an hour. I was supposed to be a hero."

Faustus' fingertips feel extremely reassuring on the Senator's forehead. The anxiety seems to melt away. Can there be anything more soothing than the voice of Faustus?

"And a hero you will be. Simply remember: When you hear the first shot, the man on your left will fall, and then you will dive to save the man on your right."

FORTY-TWO

FIFTY different views of the University Auditorium in Albany are showing on the monitor screens in the S.H.I.E.L.D. operations center within the Helicarrier. A capacity crowd has packed the venue for the presidential debate, and the attendees are anxious to hear the latest word from candidate Gordon Wright.

Smaller screens show every corridor within the building, and all the walkways and approaches, as well as every neighboring rooftop. An extra shift of S.H.I.E.L.D. operatives is on duty, assisting with monitoring and assessments.

A number of newscasters are blathering endlessly about the Senator's rapid rise in the polls and the popularity of his positions and stances.

Director Stark stands on the catwalk overlooking the monitors, and watches the sea of faces filing into the auditorium and taking their seats. In a different political climate, he would have been on the scene himself supervising the operation as Iron Man. But after the divisive agonies of the Civil War and recent public-relations disasters stemming from the riots, Stark knows it is best to keep a low profile. He reflects that transparency might be good for democracy in the long run, but that it certainly plays hell with the short game. Stark sees that same concern on all the familiar faces of his operations staff whenever they turn from their tasks to look at him. All this would be a lot simpler if Iron Man were on the job—

Familiar faces.

He makes a sudden decision.

"Run a facial-identification scan on everybody in the auditorium and within a two-block radius."

The operations staff is stunned, and one of the analysts objects: "Sir, that will hog all our computer resources, and the deep study we're running on Agent 13's pistol and the bullets that killed Steve Rogers hasn't finished. There are anomalies about the bullets that—"

"Just do it."

INTERLUDE #22

IN the underground A.I.M. facility east of Albany, the Red Skull stops by the Immersion Room to check on the disposition of his substitute Captain America, William Burnside. The same manner of containment equipment that had secured the Winter Soldier is being used to immobilize the recaptured doppelganger, and his brain has been plugged into the devices that will ensure his future cooperation. Red Skull wonders why Doctor Faustus isn't personally supervising this part of the operation. He orders the A.I.M. techs to find Faustus.

Farther down the hall, in Arnim Zola's lab, Red Skull is gratified to see the pulsing blue glow that marks the powering-up of Doctor Doom's device. He fights back the vertigo he feels as he enters the lab. When the machine is turned on, the floor seems to be constantly tipping.

"Is it ready, Zola?"

"I believe so. Of course, there is no way to tell if it works. It will either implant your essence in the new body, or it won't."

"And the other device? The one that separates me from Lukin?"

"That one I have more confidence in, since I designed it myself."

"It is inconceivable that Doom's pride would allow him to deliver faulty material."

Zola's unblinking red eye turns so the Red Skull can see his own reflection in it, distorted like a fun-house mirror.

"Yet he offered no guarantee, did he? I could have unraveled its secrets if you would have given me more time, and the doors of eternity could be open to us."

"Nobody is given more time, Zola. But it might be possible to seize enough time to meet our ends if we are audacious and risk all."

The Red Skull steps carefully toward the door.

"Call for me when you have the girl ready. I shall be in my suite watching the debate."

Frantic A.I.M. techs are running down the hall when Skull opens the door.

"Doctor Faustus is gone! He erased all his drives and took the backups with him."

Red Skull lurches, then spins to face Zola.

"We are betrayed! The schedule is meaningless. We must act now, or all is lost. Zola, go get the girl!"

FORTY-THREE

THE last time I saw Arnim Zola, as grotesque as he is, he seemed benign to me. Now, after Doctor Faustus has given me back my mind, I see what he really is: a monster.

Zola storms into the ICU—slamming the door, knocking aside the medical cart that stands in his way. He looms over me, an ugly colossus of anodized metal and black rubber. The holographic face in the robotic thorax is glowering.

He unlocks the four-point restraints that bind my wrists and ankles and pulls me forcefully from the bed.

"It is time. Come with me."

My fingers are so numb from lack of circulation that I lose my grip on the precious article I have been clutching since Faustus pressed it into my palm. It falls, bounces off the bed, and clatters across the tiled floor.

Zola knows what it is immediately.

As he bends down to retrieve my GPS unit, the floor shakes, and a massive pressure change pops my eardrums. An explosion. A big one. It would need to be sizeable to rock the foundations of this underground fortress: bunker busters. It has to be a S.H.I.E.L.D. raid.

Zola locks my wrists together with steel manacles and drags me out into the hall. Kronas security teams are rushing about toting energy weapons, while A.I.M. techs are driving mini-tractors pulling small Tesla cannons.

One of the beekeepers tells Zola that it is indeed S.H.I.E.L.D. assaulting the facility. Reports indicate Black Widow and Falcon are leading. They have already breached all the main entryways and are fighting their way to the inner-core security areas.

I know I don't have a chance in hell of getting away from Zola in my present condition. My bandages are still seeping blood, and I can barely hobble along on my numb feet. I have to play along and hold out until Sam and Natasha can reach me. My only advantage is that Zola doesn't know that Faustus gave me back control of my mind.

Zola's mechanical fingers yank at my manacles, forcing me to limp down the hall behind him.

"Our forces can hold them off long enough for us to keep our appointment with destiny, girl."

I don't know what he's talking about. But I do know that I'm going to make it through this, and I'm going to enjoy the hell out putting my foot through that ugly holographic face.

INTERLUDE #23

SIN appears very prim and proper sitting in the auditorium. She's wearing sensible glasses, with her hair tied back in a neat chignon. Her bustier and leathers have been traded for a conservative linen suit and medium-heel pumps. Her father's voice crackles with considerable static through her earpiece.

"Everything has gone to hell in a handbasket, but I am still counting on you, Sin. Faustus has betrayed us, and S.H.I.E.L.D. is at our gates, but nothing will deter me from my original plan. It is essential that you carry out your mission to the letter. Do you understand?"

"Of course, Father. I'm not an idiot."

"Senator Wright is not to be killed. Is that clear?"

"Perfectly clear."

"You are to shoot the candidate next to Wright—and when the senator pushes the other candidate to the floor seemingly to save him, you are to fire at the spot where Wright had been standing, as if he were the next target."

"I know the plan, Father."

"I've been tolerant of you despite your serial failures and egregious incompetence. This is your chance to vindicate yourself, so do not disappoint me."

Sin rises from her seat and makes her way to a media booth looking down on the stage from the second tier of seats. She has a pass card that unlocks the booth. Once inside, it is a simple matter for her to dispose of the newscaster and cameraman with the two nylon daggers she had carried through the metal detectors at the entrance. Sin notes with a little pride that she didn't even have to use the plastic squeeze bottle of disabling ammonia in her pocket. Father would be proud, if he were remotely capable of it.

Four Kane-Meyer security guards enter the booth with assault rifles, accompanied by an A.I.M. tech wearing a stagehand's overalls. The tech is carrying two long aluminum light-stand cases. Sin snaps open the locks of one case to reveal a sniper rifle nestled in foam rubber.

With the Kane-Meyer goons securing the door to the booth, Sin sets up a shooting rest, loads a round into the chamber of the rifle, and takes aim through the telescopic sight. She puts the crosshairs neatly on the meaty part of Senator Wright's left arm.

"Failures and incompetence? The hell with you, Father Dearest."

She raises the crosshairs to Wright's forehead and begins to take up the slack on the trigger.

FORTY-FOUR

A perfectly timed throw sends the red-white-and-blue shield flying out of the wings to deflect the bullet ten feet in front of the podium.

One microsecond earlier; one microsecond later; and the intersection of jacketed lead and Vibranium would not have occurred.

S.H.I.E.L.D. had given Bucky the heads-up as soon as the facial-recognition scans had spotted Sin in the audience. The Red Skull's daughter had left her seat by the time Bucky had arrived at the auditorium. It was the ex-boy-soldier's eye, trained in combat, that had spotted the distinctive silhouette of a sniper in the media booth, and it was the ballistic calculations of the trained Soviet operative that had plotted the timing. But it was a powered arm built by S.H.I.E.L.D. technicians under the command of Nick Fury that had thrown the mighty shield.

The shield hits the auditorium's far wall and bounces back across the stage, where a blur flashing out of the sidelines snatches it out of the air. The Secret Service agents have their guns drawn but are hesitant to shoot since the blur is wearing a familiar uniform.

"Who the hell are you?" they yell in confusion.

The blur coalesces into a figure they know, bounding over the first-tier seats and leaping toward the media booths.

"Can't you tell? I'm Captain America."

Sin has seen this new Cap in action and is still wearing a shoulder brace as a reminder. She knows the four Kane-Meyer agents and the A.I.M. tech are not going to hold him for long. She also knows that the Secret Service agents are hustling all the candidates out of the building and into armored limos as per their protocols. Sin grabs the second aluminum light-stand case, exits the booth, and heads for the stairs that lead to the roof.

INTERLUDE #24

SIN knows full-well that acknowledging your own faults and being able to do anything about them are two different things. She is acutely aware of the consequences of her impetuous actions. She knows from the grim experience of her entire childhood that all of her disobediences, no matter how secret, had somehow been made known to her father. She has suspected that he had her programmed to confess her misdeeds in her sleep and imagined him beside her bed bending his ear to her nocturnal *mea culpas*.

She is less afraid of being under one of the wet patches of concrete in the basement than of the process that would lead to that interment. She knows of her father's hands-on enjoyment of imaginative punishments, and his belief in the efficacy of "making good examples out of bad apples."

Throwing a monkey wrench into her father's plans by attempting to kill Wright was a mistake. She knows he will find out somehow, but her primary failure was in not killing the other candidate. That, at least, she can rectify. If she can't get satisfaction from sabotaging Red Skull's agenda, she can win back some of his appreciation for her lethal abilities.

At the top of the fire stairs, Sin convinces the agent from the Treasury Department security detail that she is a student fleeing the gunshots long enough to disable him with a squeeze from her plastic bottle of ammonia, then finish him off with one of her nylon daggers. The sniper the Secret Service placed on the roof is so intent on the updates coming through his earpiece that he doesn't hear Sin until she slams the nylon dagger through his spine at the base of his skull.

Opening the long aluminum case, Sin is at first taken aback by the sight of an actual folding light stand nested in the gray foam rubber. She removes the stand, peels back the foam, and smiles at what is revealed beneath.

She thinks her father's contingency plans are always just as good as the main event. If this doesn't put her back in his good graces, nothing will.

The weapon she lifts out of the case has been a favorite of insurgents and terrorists as far back as the Vietnam War and is still in use by Al Qaeda and others: an RPG-7 Russian-designed, rocket-propelled, shoulder-fired anti-tank missile launcher.

The RPG-7's piezoelectric-detonated shaped-charge warhead is more than enough to punch through the roof of an armored Secret Service limousine, like the ones now parked in front of the auditorium awaiting their illustrious passengers.

Sin peeks over the parapet. Her only question now is, "Which one first?"

FORTY-FIVE

ZOLA told me it was going to hurt, and it was like getting a root canal on my whole body. That psychotic brain-in-a-box zapped me with something as he dragged me into a room at the end of his lab that pulsated with a blue light. I think it was supposed to knock me out—and it almost did, while sending a jolt through my entire nervous system. The world turned into white light and unspeakable pain, but I could hear Zola and Red Skull clear as a bell through it all.

They are strapping me into a machine that holds me upright. I can't see through the white light, but I know there's something in front of me that's giving off a cold glow. I feel dizzy, like I'm on the sloping deck of a ship in rough seas.

The Red Skull is telling Zola to hurry up—that he doesn't want to be caught by his enemies, trapped in the body he's in.

I feel needles piercing me in several places. The hum of the machinery gets louder, and the rate of the light pulses increases.

"Is the connection to the Immersion Room complete?"

That's the Red Skull. What is he talking about? What's the Immersion Room?

"Don't worry about that, Herr Skull. The connection will be intact when we need it. Right now, the catalyst is in place and working perfectly."

"How can you be sure of that, Zola? Can it all work properly without the baby? You said the DNA of the fetus was important."

Now, they've got my attention. There's a baby involved? I have to save it! Now they've given me the impetus to will my consciousness back into control.

Now I'm determined to fight back.

"The process will probably work without the baby's DNA. As long as we have the Constant, we are in safe waters, and we still have our contingency plan ready for containment in the Immersion Room."

The Constant? They keep talking about the Constant—wait, am *I* the Constant? And Zola knows a lot about transferring his consciousness to other bodies...

They're going to put the Red Skull in my body!

They're going to—

No

That doesn't make sense.

The white light is fading, and I can see something coming together in the pulsing blueness right in front of me.

"This is taking too long, Zola. How do we even know he is actually in the timestream, and that we can extract him?"

What? Who are they talking about now?

"The temporal-distortion bullets in her gun did their job, Herr Skull. We know what they buried in the casket wasn't what they thought."

Oh, my god. I know who they're talking about. I know—

And I see him.

He's materializing in the blueness. It's him, it's him, it's him...

"There you are, Skull. You can see for yourself that it's working. You will have no need of your 'contingency plan' in the Immersion Room."

They don't know I'm still conscious. They don't know that

DEATH OF CAPTAIN AMERICA

Doctor Faustus released me from his command. They don't know
I'm back in control and no longer passively following their game
plan. They don't know how much I can push back right now.

I am only the Constant if I am not in command of myself.
That was why they needed Doctor Faustus. But that's changed now.

Go to hell, Red Skull. You are not getting your way.

*"What's going on, Zola? He's fading away. He's supposed to be
phasing back into our continuum—"*

The blueness goes away.

The white light consumes everything, and the room goes silent.

Colors begin to reconstruct as motes float into the light
and grow larger. Sounds creep in, turning from barely audible
mutterings to real words. I'm no longer upright, confined in a
machine, but on my hands and knees with the stink of burning
metal in my nose.

*"She did this on her own, Zola? She destroyed the device? This
insignificant girl?"*

*"Complete failure of Faustus' control protocols. She was
supposed to have no will. She broke the connection and shorted out
the device."*

"Fix it, Zola!"

"There's no time. S.H.I.E.L.D. forces will be here any moment."

Pain.

Now I'm feeling real pain. The Red Skull is kicking me, over
and over again.

"My plans are ruined!"

*"There's no time for this, Herr Skull. We are not ruined, but
delayed for a time. We must get out of here."*

"There is no way out for me, Zola. No way out of Lukin's head."

I roll over on to my back and try to gather my strength. I hear their footsteps fading through Zola's lab and down the corridor. Zola's metallic voice carries over the increasing volume of gunfire.

"That is not exactly true. We can still accomplish part of the plan."

I force myself to my feet and stumble through the lab, out into the hall. The bitter stench of whatever they use as propellant these days is everywhere. A Kronas security trooper is sprawled motionless in the doorway, so I relieve him of his pistol and make sure there's a live round in the chamber. I proceed down the hallway and away from the sound of shooting.

FORTY-SIX

FALCON and Black Widow are functioning as point for a S.H.I.E.L.D. heavy-weapons team. Eighty percent of the facility is cleared and under friendly control. The sound of intermittent fire can be heard from isolated pockets of hard-liners. Spearheading straight through the defenders, Falcon and Black Widow fought their way into the medical bay where their GPS locaters had honed in on Sharon Carter. But all they found was Sharon's GPS unit itself, amid the rubble in the ICU.

The power has been cut off to most of the facility, so the only illumination is from the tactical lights on the helmets of the weapons team and battery-operated red lockdown lights in the corridors.

Farther down the hall and through two security doors, they have a dicey moment when they enter Arnim Zola's lab and their lead weapons squad opens fire on what appears to be Zola himself. Falcon steps over the smoking remains of the "spare" Zola bodies and enters the room at the lab's far end. The wreckage of Doctor Doom's device is still smoldering, and parts of it have not lost their pale-blue glow.

Black Widow follows Falcon and says, "That's what this was all about. That's what Zola was building for Red Skull, and Sharon was supposed to be a part of the process. Doctor Faustus' only job was to get Sharon ready for this."

Falcon can only surmise that Black Widow has had access to far more intel than he has to be able to make those deductions.

A S.H.I.E.L.D. agent in pocked-and-charred battle armor reports breathlessly that Falcon and Black Widow need to see what's been found in the next room.

The room has been torn apart, from the inside.

A large superhuman containment device dominates the room—or rather, what's left of the device. Whoever had been locked in it had torn it apart when the power cut out and the strength dampers went dead. The steel flanges that supported the device have been bent back, and some appear to be missing.

"Are you thinking what I'm thinking about who was confined in here, 'Tasha?"

"The guy you and Bucky were tailing from Minneapolis, Burnside, the Skull's fake Captain America."

Large cables lead from the device to the wall that abuts Zola's lab and the room where Doctor Doom's machine was housed. Falcon notes that judging by their newness, the cables were added relatively recently.

"And what do you make of the renovations?"

"I think we'd better get cracking and find Sharon."

FORTY-SEVEN

I catch up to Zola and the Red Skull near the end of a hidden security corridor. I don't think I could have if they hadn't stopped in a room filled with more of Zola's bizarre equipment. Luckily, I got there just as they were leaving it. No idea what they were doing in there. When I took a quick peek inside, the only thing that caught my eye was a bank of monitors, all frozen with the big digits 0.000.

It takes everything I have to keep going. Passing out is not an option. What if they're going after the baby they were talking about?

I creep after them, scurrying from doorway to doorway until I can hear what they're saying. Zola is doing most of the talking now.

"We have to hurry. The entire facility is overrun by our enemies. Pull yourself together, or I will be forced to leave you behind."

The Red Skull is tugging at his mask, trying to get it off.

"I have to get my bearings. I can't breathe in this damn mask."

He pulls the gross red-rubber thing off his head, and I can see that it's Aleksander Lukin. My first reaction is that he's too young. But Steve was almost as old as the Red Skull, and the same with Nick Fury and Black Widow. It's possible. The odd thing is how he sheds the accent with the mask and becomes Lukin entirely. Is he a multiple-personality as well as a paranoid psychopath?

It doesn't matter.

He used me to kill Steve Rogers.

At least I caught up to him before he got to that baby he was talking about.

I step out into the corridor and call his name.

"Red Skull!"

At first, he doesn't respond. Then he turns to face me, an odd look of surprise on his face.

"*You*, girl? Are you talking to *me*?"

I pull the trigger, and I keep pulling the trigger until the pistol is empty. The man holding the Red Skull mask is dead on the floor.

I didn't save a bullet for Zola, or for myself. But I know that I am done with killing. I know that Steve would never condone what I have done. But I am not Steve, and Steve was never compelled to kill somebody he loved. I am forced to judge Steve for how I know he would judge me, and I hate that. I can't live with what Steve would think of me, and I can't live with the monster responsible for making me kill Steve still being alive.

Arnim Zola's expressionless voice drones from behind me: "The magnitude of the futility of your actions is beyond your perception."

He is lifting his black-rubber-coated hands toward me.

A jagged shard of blackened metal punches through Zola from behind and emerges between the eyes of the holographic face on his chest. The holographic field flickers for an instant and goes blank. The robotic body collapses in an inert pile to reveal the man who was behind Zola: the man who just killed him.

He's wearing a Captain America suit without the mask. It's Burnside—the Cap from the fifties that I tried to rescue and then tried to shoot.

I only have one question for him:

"Are you one of the good guys now?"

FORTY-EIGHT

IT takes Bucky all of ten seconds to deal with the Kane-Meyer toughs and the single A.I.M. tech in the media booth, but the Red Skull's daughter is already gone. Bursting into the hallway, he is confronted by a panicking crowd, all trying to get to the exits at the same time.

"Help me out, Stark. I've got nothing here."

"She's on the roof."

Bucky jumps over one of the dead Secret Service agents at the top of the fire stairs and sprints toward the parapet, where Sin is taking aim with a rocket launcher at one of the limos below.

She glances back for a second and laughs, "Too late, Captain Moron," and she fires the rocket.

Bucky has been airborne since before Sin started talking. He knew that with her finger on the trigger, she could still fire the rocket as he tackled her. So he calculated his own trajectory to pass over her and placed himself and his Vibranium shield between the rocket and the limo.

The rocket hits dead-center on the shield. The concussion from the explosion knocks Sin backward on the roof, and Bucky is blown straight downward.

The empty limo acts as big air bag, collapsing under the impact of the hero in the red-white-and-blue uniform. He lies still for a moment on the crumpled vehicle like a carved figure atop the sarcophagus of a Crusader knight, clutching his shield.

Two-dozen Secret Service agents circle and approach the semi-flattened limo, guns drawn and pointed.

The S.H.I.E.L.D. earpiece was damaged in the explosion. Stark's voice had cut off in mid-sentence: "Our people on the roof have Sin in custody, and—"

The agents around the limo try hard to assess the situation.

"Is that—"

"Who the hell do you think it is, dummy?"

The Agent In Charge of the Secret Service detachment speaks out with the voice of authority.

"Stand down. Weapons on safe and holstered. Somebody give Captain America a hand down from there."

Captain America.

A dozen hands reach out to ease the hero to his feet on the pavement. A dozen more hands reach out to clap him on the shoulder, or just to touch the shield.

A voice from the crowd beyond the agents rings out.

"Hey, Cap! Over here!"

Hundreds of mini-flashes from phone cams go off.

A thousand people are cheering and shouting.

The man who used to be a boy-soldier—who was once a Soviet assassin and thought he was lost—discovers that he is, in fact, found.

FORTY-NINE

I'M staring at a steel-reinforced concrete ceiling. Smoke is swirling around me. I hear sporadic gunfire and muffled explosions.

I sit up, and a wave of dizziness passes over me. I must have passed out for a short while. I don't know how I had the strength to get as far as I did. The fake Steve in the fake Captain America suit is nowhere to be seen.

I fall back on my elbows as two figures approach through the dust and smoke: Black Widow and Falcon, followed by a squad of S.H.I.E.L.D. agents.

"Oh, Sam. And Natasha...I am so glad to see the both of you."

Falcon kicks the inert Zola and pulls the red mask from the dead hand of the other body on the floor.

"Arnim Zola and the Red Skull. Not too shabby, Sharon."

I think I start to cry as Sam kneels to hold me.

"I did it, Sam. I killed Steve. I didn't mean to, but..."

Sam holds me even tighter.

"We know. Zola was controlling you. It's all over."

Natasha takes my free hand.

"It's over, Sharon—and the good guys won."

EPILOGUE 1

SHE sits on a lounge chair on the Helicarrier's observation deck with her bare feet tucked under her. Her eyes focus inward, not on the panorama of New York City stretched out before her.

One level above, on a spidery catwalk, Tony Stark and Sam Wilson watch her and talk.

"Sharon had a miscarriage, Sam. The medical report says it was caused by a knife wound."

"And she doesn't remember being pregnant?"

"We think Doctor Faustus erased selective memories. He must have done that when he turned on the Red Skull."

"Why would he do that, Tony? He set her up in the first place."

"Who knows? People have remorse. Maybe it's Stockholm Syndrome in reverse. Could be, he thought he was helping her. Or it's an early move in a complicated gambit that Faustus thinks will pay off much later. The important thing is that Sharon deserves to know the truth, but I just can't bear to be the one to tell her."

Sam Wilson leans on the railing and takes a deep breath.

"I'm going to take care of her for a while. I think Steve would have wanted that. And when she's strong enough to handle it, I'll be the one who tells her—but not today."

EPILOGUE 2

"...AND in breaking news, Senator Wright has announced his resignation from his congressional seat and withdrawn from the presidential race, for 'deeply personal reasons' and to spend more time with his family—"

The cable-TV newscaster blathers on as Natalia Romanova snuggles farther into the chest of James "Bucky" Barnes on her comfortable couch in her comfortable apartment overlooking the East River.

"You're good, Natasha. Did he even blink?"

"He knew the game was up when I showed him the copies of all the bank transfers from Kronas Corporation to his various offshore accounts—oh, look, they're playing it again."

On the screen, the now-famous footage of Captain America being helped off the crushed limousine and cheered by the crowd is running over the newscaster's enthusiastic commentary. Bucky clicks off the TV.

"If I watch it one more time, I'll turn into Gloria Swanson in *Sunset Boulevard.*"

"Please. You're a star now. The people love you."

With anybody else, she would have suppressed the yawn. But she's at home with Bucky, and feels completely at ease.

"They loved Senator Wright until this afternoon. I can't stop thinking how close the Red Skull got to owning a president."

Natasha perks right up.

"I enjoy seeing you like this, James—struggling with the whole Captain America thing. Remember, it's never supposed to be easy."

"Steve made it look that way. He made it look natural."

"You will, too," she says. She pulls him down on the sofa. "Someday."

EPILOGUE 3

IN Times Square, the man in the anonymous raincoat stops in the constant flow of pedestrian traffic. He looks up at the giant screens showing Captain America accepting the accolades of the crowd after the incident in Albany.

A drunken teenager bumps into the man, pulls back, and squints at his face. "Anybody ever tell you that you look like Steve Rogers, dude?"

"All the time."

The inebriated teen staggers on. William Burnside continues uptown, deep in thought. He thinks that being Captain America is the toughest job in the world, and that world is completely different from the one he knew. He thinks that his old world made sense, that this new world is too decadent and wrong. He thinks that this isn't his America.

But tomorrow will be different.

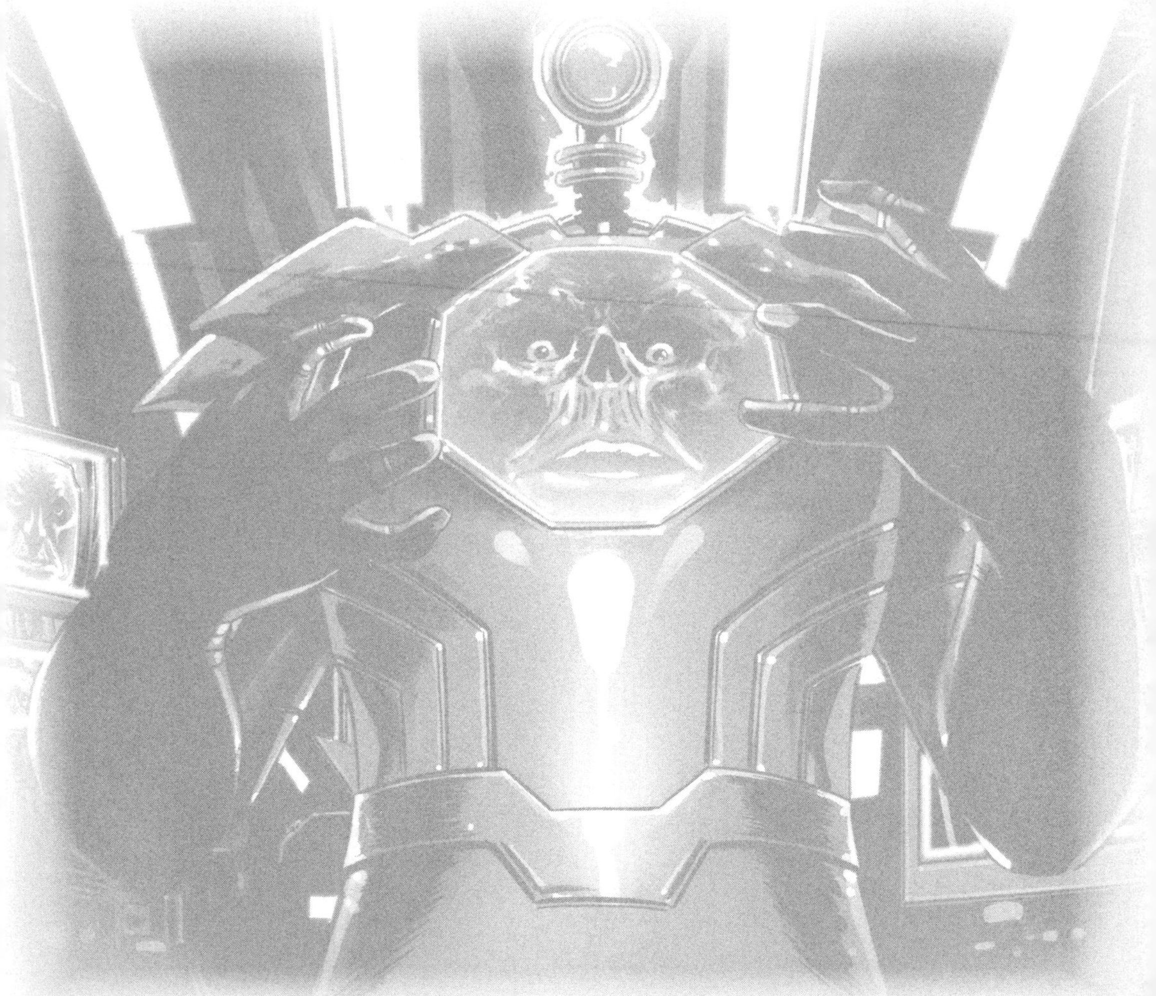

EPILOGUE 4

THE laboratory is well-hidden. There are sound baffles and passive arrays that defy all manner of sensors and detectors. It is a place that cannot be penetrated by even the most sophisticated S.H.I.E.L.D. spy devices.

Arnim Zola's face flits across multiple monitors between bursts of static in the dark and claustrophobic space.

"There was no choice, no time for options. I assure you this is only temporary. We have had our differences, Herr Skull, but Arnim Zola is always true to his word. I swear I will be back for you, and I will alleviate these circumstances."

One of Zola's robotic bodies rises from the transference table, its red eye scanning the monitors. The face in the holographic chest plate is not Arnim Zola's. It is the Red Skull.

The expression on the face is sheer horror.

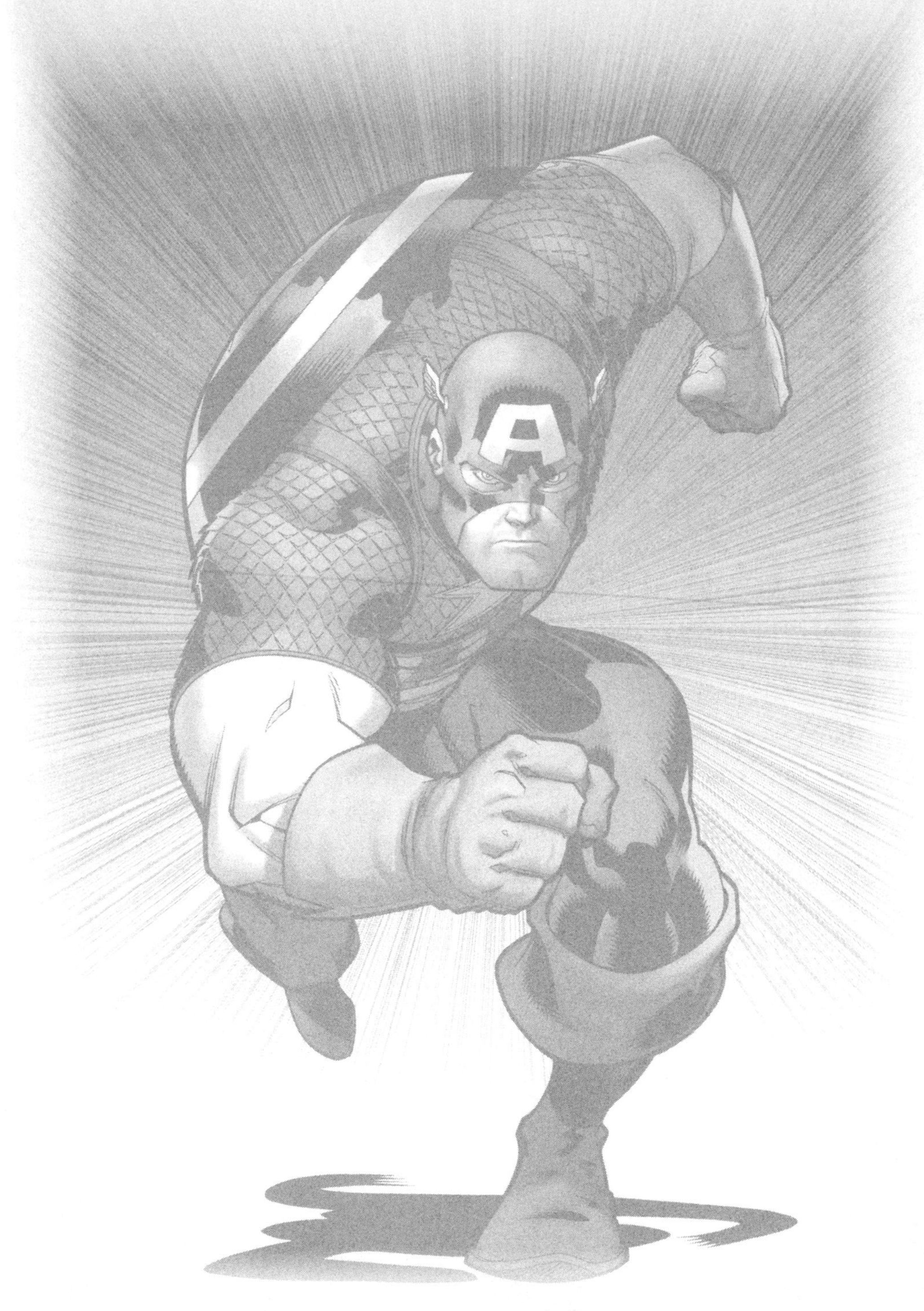

EPILOGUE 5

I know that Doctor Faustus played fast and loose with my memory. There's not much I can do about that. But he couldn't erase memories that hadn't been made yet. He had no idea what I was going to see when Doctor Doom's machine started to warp time and space.

He couldn't erase the fact that I was going to see Steve Rogers still alive, but lost in the timestream. He couldn't foresee that I would be capable of thwarting Red Skull's plan to bring Steve back and plant himself in Steve's body.

He couldn't erase the feeling that I have right now, knowing that Steve is still out there. If Red Skull could pull him back, then it's possible for Tony Stark or somebody else to do the same.

Possibilities are hope, and hope is life.

And so I allow myself to smile again.

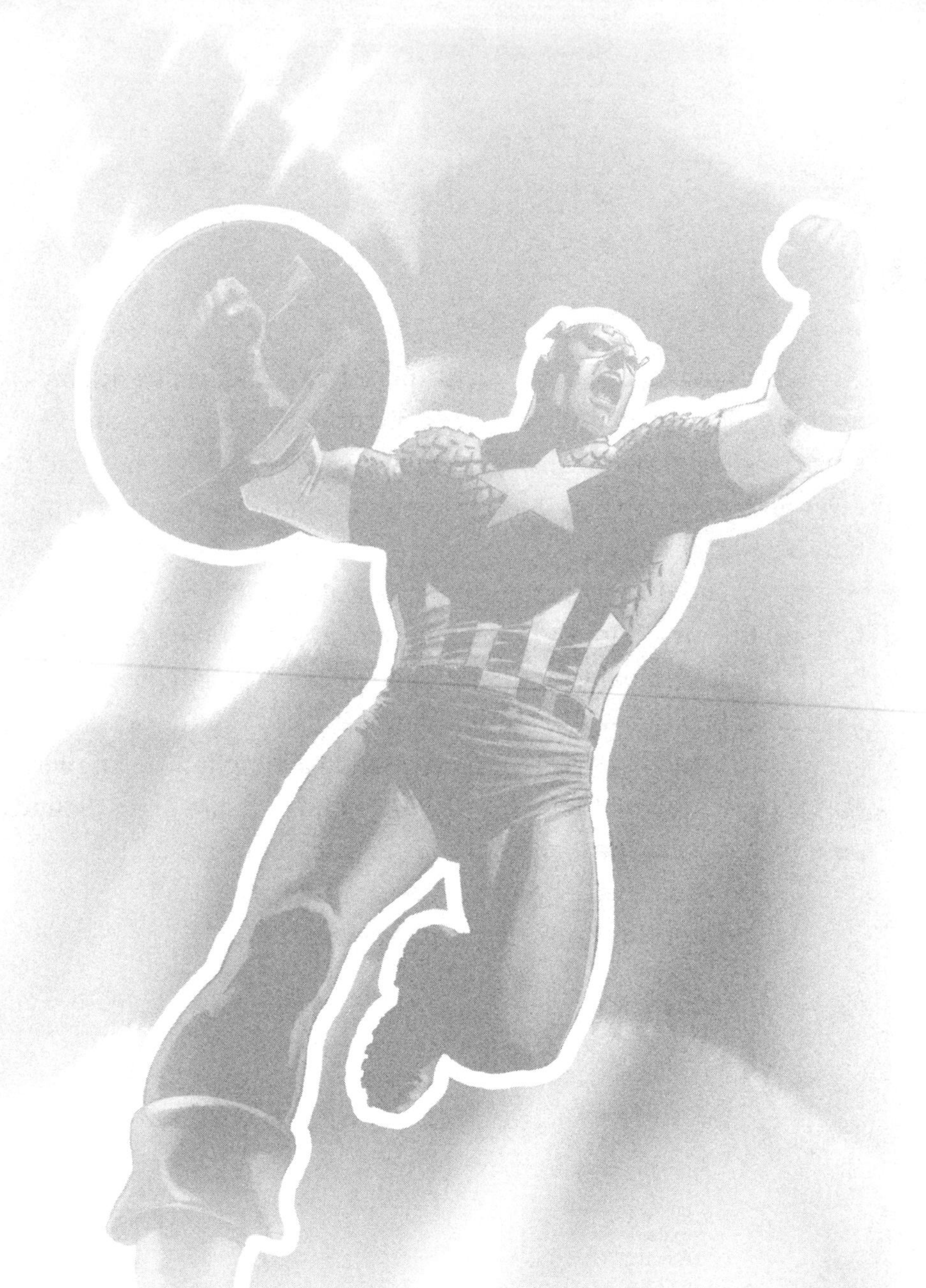

CIVIL WAR prose novel
Written by STUART MOORE
Adapted from the graphic novel by MARK MILLAR & STEVE McNIVEN
The Marvel Universe is changing. In the wake of a tragedy, Capitol Hill proposes the Super Hero Registration Act, requiring all costumed heroes to unmask themselves before the government. Divided, the nation's greatest champions must each decide how to react — a decision that will alter the course of their lives forever! Experience Marvel's blockbuster event like never before in this new adaptation!
TPB ISBN: 978-0-7851-6036-6

NEW AVENGERS: BREAKOUT prose novel
Written by ALISA KWITNEY
Adapted from the graphic novel by BRIAN MICHAEL BENDIS & DAVID FINCH
Fantasy/romance/comics author Alisa Kwitney (*A Flight of Angels, Moonburn*) reveals the secret history of Avengers couple Hawkeye and the Black Widow. Under secret orders to assassinate the Widow, the rough-edged marksman finds himself caught up in a violent prison break that releases some of the world's most vicious and powerful criminals. Defying his superiors, Hawkeye joins forces with the sultry Russian spy — and with a mismatched group of personalities that includes Spider-Man, Spider Woman, Luke Cage, Captain America and Iron Man, in a dramatically different take on Brian Michael Bendis' Avengers comics debut. Learn the sizzling backstory of your favorite big-screen heroes in this adaptation, inspired by the best of page and screen!
TPB ISBN: 978-0-7851-6517-0

ASTONISHING X-MEN: GIFTED prose novel
Written by PETER DAVID
Adapted from the graphic novel by JOSS WHEDON & JOHN CASSADAY
The X-Men: outcast heroes, banded together to defend the rights of mutants everywhere. But what if no one had to be a mutant anymore? Would that be a curse, or a blessing? And what price would mutantkind pay for this "cure"? The X-Men go head-to-head with the enigmatic Ord, with an unexpected ally — and some unexpected adversaries — tipping the scales in this full-length novel based on the acclaimed comics series by the writer/director of *Marvel's The Avengers!*
TPB ISBN: 978-0-7851-6515-6

IRON MAN: EXTREMIS prose novel
Written by MARIE JAVINS
Adapted from the graphic novel by WARREN ELLIS & ADI GRANOV
Iron Man was forged out of advanced technology, but now that same future tech threatens to doom Tony Stark. A dangerous terrorist has ingested a techno-organic virus called Extremis, transforming him into a superhuman killing machine. Now immensely powerful, but driven mad by the virus' effects, the Extremis creature seems unstoppable. To halt this madman's psychotic rampage, Iron Man must face the Extremis virus head-on — in a life-or-death battle that will drive Tony Stark closer than ever to the thin line between man and machine. Experience Warren Ellis's blockbuster reimagining of the armored Avenger like never before in this new adaptation!
TPB ISBN: 978-0-7851-6519-4

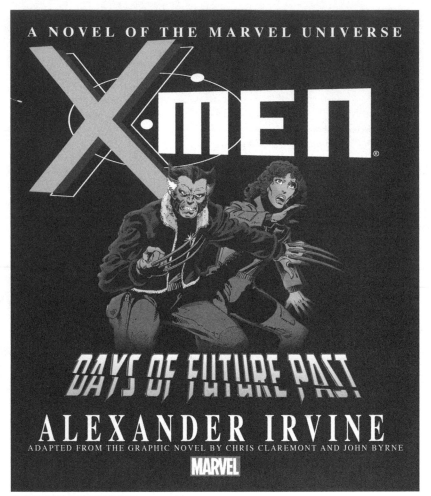

A NOVEL OF THE MARVEL UNIVERSE

X·MEN

DAYS OF FUTURE PAST

ALEXANDER IRVINE

ADAPTED FROM THE GRAPHIC NOVEL BY CHRIS CLAREMONT AND JOHN BYRNE

MARVEL

X-MEN: DAYS OF FUTURE PAST prose novel
Written by ALEXANDER IRVINE
Adapted from the graphic novel by CHRIS CLAREMONT & JOHN BYRNE
In a dark and dangerous post-apocalyptic future, the mutant-hunting killing machines known as the Sentinels rule America with an iron fist. Almost all mutants, super heroes and villains have been exterminated. Only a handful r main to fight against their oppressive robotic overseers and most of those are powerless, locked in mutant conce tration camps. Now, Kate Pryde must travel back in time and warn the present-day X-Men of the coming danger — and hopefully prevent this horrible future from ever taking place! Experience the classic, genre-defining X-Men event like never before in this new adaptation!

HC ISBN: 978-0-7851-8975-6